FALKLAND
ISLA~~ND~~

WILL WAGSTAFF

www.bradtguides.com

Bradt Guides Ltd, UK
The Globe Pequot Press Inc, USA

Bradt GUIDES
TRAVEL TAKEN SERIOUSLY

West Point Island: with its sheltered cove, rugged cliffs, and the opportunity to sit in the tussac grass watching black-browed albatrosses gliding by, this feels like a very special place
page 171

Carcass Island: the abundance of small birds around the settlement makes this a birdwatcher's paradise
page 165

Jason Islands

Keppel Sound

Carcass Island

Saunders Island

Keppel Island

Pebbl

West Point Island

Storm Mountain 521m

Dunbar

Byron Sound

Hill Cove

Roy Cove

Mount Adam 700m

Hill Cove Mountains

Watrah

Port H

Mount Marie 660m

WEST FALKLAND

Chartres

Chartre

Passage Islands

King George Bay

New Island

Grey Channel

Queen Charlotte Bay

Mount Sulivan 469m

Hornby Mountains

Mount Moo 554m

Beaver Island

Weddell Island

Mount Weddell 383m

Staats Island

Smylie Channel

Fox Bay West

Fox Bay East

Falkland

Port Stephens

Port Edgar

Mount Young 340m

Eagle Passage

Albemarle

Port Albemarle

Mount Young 340m

Arch Islands

Speedwell Island

Cape Meredith

N

Bradt

0 _____ 40km
0 _____ 20 miles

New Island: generally only accessible to cruise ships, the mix of penguins, albatross and superb scenery makes a visit here very memorable
page 173

Port Howard: the perfect place to experience *camp* life and a superb base from which to explore West Falkland
page 129

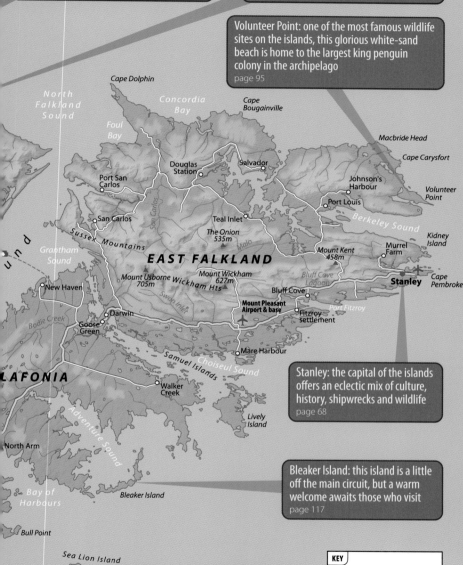

Saunders Island: although this island is best known for its black-browed albatross colonies, it is also home to the first British settlement on the Falklands
page 156

Pebble Island: from open pools often teeming with waterfowl to rocky cliffs where you'll find noisy rockhopper penguin colonies, this large island has it all
page 145

Volunteer Point: one of the most famous wildlife sites on the islands, this glorious white-sand beach is home to the largest king penguin colony in the archipelago
page 95

Stanley: the capital of the islands offers an eclectic mix of culture, history, shipwrecks and wildlife
page 68

Bleaker Island: this island is a little off the main circuit, but a warm welcome awaits those who visit
page 117

Sea Lion Island: sit outside at dusk listening to magellanic penguins calling, while yards away elephant seals are hauled up on the beach
page 122

North Falkland Sound

Cape Dolphin

Concordia Bay

Cape Bougainville

Macbride Head

Cape Carysfort

Foul Bay

Douglas Station

Salvador

Johnson's Harbour

Volunteer Point

Port San Carlos

Port Louis

Berkeley Sound

San Carlos

Teal Inlet

The Onion 535m

Kidney Island

Grantham Sound

Sussex Mountains

San Carlos

Molo

Mount Kent 458m

Murrel Farm

EAST FALKLAND

Mount Usborne 705m

Mount Wickham 627m

Wickham Hts

Bluff Cove Lagoon

Stanley

Cape Pembroke

New Haven

Swan Inlet

Bluff Cove

Mount Pleasant Airport & base

Fitzroy settlement

Port Fitzroy

Bodie Creek

Darwin

Goose Green

Mare Harbour

Samuel Islands

Choiseul Sound

LAFONIA

Walker Creek

Lively Island

North Arm

Adventure Sound

Bay of Harbours

Bleaker Island

Bull Point

Sea Lion Island

FALKLAND ISLANDS
DON'T MISS...

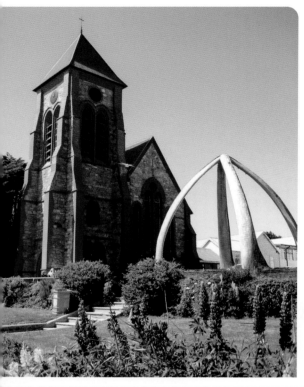

STANLEY
Christ Church Cathedral, and its whalebone arch, is one of the most photographed sites in the islands' capital PAGE 80
(B/S)

VOLUNTEER POINT
This scenic site is most famous for its king penguin colony where over 1,500 adults have been counted in recent years PAGE 95
(WW)

HISTORIC SITES
One of many memorials found on the islands, Stanley's Liberation Monument serves as a reminder of those who lost their lives in 1982 PAGE 78
(JSM/S)

RARE BIRDS
The endemic Falkland steamer duck, often spotted waddling along beaches, is one of several species of rare bird that can be seen across the islands PAGE 38
(GP/S)

WILD FALKLANDS
The islands are home to a multitude of spectacular wildlife sites, with one of the most impressive being The Neck on Saunders Island PAGE 162
(JR/S)

FALKLAND ISLANDS
IN COLOUR

above
(FITB)

White-sand beaches, such as Carcass Island's Leopard Beach, are common across the islands and are often dotted with penguins PAGE 168

left
(K/S)

Cape Pembroke's restored lighthouse offers many cruise-ship passengers their first glimpse of the Falkland Islands PAGE 89

below
(K/S)

Quartzite hills, such as those seen from Kidney Island, are typical across East Falkland PAGE 3

In *camp*, farms are busy during the summer months as sheep gathering takes place prior to the shearing season PAGE 19

above
(SA/S)

Although never easy to spot, on a sunny day the queen of Falklands fritillary will find a sheltered location and bask in the sun PAGE 45

top right
(WW)

Pale maiden, the national flower of the Falkland Islands, is one of the most characteristic sights of spring PAGE 27

bottom right
(WW)

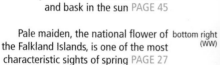

Gorse, such as that seen around the Carcass Island settlement, was introduced to the islands by early European settlers and provides a wonderful splash of colour PAGE 25

below
(JR/S)

above (JR/D) A typical stand of tussac grass, here fringing the coast of Bleaker Island with diddle-dee heath growing alongside PAGE 25

below left (KN/D) Sea cabbage is usually found growing in the loose sands at the top of beaches above the high water mark; its attractive yellow flower glows in midsummer PAGE 28

below right (FITB) Tea berry fruit are often gathered by the islanders in the autumn and used in the making of cakes and jam, or just eaten raw with cream; the leaves are used to make a tea, hence the name PAGE 26

bottom right (RLC/D) *Acaena ovalifolia*, one of several species locally called prickly burr, whose seeds can get well embedded in one's socks! PAGE 23

AUTHOR

Will Wagstaff is originally from Cardiff, South Wales and, having graduated with a BSc Joint Honours in Biology and Geology, he settled in the Isles of Scilly in 1981. His main passion has always been ornithology, but over the years his interests have encompassed all aspects of wildlife. In the Isles of Scilly he has set up his own business, Island Wildlife Tours, through which he has been able to share his love of the islands with many hundreds of visitors who stay in Scilly. His regular contributions to wildlife programmes on radio and on television have also helped him foster interest in the islands. A regular agenda of walks, talks and boat excursions throughout the summer keeps him very busy but leaves him free to lead tours all over the world during the winter months. The Falkland Islands have been the most frequently visited and favourite location where he has been able to communicate his love of wildlife to many.

AUTHOR'S STORY

Like many people in Britain I watched the television coverage of the 1982 war, little realising that I would one day visit those far-away islands. My chance came out of the blue one Saturday afternoon in January 1994. I had led some tours here on the Isles of Scilly for Libby of Island Holidays and had said that I should be pleased to lead tours elsewhere. She rang that afternoon to say 'You know you said you'd like to go to the Falkland Islands? Could you go on Monday?' Well, to cut a long story short, a few phone calls later it was all sorted and I was ready to go.

Reaching the islands for the first time was a magical experience, from watching upland geese and meadowlarks to admiring the huge expanses of white grass on the bus ride into Stanley. I shall always remember my first walk along Stanley seafront with the faint smell of peat smoke in the air, and the first penguin I saw swimming just offshore.

Since that first tour in 1994 I have led groups around the islands on many other occasions and have managed to visit a large part of the archipelago. Every trip brings something new, whether birds, flowers or seeing familiar places at different times of year. There is tremendous pleasure in taking people around the Falkland Islands and watching their reactions to the sights and sounds. I have been lucky in that some people have visited the islands with me more than once and are therefore able to share my memories of what we have seen and the events of particular trips. The welcome in each of the places we stay makes it so much easier to settle in and enjoy the highlights of each area.

Having visited the islands almost every year since 1994, I still find them to be one of the most amazing places in the world. Hopefully by reading this guide and visiting the islands you will agree.

Third edition published November 2024
First published 2001
Bradt Travel Guides Ltd
31a High Street, Chesham, Buckinghamshire, HP5 1BW, England
www.bradtguides.com
Print edition published in the USA by The Globe Pequot Press Inc,
PO Box 480, Guilford, Connecticut 06437-0480

ISBN: 9781804692042

British Library Cataloguing in Publication Data
A catalogue record for this book is available from the British Library

Photographs Alamy Stock Photo: blacklabphotos (B/A); Dreamstime.com:
Hel080808 (H/D), Jeremy Richards (JR/D), Kim Nelson (KN/D), Ondřej Prosický
(OP/D), Rob Lumen Captum (RLC/D), Steve Allen (SA/D); Falkland Islands
Tourist Board (FITB): Derek Pettersson (DP/FITB), Neil Golding (NG/FITB);
Georgina Strange, Design In Nature Falklands (GS); Shutterstock.com: Anton_
Ivanov (AI/S), Barnes Ian (BI/S), benmoat (B/S), bumihills (B/S), Giedriius (G/S),
Goldilock Project (GP/S), GybasDigiPhoto (GDP/S), Jeremy Richards (JR/S), Joel
dos Santos Matos (JSM/S), kwest (K/S), Leksele (L/S), Ondrej Prosický (OP/S),
Steve Allen (SA/S), Steve Heap (SH/S), Vladislav T. Jirousek (VTJ/S); SuperStock
(SS); Will Wagstaff (WW)

Front cover King penguins at Volunteer Beach (GS)
Back cover, clockwise from top left Marmot Row, Stanley (H/D), Gypsy Cove
(GDP/S), sea lion (DP/FITB), tea berries (FITB)
Title page, clockwise from top left Lady Elizabeth wreck, Stanley Harbour (L/S),
Christ Church Cathedral, Stanley (B/S), imperial shag (OP/D)

Maps David McCutcheon FBCart.S. FRGS, assisted by Pearl Geo Solutions

Typeset by Ian Spick, Bradt Guides and Dataworks, India
Production managed by Imprint Press; printed in India
Digital conversion by www.dataworks.co.in

Acknowledgements

Thanks must go to John Fowler in the Falkland Islands and also to the late Robin Woods in the UK for answering my many queries for the first edition. Thanks also go to those in the Falklands and in the UK who have patiently answered any other queries I have had for each of these editions. I am very grateful to the late Libby Weir-Breen of Island Holidays for sending me to the Falkland Islands so often.

DEDICATION

This book is dedicated to the memory of Robin Lee, a true Falkland gentleman, who shared his love of the islands with so many people.

FEEDBACK REQUEST

At Bradt Guides we're aware that guidebooks start to go out of date on the day they're published – and that you, our readers, are out there in the field doing research of your own. You'll find out before us when a fine new family-run hotel opens or a favourite restaurant changes hands and goes downhill. So why not tell us about your experiences? Contact us on ☎ 01753 893444 or e info@bradtguides.com. We will forward emails to the author who may post updates on the Bradt website at w bradtguides.com/updates. Alternatively, you can add a review of the book to Amazon, or share your adventures with us on social:

🅵 BradtGuides & Island Wildlife Tours
𝕏 BradtGuides & IWTScilly
📷 BradtGuides

Contents

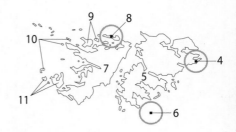

	Introduction	**vii**
PART ONE	**GENERAL INFORMATION**	**1**
Chapter 1	**Background Information** Geology and geography 3, Climate 5, History 6, Government and politics 16, Economy 16, People 19, Language 19, Education 20, Culture and sport 20	**3**
Chapter 2	**Natural History** Flora 23, Marine algae 29, Fauna 29, Conservation 46	**23**
Chapter 3	**Practical Information** When to visit 49, Highlights and suggested itineraries 49, Tour operators 51, Red tape 52, Embassies 53, Getting there and away 53, Health 55, Safety 55, Travelling with children 56, What to take 56, Money and budgeting 57, Getting around 57, Accommodation 59, Eating and drinking 61, Public holidays and events 61, Shopping 62, Arts and entertainment 62, Media and communications 64, Cultural etiquette 64, Travelling positively 65	**49**
PART TWO	**THE GUIDE**	**67**
Chapter 4	**Stanley** History 69, Getting there and away 71, Getting around 72, Tourist information and local tour operators 72, Where to stay 73, Where to eat and drink 74, Entertainment and nightlife 76, Shopping 76, Other practicalities 76, What to see and do 77	**68**
Chapter 5	**East Falkland** Gypsy Cove, Cape Pembroke and Surf Bay – a driving tour from Stanley 85, Kidney Island 90, Kidney Cove 94, Volunteer Point 95, Cape Bougainville 105, Cape Dolphin 105, San Carlos and Port San Carlos 107,	**85**

Darwin and Goose Green 110, Lafonia 114, Bleaker
Island 116, Bertha's Beach 118, Bluff Cove Lagoon 120

Chapter 6   **Sea Lion Island**   **122**
                   History 122, Getting there and away 123, Where to
                   stay 124, What to see and do 124

Chapter 7   **West Falkland**   **129**
                   Port Howard 129, Fox Bay and around 136, A circular
                   tour to the north of West Falkland 140, A circular tour
                   from Port Howard to Hill Cove, Main Point and Turkey
                   Rocks 141, Gladstone Bay 144

Chapter 8   **Pebble Island**   **145**
                   History 145, Getting there and away 147, Where to
                   stay 147, What to see and do 148

Chapter 9   **Saunders Island and Keppel Island**   **156**
                   Saunders Island 156, Keppel Island 163

Chapter 10   **Carcass Island, West Point Island and New Island**   **165**
                   Carcass Island 165, West Point Island 171,
                   New Island 173

Chapter 11   **Weddell, Staats and Beaver islands**   **179**
                   Weddell Island 179, Staats and Beaver islands 182

Appendix 1   **Selected Flora and Fauna**   **184**

Appendix 2   **Further Information**   **188**

Index   **195**

Index of Advertisers   **199**

LIST OF MAPS

Bleaker Island	116	Port Howard	132
Carcass Island	166	Saunders and Keppel islands	157
East Falkland, North	96	Sea Lion Island	123
East Falkland, South	111	Stanley	68
Falkland Islands	1st colour section	Stanley area	84
Falkland Islands location	4	Weddell, Staats and Beaver	
Kidney Island	90	islands	180
New Island	174	West Falkland	130
Pebble Island	146	West Point Island	171

═══	Main road	⚑	Cemetery
══	Minor road	⚑	Golf course
--⛴--	Ferry route (vehicular)	✝	Place of worship
✈	Airport	⬤	Hut
✛	Car park	※	Lighthouse
ℤ	Tourist information office	⚓	Shipwreck
♨	Museum/art gallery	℺	Communications dish
⊞	Important/historic building	➤	Bird colony
$	Bank/ATM	▲	Summit (height in metres)
⊠	Post office		Out of bounds/restricted area
⊞	Hospital		Wood
⬥	Statue/monument		Urban park
⚘	Sports facility		Beach

PRICE CODES Throughout this guide we have used price codes to indicate the cost of those places to stay and eat listed in the guide.

Accommodation price codes Average price of a double room per night including breakfast.

££££	Expensive	£120+
£££	Moderately expensive	£80–120
££	Moderate	£30–80
£	Inexpensive	< £30

Restaurant price codes Average price of a main course, per person exclusive of drinks.

££££	Expensive	£20+
£££	Moderately expensive	£15–20
££	Moderate	£10–15
£	Inexpensive	< £10

MAPS

Keys and symbols Maps include alphabetical keys covering the locations of those places to stay, eat or drink that are featured in the book. Note that regional maps may not show all hotels and restaurants in the area: other establishments may be located in settlements shown on the map.

Grids and grid references The Stanley map uses gridlines to allow easy location of sites. Map grid references are listed in square brackets after the name of the place or site of interest in the text, with page number followed by grid number, eg: [68 B2].

Introduction

The Falkland Islands are situated between latitude 51° and 53°S and longitude 57° and 62°W in the South Atlantic, some 300 miles to the east of southern Argentina. There are two large islands, East and West Falkland, and over 700 smaller islands, which combine to create a total land area of 4,700 square miles (12,173km²). Most of the islands' population of over 3,400 now live in Stanley, the islands' capital. The remainder are spread over East and West Falkland and 12 of the smaller islands. Stanley has grown considerably since my first visit with new houses now east and west of the original town and more being built as I write. However, the relaxed pace of life is still the same, even if the smell of peat smoke does not linger over the town as it did in the past. Away from Stanley the drop in wool prices has led to a steady increase in the numbers of islanders leaving the *camp* and moving to work in the capital, although there is still very much a community feel there.

The islands hit the international headlines when Argentina invaded in April 1982, and the subsequent recapture by the British Forces raised the Falklands' profile in the world at large. A fledgling tourist industry took advantage of this post-war interest to offer holidays to these wild and beautiful places. The numbers of cruise ships visiting is still increasing, enabling more visitors to reach this isolated archipelago. Income generated by the advent of the fishing industry and tourism has increased the standard of living, thus encouraging more to make the islands their home.

Stanley and New Island are at opposing extremes, east and west, 148 miles (238km) apart. The coastline is highly indented with many rocky headlands and sandy beaches. Large inland bodies of water are absent but there are many small lakes and pools. Mount Usborne at 2,312ft (705m) in the Wickham Heights range on East Falkland is the highest point on the islands. Standing on the hilltops gives one a feeling of being on top of the world as the Falklands are laid out at one's feet. The amazing clarity of light in these islands never ceases to amaze me.

Natural woodland is not a feature of the islands, the only trees having been introduced around the settlements. Low grasses, ferns and shrubs provide the most typical ground cover, with a fringe of tussac grass around the coast away from any grazing animals.

Geographical isolation has limited the numbers of animals that have reached the islands by their own means and has restricted the birdlife to long-distance migrants and strong fliers. The flora of the Falklands is equally restricted, although isolation has created a number of endemic species and subspecies. Five species of penguin breed around the coasts, making this one of the best places in the world to observe this family. The prospect of seeing elephant seals, killer whales and penguins attracts many visitors to the islands. The Falklands, although not as rich in species of flora and fauna as nearby South America, offer an abundance of spectacular wildlife to gratify humankind's continuing fascination with nature. Sitting quietly not far from a penguin colony and watching them come out to see you is a magical and memorable experience. Every time I leave the islands I realise I have taken yet more photos of the scenery and wildlife.

The Falkland Islands are one of those magical places in the world that capture the imagination, and although the weather is not always clement, the overriding memory is of blue sea, blue sky, teeming wildlife and *smoko* as soon as you get back indoors.

Part One

GENERAL INFORMATION

Location Between latitude 51° and 53°S and longitude 57° and 62°W in the South Atlantic

Area 4,700 square miles

Capital Stanley

Population 3,662 (2021 census), plus around 1,400 military personnel and civilian contractors

Status Dependent territory of the United Kingdom

Executive authority His Majesty King Charles III, represented by the governor

Flag Blue, with Union Jack in the top left-hand corner and a white shield containing the coat of arms in the centre of the distal half

National anthem 'God Save the King'

Language English

Religion Predominantly Christian

Main industries Fishing, tourism, wool production

Currency Falkland Islands pound (equivalent to and interchangeable with GB pound)

Exchange Rate US$1 = £0.76, €1 = £0.85 (August 2024)

Time 3 hours behind GMT (4 hours out in parts of *camp*)

International dialling code +500

Electricity supply 240V using three-pin UK-type plugs

1

Background Information

GEOLOGY AND GEOGRAPHY

The islands were created by folding layers of rock which were uplifted as a result of tectonic plate movements during the Palaeozoic and Mesozoic eras. The most obvious results are the three principal mountain ranges, all in the northern half of the islands. On East Falkland, Wickham Heights run from east to west, culminating in the highest point in the islands, Mount Usborne (2,312ft/705m). This range is very rugged; many peaks are tipped with jagged outcrops and many stone runs occur along the slopes. On West Falkland the other two ranges are more rounded, stone runs being comparatively rare. Byron Heights run from east to west, while the Hornby Mountains run almost north–south parallel to Falkland Sound, the channel between East and West Falkland. Mount Adam, the second-highest point on the islands, reaches 2,297ft (700m) in the Hornby Mountains. The greatest part of the islands is composed of Palaeozoic sedimentary rocks incorporating quartzite, sandstone and shale. Lafonia, the southern part of East Falkland, is composed of Mesozoic sandstone and shale. These younger rocks have created a landscape that is the most low-lying in the islands, as its greatest elevation is only 196ft (60m). Some of the rocks contain large numbers of fossils indicating that shallow warm seas must have covered the area at some point in its past. *Trilobites, brachiopods* and *crinoids* are among the many species of fossil that have been found.

Higher mountains show some signs of localised glaciation in certain areas over 2,000ft (600m). When flying over these areas it is possible to see small corries containing lakes, which probably indicate glacial action. The formation of stone runs has been linked to some form of periglacial activity. The actual mechanism by which these grey rivers of stone were formed is not fully understood. They can run for several miles downhill from the jagged peaks. Some of those on the lowest slopes are steadily disappearing under the encroaching undergrowth, whereas those on higher ground stand out against the local vegetation. It is generally agreed that mud created by the breakdown of the softer rocks carried these hard quartzite boulders down the hill from their point of origin by a process called solifluction, the gradual movement of mud or soil down a slope. It is also thought that freeze-thaw action had some impact upon this process. Suffice to say, there are still several proposed theories for the formation of stone runs, in particular the layering that remains constant whatever the angle of the slope.

There are many small ponds and lakes on the islands. Away from the coast they tend to be shallow, peaty pools, formed by localised subsidence in the peat or by erosion hollows filling with water, some of which are connected to the sea via small streams. There are three major rivers on the Falkland Islands: the San Carlos River on East Falkland, and the Warrah and Chartres rivers on West Falkland. Some bodies of water have been created by sand having been blown across the mouth of a

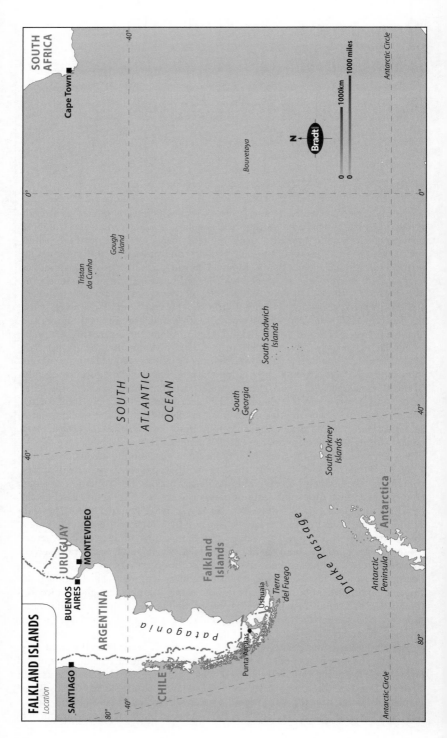

FALKLAND ISLANDS
Location

river or inlet thus forming a lagoon or lake. The islands' jagged coastline favours the formation of these features. Rocky headlands protect the many sheltered harbours around the archipelago, often with long sandy beaches on the innermost part of these inlets.

The coastline varies from the low-lying shores of Lafonia and Port Salvador on East Falkland to the high cliffs and rocky bluffs that typify the outer reaches of West Falkland and West Point Island, where the cliffs can rise to 700ft (213m).

Away from the Stanley area it is possible to travel for many miles without seeing any houses or other artificial structures apart from fences and tracks. The rolling landscape with its relatively uniform flora creates a unique habitat.

CLIMATE

The paramount climatic feature of the Falkland Islands is wind. The islands are usually described as having an oceanic climate dominated by the prevailing westerlies. Footage of the events of April, May and June 1982, showing the military in action in snow and ice, have resulted in a public perception that the islands are snow-covered throughout the year, as though comparable with the Antarctic. In fact, the islands have a rather narrow temperature range from 19°C in January to 2°C in July, with an average annual mean temperature of 6°C. Very warm days are rare during a Falkland summer, although the islands enjoy more sunshine hours than the south of Britain. The general lack of pollution and dust in the atmosphere increases the penetration of ultraviolet rays, so a high-factor suncream is an essential part of any visitor's travel pack. The sea temperature varies very little during the year on average, with a range of between 6°C and 7°C.

The islands lie just to the north of the main belt of depressions, which pass through the Drake Passage between the Antarctic and the tip of South America. These continually moving air masses cause frequent changes in the islands' weather. Forecasting is very difficult on the Falkland Islands as the proximity of the South American continent modifies the effect of each weather system locally. The Falklands' saying of, 'if you don't like the weather, wait 15 minutes', can often hold true. Visitors to the islands have to be prepared for sudden changes in weather and local variations; it is possible to be in sunshine on one island and for it to be wet and windy only a few miles away.

The predominantly westerly winds have created a noticeable difference between the western and eastern halves of the islands. Those islands out to the west tend to be drier and have more sunshine hours than those to the east. Stanley and Port Howard are two of the wettest places on the islands, having in the region of 25 inches (630mm) of rain per year, whereas West Point Island on the western side of the islands has an annual rainfall of 17 inches (431mm). This rainfall affects the flora of the islands in that tussac grass and ferns do not grow as well in the west as they do in the wetter east. There is a fairly even level of precipitation throughout the year. In summer months the wind dries the ground, whereas the slightly calmer conditions in the winter result in water lying on the ground for longer periods of time. The average wind speed for the year is 16 knots. Calm days are rare in the summer months and are infrequent in wintertime. Fog is therefore quite uncommon in the islands, but can occur in any season.

Falkland winters are comparable with those in southern Britain in terms of average temperature, and although snowfall occurs most years, it does not often lie on the ground for any length of time. The one factor that differs from southern Britain is that the Falklands' winters are longer and the summers shorter. There are records of snow in all months of the year, but any such snowfall is usually brief and generally localised, often falling on the peaks over 2,000ft (600m).

HISTORY

DISCOVERY AND EXPLORATION Quite when the Falkland Islands were first discovered is rather unclear. A group of islands roughly in the area now occupied by the Falklands were drawn on maps from the early 16th century. It is possible that Italian explorer Amerigo Vespucci may well have seen them in 1502, or that one of the ships' companies participating in Fernando de Magellan's Spanish expedition, on board the *San Antonio,* may well have seen the islands after deserting. They are thought to have given the islands the name Sanson, from an abbreviation of the ship's name. The islands were included on maps of South America from 1507, although their number and exact locations varied greatly from map to map. The Portuguese cartographer Pedro Reinel drew one of these early maps in c1521–22. The name most commonly used by cartographers during the mid 1500s was the Sanson Islands, although it would appear that very few ships actually saw the islands during this period.

The first British claim to the discovery of the islands was on 14 August 1592 by Captain John Davis of the *Desire*, which was part of Thomas Cavendish's second expedition. Two years later Sir Richard Hawkins thought he had found the islands and named them Hawkins Maydenlande after himself and Queen Elizabeth I of England. Yet another name for the islands came about after a sighting of them in 1598 by the Dutch Captain Sebald de Weert, who promptly called the islands the Sebaldines. This probably accounts for the name Sibbel de Wards, given to the islands by William Dampier who reached Falkland in 1684 with John Cook and Ambrose Cowley. Dampier gave remarkably accurate bearings for the islands. Ambrose Cowley's version was somewhat different and invented the legend of Pepys Island, named after the famous English 17th-century diarist and secretary to the Admiralty. Generations of mariners sought this archipelago in vain, handicapped by the inaccurate descriptions and bearings supplied by hopeful explorers.

EARLY SOVEREIGNTY DISPUTES It has been suggested that humans had reached the islands long before the arrival of the first Europeans. The discovery of the presence of large fox-like animals, now known as the *warrah*, by John Strong in West Falkland in 1690 raises some unanswered questions. These creatures, now extinct, were closely related to the Fuegian fox of South America. It is possible that the Yaghan indigenous peoples might have brought a domesticated fox to the islands for hunting purposes. The presence of the warrah on Falkland remains a mystery but could well be a clue as to who first discovered the islands.

Captain John Strong of the sloop *Welfare* made the first landing on the Falkland Islands in 1690. He landed at Port Howard on West Falkland in an archipelago known as Hawkins Maiden Land. His claim to fame was naming Falkland Sound, the strait between East and West Falkland, in honour of Viscount Falkland, the Treasurer of the English Navy. This landing is regarded as crucial by the Falkland Islands Government in the long-running dispute over sovereignty. Other ships reached the islands at the end of the 17th and the beginning of the 18th centuries. William Dampier (see above) circumnavigated the islands in 1696, and in 1701 Captain Beauchene discovered the island which now bears his name. The name Falkland being applied to the whole archipelago was first noted in Captain Woods Rogers' account of his exploration of the islands during 1708. Other expeditions that reached the Falklands included one by Lord Anson in 1740, when he suggested using the islands as a base for further exploration of the Pacific Ocean. He then drew up a plan to explore Falkland and its surrounding seas in the hope of locating Pepys Island. It appears that the Spanish rejected this plan when it was put before them, as it could have caused instability in the region. The Spanish claim to the area came as a result of the decision by the Spanish Pope Alexander VI in 1494 to draw a line north to south down the Atlantic, one hundred leagues west of the Azores. He was responding to the question of ownership of the recently discovered New World. He decided that everything to the west of this imaginary line, which included the Falklands, would belong to Spain; everything to the east would be Portuguese. Britain disagreed with this edict, which was arguably the motive for the subsequent voyages of the English explorers Drake, Raleigh and Cavendish.

Another major event in the islands' history was the arrival of the French navigator Louis-Antoine de Bougainville in East Falkland on 5 April 1764. He had left his base at St Malo in northern France in 1763 with the aim of establishing a colony at Port Louis. The French name for the islands, Îles Malouines, derives from the name St Malo (as does the Argentinian name Islas Malvinas), and was first coined by the French geographer De L'Isle in the late 1710s to early 1720s.

A further English expedition, under the command of Commodore John Byron, set off to search for the mythical Pepys Island and to explore the Falkland Islands, reaching the archipelago in mid-January 1765. They made their base at Port Egmont on Saunders Island in the northwest of the islands before starting to survey the coastline, leaving Captain John McBride to create a proper settlement there on 8 January 1766. In the interim Spain offered to purchase the settlement from the French in an attempt to avoid giving the British the wrong impression regarding sovereignty. Bougainville, having returned to Europe to negotiate terms with the Spanish Court, agreed to transfer ownership to the Spanish in return for £25,000. Meanwhile, on 4 December 1766, the British ascertained the French presence at Port Louis and informed the French that they had had a colony at Port Egmont since 1765. The transfer of the settlement at Port Louis from Bougainville to a Spanish Governor, Don Felipe Ruiz Puente, took place on 1 April 1767. Two years later English and Spanish ships met while undertaking surveying work. Each regarded the other as being there unlawfully; letters to this effect were exchanged between the two vessels.

In 1770 a Spanish force, commanded by Don Juan Ignacio de Madariaga, arrived at Port Egmont and occasioned another exchange of letters. The officer in charge of the garrison on Saunders Island, Captain Hunt, stated categorically that the Falkland Islands belonged to Britain. The British forces were removed from Port Egmont when the Spanish returned with a much larger force on 14 July 1770. It took the threat of war – after lengthy negotiations – to get an agreement on 22 January 1771, whereby the Spanish gave Port Egmont back to the British. The surrender took place at Port Egmont on 15 September 1771 with Captain Scott, the commander of the frigate *Juno*, representing the British. The British withdrew from the islands in 1774, leaving behind a flag and a plaque representing their claim to ownership. Argentina subsequently claimed that the British withdrawal was the consequence of a secret deal within the treaty of 1771. The Spanish evacuation of the islands took place in two stages as Spain progressively lost control of its colonies. Spanish troops remained at Port Louis, known then as Port Soledad, until 1806, when the governor Juan Crisostomo Martinez departed, leaving behind a plaque claiming sovereignty for Spain. The Spanish commander of Port Louis, who was based in Montevideo at that time, withdrew the remaining Spanish settlers in 1811.

In the early part of the 19th century, ships of many nationalities called in at the Falkland Islands. Some, mainly whalers and sealers, used the islands as their base. Argentina, having gained its independence from Spain in 1816, claimed sovereignty over the Falkland Islands in 1820 and dispatched David Jewett, commander of the *Heroina*, to assert their ownership, although there is little written evidence of this or of his being given the title of governor. Don Jorge Pacheco, an associate of Louis Vernet, was granted land in the Falklands by the United Provinces Government in 1823. Don Pablo Areguati, an employee of Don Jorge Pacheco, became the unpaid *comandante* of Port Louis. Vernet and Pacheco's first attempt at colonisation lasted less than a year, but Vernet was determined to be more successful with his second expedition in 1826. By 1828 he had been given permission to form a colony and had been granted all of East Falkland together with comprehensive fishing and sealing rights. A small settlement was well established at Port Louis by the time Vernet became unpaid Comandante Politico y Militar in 1829. This appointment was countersigned by the British consul at that time, but his appointment caused Britain to protest to Argentina over what was viewed as an Argentinian position of authority on British Crown land. Vernet ordered the arrest of three American schooners for supposed illegal sealing in 1829.

The discovery of the arrests of these ships only reached the United States when one of the boats, the *Breakwater*, escaped and carried the news back home. Another of the ships, the *Superior*, was released, but the captain of the third ship, the *Harriet*, was taken for trial in Buenos Aires. The US consul in Buenos Aires arranged for the dispatch of the corvette USS *Lexington* under Commander Silas Duncan, which arrived on 28 December 1831, destroying the settlement at Port Soledad and declaring the islands to be free of any government. The man left in charge by Vernet, Matthew Brisbane, was arrested and taken to Montevideo. Mutineers murdered the new governor, Don Juan Esteban Mestivier, sent to the islands by Argentina in 1832, shortly after he took up his appointment. The officer in charge of the Argentinian warship *Sarandi*, Don José María Pinedo, was then in command of the settlement until the arrival of the British in 1832. On 20 December the British reached Port Egmont and posted a notice of possession, then moved on to Port Soledad to take control of the islands on 2 January 1833. The British commander, Captain Onslow, gave Pinedo written notice that he was exercising British sovereign rights, would be raising the British flag the next day and that Pinedo was expected to lower the Argentinian flag and leave immediately. Pinedo refused to comply with these demands. Nonetheless, the Argentinian flag was removed the next day and presented to him by the British before he left the islands with all his troops.

By the time Matthew Brisbane returned to the islands in April 1833, the settlement had been left in the hands of William Dickson, who had been Vernet's bookkeeper. Brisbane and Dickson were murdered during a mutiny by a group of *gauchos* – the South American cowboys brought to the islands to manage the cattle imported to the islands from South America – in August 1833. The surviving settlers managed to escape from the settlement and live on some of the small islands offshore until their rescue by the sealer *Hopeful* in October 1833, under the command of Lieutenant Rea, and by HMS *Challenger* in January 1834. The gauchos were arrested and taken for trial in England but were released and returned to Montevideo. Lieutenant Henry Smith, the first officer of *Challenger,* and a ship's crew were left in charge of Port Louis.

BRITISH COLONISATION The decision of The Colonial Land and Emigration Commissioners that the Falkland Islands were suitable for colonisation in 1840 heralded the arrival of the first settlers from Britain. The first British Governor, Richard Moody (page 11), initially used Port Louis as his base. In 1842 he was instructed by Lord Stanley, the British Secretary of State, to investigate the potential of the Port William area as a location for a new town on the islands. The survey work was done from the *Erebus* and the *Terror*, two ships taking part in the Ross Expedition. Captain Ross advised that Port William would make a good deep-water anchorage for naval vessels and that the shores of Port Jackson would be ideally suited for the new settlement. It had everything they needed: shelter, fresh water, a natural harbour and a plentiful supply of peat. The work of creating the new town was completed in just under a year on 18 July 1845. The capital of the islands was named Port Stanley in honour of the current Secretary of State. Not everyone was in favour of this site; one well-known inhabitant, J W Whitington, is quoted as saying:

> ...of all the miserable bog holes, I believe that Mr Moody has selected one of the worst for the site for his town.

Despite this opposition the population increased rapidly, to the extent that some 200 residents were present in 1849.

There was a dramatic increase in the number of ships calling into the islands, and Port Stanley in particular, from the mid 1850s, the time of the Californian Gold Rush. These ships had been trying to round Cape Horn but were forced to retreat to the islands for repair after being battered by the severe weather around the Cape. The original settlers were soon making a good living as shipwrights or in supplying provisions for these stricken vessels. Many of these boats were condemned on the islands and ended their days as floating warehouses in Port Stanley Harbour, which became one of the busiest ports in the world during the second half of the 19th century. This boom lasted until the increasingly reliable steamships began to take over in the late 1890s, the final blow being the completion of the Panama Canal in the early 1900s, which drastically reduced the number of boats needing to call into the islands for repair. However, as a consequence of this boom, the population of the Falkland Islands numbered 1,510 in 1881.

ECONOMIC EXPLOITATION Changes were also occurring on the land in *camp* at this time, although not at such a great rate as in Port Stanley. The first attempt at sheep farming was made on East Falkland in about 1840. The only other stock were large numbers of cattle roaming wild. A merchant from Montevideo, Samuel Lafone, signed a contract with the Falkland Islands Government in 1846 to take charge of all the wild cattle in East Falkland. He also bought up all the land south of Darwin that is now called Lafonia, a derivation of his name. The Falkland Islands Company, which had been set up by Royal Charter in 1851, bought out Lafone and set up a trading company, which was soon to become the largest owner of livestock on the islands. West Falkland was opened to settlers in 1867 and, only one year later, all available land was taken up for sheep farming. The larger, outer islands were the next to be taken over by the sheep farmers. The Falkland Islands Company continued to expand so that by 1880 the company had 100,000 sheep and several thousand cattle on East Falkland alone. (The company continues to exist although it sold the majority of its land in 1991 to the Falkland Islands Government, who set up Falkland Landholdings Limited to run its farms.)

In the latter years of the 19th and the early 20th centuries attempts were made to export frozen sheep carcasses. Prior to this time sheep had been exported live and surplus stock was converted into fat for the soap, candle and lubricant industries.

At first the frozen mutton was deemed to be of insufficient standard for the European market, but in 1910 two meat canneries were set up on East Falkland. The good British market stimulated trade during World War I and finance was offered to set up a freezer in the islands at Ajax Bay on East Falkland. This building operated for just two seasons before closing down. High wool prices led to a demand for Falkland Islands' fleeces, which were brought in from the outlying farms before being shipped to the northern hemisphere. (Wool still remains the main farm export from the islands.)

Whale oil is recorded as having been shipped back from the islands from as early as the late 1700s. Whalers sailing from North America were based in West Falkland when this area became the principal region to hunt southern right whale and sperm whale. It is thought that oil was taken from elephant seals, fur seals and southern sea lions when there was a shortage of whales. It is not believed that many whales were caught in these waters at that time, but the islands provided the ideal base to obtain provisions. Penguin and albatross eggs and the abundance of geese, along with a plentiful supply of fresh water, were all within easy reach of sheltered harbours. Livestock was kept on some islands, thus creating a valuable food source that could be drawn upon between expeditions. There was massive hunting of fur seals for their skins by 1784 when one vessel was reported to be carrying 13,000 pelts. This trade tailed off later in the century, probably as a result of excessive hunting, although it was not completely banned until 1921 following the protective legislation created by the Falkland Islands Government in 1881. Elephant seals were culled for their oil from the late 1700s until the early 1800s but had become virtually extinct on the islands by the late 19th century, only starting to breed again in the early 1900s. Fur seal populations had also been almost eliminated by the late 1850s, and attention was switched to the much more common southern sea lions. These animals were skinned and rendered for their oil until the population became so diminished that the operation became uneconomical. There were three further attempts at commercial sealing on the islands during the 20th century but all failed due to the scarcity of seals.

The dearth of seals gave rise to the penguin oil industry in the early 1860s. Rockhopper penguins and occasionally gentoo penguins were the species taken. This activity reached a peak in 1864, when no fewer than seven vessels were registered locally to catch penguins. The actual number of birds taken is not recorded but between 1864 and 1866 some 63,000 gallons of penguin oil was shipped out of Port Stanley. At the time it was reckoned that eight rockhopper penguins yielded one gallon of oil; gentoo penguins being slightly larger would have yielded a little more. It has been estimated that more than half a million birds were killed during this period. The industry began to decline, although there was a slight recovery in the later 1870s, until its final demise in c1880.

Some 50 years later, the southern oceans witnessed the swift expansion of the whaling industry. New Island, to the southwest of the archipelago, became the centre of operations during its brief lifespan on the islands. The whaling boats operating out of New Island doubled up as mail and passenger boats in the initial phases of the industry before being replaced by a purpose-bought ship. The greater profits being realised further south in the Antarctic saw the closing and removal of the whaling station to South Georgia only just over ten years after it opened.

The activities of these whalers and the export of wool from Port Stanley brought about an escalation in shipping activity around the islands, as imports and exports increased.

BRITISH MILITARY PRESENCE Throughout the history of the islands there has been a strong connection between the British military and the Falklands. The first British governor of the islands, Richard Moody, was a Royal Engineer and his expeditionary force was composed of men from the Royal Sappers and Miners Regiment. The British Government proposed that a local force be set up using civilians; Governor Moody thus created what he called 'the Militia Force of the Falkland Islands', which consisted of a mounted corps, an artillery corps and two infantry platoons. Once the Sappers and Miners had completed their tour of duty on the islands in 1849, a new force was needed to protect the islands. A group of 30 married Chelsea Pensioners were sent out to become settlers and to act as the local police force the next year. Some of the houses they brought with them are still standing in Stanley. What were known locally as the 'Stanley Volunteers' were set up in 1854 only to be disbanded two years later and replaced with civilian constables. In 1858 a group of 35 marines, to be called the Falkland Islands Garrison Company, arrived to take over from the pensioners. These in turn were replaced in 1863 by a new detachment of marines. In 1892, a steamer carrying some 200 armed men involved in the civil war in Chile arrived in Port William for repairs. Sir Roger Goldsworthy, the governor at that time, was concerned about the security of the islands so formed a volunteer force that became known as the Falkland Island Volunteers. This force became the Falkland Islands Defence Force in 1919 and still exists to this day. These volunteers saw active service during the Battle of the Falklands in World War I (see below) and manned watch posts on the islands during World War II, with some leaving the islands to fight with the British Forces.

WORLD WARS I AND II The strategic value of the islands in the South Atlantic became apparent during World War I. Shortly after the declaration of war in the autumn of 1914 the British Rear Admiral Sir Christopher Cradock visited Port Stanley with his squadron of ships, after having chased three German cruisers, *Leipzig*, *Dresden* and *Nürnberg*, near the Magellan Straits. On 1 November 1914 the German cruisers were sighted off the Chilean coast along with the *Gneisenau* and *Scharnhorst*. The two squadrons then engaged in battle. Cradock's flagship HMS *Good Hope* and HMS *Monmouth* were sunk with all hands and the rest of the fleet driven off. Prior to this event Vice Admiral Frederick Sturdee had set sail from England on HMS *Invincible* with a fleet of cruisers and instructions to defeat the German squadron under Vice Admiral Graf Von Spee. Sturdee's fleet reached Falkland waters on 12 November 1914. On 8 December 1914 two of Von Spee's ships, the *Gneisenau* and the *Nürnberg*, were sighted near Port Stanley where Sturdee's ships lay at anchor. Some of the British fleet opened fire but the range was too great. The two German ships rejoined the rest of their squadron and headed east away from the islands. The British fleet set sail and caught up with the rearguard of the Germans by early afternoon. The ferocious Battle of the Falklands ensued, the outcome of which was that almost all of the German squadron, apart from the *Dresden*, was sunk with the loss of 2,000 lives. This victory gave Britain control of the ocean routes around Cape Horn and 8 December lives on as a public holiday in the islands.

The most famous incident during World War II near the islands was the Battle of the River Plate. At the start of the war HMS *Ajax* and HMS *Exeter* were patrolling Falkland waters. With HMS *Achilles*, under the command of Rear Admiral Harwood, they made for the River Plate estuary in December 1939. The British ships were outgunned by the German pocket battleship *Graf Spee* during the Battle of the River Plate, but still managed to trap it in the neutral port of Montevideo where it was later scuttled. The British fleet, including the badly damaged HMS *Exeter*, returned to Port Stanley. The South Atlantic routes remained in British control. Throughout World War II the Falkland Islands Defence Force manned shore batteries and observation posts around the islands. A battalion of the 11th West Yorkshire Regiment supplemented these men in 1942 and were succeeded by a detachment of Royal Scots, who were the garrison force until the end of the war. The Royal Navy presence in the islands was maintained by HMS *Poursuivant*, which acted as the Naval Office in Port Stanley.

Argentina, in common with so many other countries, experienced the growth of nationalist movements between the two world wars. The nationalists envisaged the Falkland Islands as belonging to Argentina. Although nationalist pride was superseded by the events of World War II, this issue regained significance after 1945.

FURTHER SOVEREIGNTY DISPUTES Discussions about the islands' sovereignty continued through the 1960s. The islands were discussed by a United Nations committee on decolonisation in 1964. The Argentinian claim was based on the papal bulls of the 15th century, while the British position rested on having the first recorded landing on the Falkland Islands in 1690 and the 'open, continuous effective possession, occupation and administration' of the islands since 1833. Britain was resolved that it would grant the Falkland Islanders self-determination as recognised in the United Nations Charter. Britain claimed that Argentinian control would create a colony rather than remove one. A year later the United Nations general assembly agreed a resolution inviting Britain and Argentina to hold discussions aimed at a peaceful solution to the dispute – talks that would continue until just a few months before the Argentinian invasion. This high level of international diplomatic activity led to a series of incidents on the islands. The first of these, on 8 September 1964, saw a light aircraft circle Stanley before landing on the racecourse. The pilot jumped out of his plane, planted an Argentinian flag, and handed a letter stating Argentinian sovereignty over the islands to one of the islanders before hopping back in his plane and flying off again.

More dramatic was the 1966 hijacking of a DC4 on an internal flight in Argentina by 20 nationalists calling themselves the Condors. The plane flew up Stanley Harbour before landing on the racecourse, missing the grandstand but hitting some telegraph poles and then sinking into the mud. The nationalists took four hostages before being surrounded by the local defence force accompanied by the only six marines on the islands. They vowed never to surrender but 32 hours later, after a cold night, they gave themselves up to the local priest and were moved to the local church. The heavy swell off Mengeary Point prevented their embarkation on to an Argentinian naval ship in the first instance, but they were eventually taken back to Argentina where nominal prison sentences awaited them. It later turned out that this had been the first of three planes planning to land on the islands. The other planes, with reinforcements and press, were grounded when the President of Argentina was informed of the scheme and temporarily banned all civilian flights.

Later that year one other landing took place, which was to remain a secret for many years. A small detachment of Argentinian marines landed via submarine near Stanley for a few hours over a period of nights. Their remit was to explore potential landing beaches near the capital. The second officer on board, Juan José Lombardo, rose through the ranks to become Chief of Naval Operations and as such was the man responsible for planning the 1982 invasion by Argentina. In November 1968, the Argentinian press sponsored a plane to reach the islands, but the scheme ended in a crash landing on the road to Eliza Cove, south of Stanley. The three Argentinians on board wanted to attract publicity for their cause during the visit to the islands of Lord Chalfont, the Minister of State at the Foreign and Commonwealth Office. As the plane flew over he was talking at a public meeting, called to allay islanders' fears after news had leaked that Britain was negotiating sovereignty with Argentina.

Matters were a little quieter until 1976, when a British research ship, the *Shackleton*, was fired upon by an Argentinian gunboat near Stanley, and an illegal military base was set up on Southern Thule, a dependency of the Falkland Islands situated to the south of South Georgia. Despite these incidents, trade with Argentina continued to expand. The only way to reach the islands by air was via South America, departing from Comodoro Rivadava in Argentina. It was possible to reach the islands by cargo ship from Britain, but this took several weeks of sailing through what could be very rough seas.

THE FALKLANDS WAR 1982 As far as the general public were aware, the first incident of the 1982 war was the landing on South Georgia of an Argentine scrap-metal merchant accompanied by some military personnel on 18 March. It was revealed later that concerns about a possible invasion had been raised in the weeks prior to this event. Britain called for the removal of the military men with little response from Argentina. On 26 March the head of the military junta in Argentina, General Galtieri, decided to invade the islands. The first land forces reached the islands on 2 April and took control of Stanley after a short battle with the Royal Marines garrisoned on the islands. These soldiers and the governor were taken off the islands and flown to Montevideo.

Over the next few days, Argentinian troops consolidated their positions on the islands, also landing on South Georgia and the South Sandwich Islands. The United Nations passed Resolution 502 calling for the cessation of all hostilities, the withdrawal of Argentinian troops from the islands and the resumption of talks between Argentina and Britain. In London, the House of Commons was convened at an emergency session on 3 April and informed that a task force would be sent to liberate the islands. The first British Navy ships left the following week for the South Atlantic, and Britain declared a 200-mile exclusion zone around the Falklands.

The American Secretary of State, Alexander Haig, began shuttle mediation between the two countries and Argentina landed over 10,000 troops on the islands. In Europe, the European Economic Community supported Britain by approving trade sanctions against Argentina on 10 April. The main task force, under the command of Rear Admiral Sandy Woodward, departed from Ascension Island. Wideawake Airfield on Ascension was the busiest airport in the world on 16 April. Alexander Haig's efforts in mediation eventually failed on 17 April, and five days later the British Government advised all British nationals to leave Argentina. In late April many more ships headed towards the South Atlantic carrying troops and the first action took place involving British forces. After several exploratory landings, the Royal Marines and the SAS retook South Georgia on 25 April. At the end of April, President Ronald Reagan of the United States declared his country's support for the British and enforced trade sanctions against Argentina.

Hostilities increased on 1 May when members of the SAS and SBS landed reconnaissance forces on the Falkland Islands for the first time and Stanley airfield was bombed by a Vulcan bomber based on Ascension Island. This was followed by a naval bombardment and Sea Harrier attack on Argentinian installations at Stanley and Goose Green. The first aerial combats took place that day when two

Argentinian planes were shot down and two others damaged without any British losses. These events were to be overshadowed a few days later when the Argentinian warship, *General Belgrano*, was sunk by torpedoes fired from the submarine HMS *Conqueror* on 2 May and an Exocet missile hit the British Warship HMS *Sheffield* on 4 May. Naval bombardment and air battles began to occur more regularly as the British forces neared the islands. 'Active Service' – full-time service in the forces – was declared on 14 May. That night Pebble Island was raided by the SAS, which successfully destroyed 11 Argentinian aircraft on the ground. Political activity continued until 19 May when the United Nations peace initiative foundered, and on the same day the British Cabinet gave approval for the task force to land.

The night of 21–22 May witnessed the landing of the British Task Force, under the command of Major General Jeremy Moore, on the western side of East Falkland at San Carlos Water. Several of the British warships were damaged or, in the case of the *Ardent*, sunk, but the land forces were able to get ashore relatively unscathed. Over the next two days attacks continued on the warships in Falkland Sound and San Carlos Water while the bridgehead was consolidated. Some 5,000 men were entrenched on East Falkland by dawn on 24 May. The second parachute regiment began their advance on Goose Green on 26 May, eventually attacking that settlement and Darwin on 28 May. Despite being outnumbered two to one, the soldiers of the parachute regiment were victorious at a critical stage of the war.

It was during this fighting that Lieutenant Colonel 'H' Jones was killed. Colonel 'H' Jones was the commanding officer of the second parachute regiment which was in the forefront of the battle of Goose Green. His forces were pinned down at the bottom of a slight valley by gunfire from the Argentinians dug-in at the crest of the next hill. Under covering fire, with very little in the way of shelter, he attacked the Argentinian forces. His extreme bravery and that of his men saw the overrunning of the Argentinian forces occupying Goose Green. He was posthumously awarded the Victoria Cross in recognition of his bravery. During this period the British Task Force was being regularly attacked at sea, with losses including HMS *Coventry* and MV *Atlantic Conveyor*. The last few days in May saw the British troops advancing over East Falkland towards Stanley. Special forces had taken over Mount Kent so that by 31 May Stanley was surrounded.

In early June the British Government vetoed the Panamanian–Spanish ceasefire resolution at the United Nations Security Council and gave Argentina one last chance to withdraw from the Falklands. Some of the most dramatic images of the war came from the British landings at Bluff Cove. The attacks made by the Argentinian aircraft on the *Sir Galahad* and the *Sir Tristram* created scenes resembling Dante's inferno. Fifty men were killed on 8 June. The battles were fought closer to Stanley on 11 June, when fighting commenced on Mount Longdon, Mount Harriet, and the Two Sisters. HMS *Glamorgan* was hit by an Exocet missile while withdrawing to sea, after having supported these attacks with its heavy guns.

The fighting reached Wireless Ridge and Mount Tumbledown on 13 June. The capitulation of the forces of General Menendez, the Argentinian commander, meant that these were the last battles of the war. British forces were welcomed with open arms in Stanley later that day. Over the next few days some 10,254 Argentinian prisoners were brought into Stanley. The British forces established a headquarters at Government House and began the consolidation of the Stanley area. General Galtieri was removed as head of the military junta in Argentina on 17 June, to be replaced by General Bignone on 21 June, who announced that the ceasefire would be observed by all Argentinian forces. Britain formally declared an end to hostilities as soon as the South Sandwich Islands had been reoccupied on 20 June 1982.

POST-WAR TO PRESENT The aftermath of the war saw many changes on the islands, the greatest of which was the construction of Mount Pleasant Airport (MPA), later to become the main base for the British forces on the Falkland Islands. Stanley was very busy during the post-war years and the population quadrupled immediately after the ceasefire as most of the British troops came into town. The accommodation problem was initially eased by billeting troops on ships anchored in the harbour. Thereafter, three floating 'coastels' were imported to house all the forces involved in building the air base at Mount Pleasant and generally stationed on the islands. These coastels were anchored to the east of Stanley (page 71) and remained in use until MPA came into service in May 1985, only 14 months after construction had begun. Previously, aircraft had had to use the temporarily extended runway at Stanley Airport, from which it was possible to fly to Ascension Island on Hercules transport planes and then on to the UK. The need for a deep-water dock in Stanley was solved by the building of the Floating Interim Port and Storage System (FIPASS) in 1983–84, which still serves as the main quay for Stanley although it is due to be replaced in the near future. The Royal Navy constructed its own dock at Mare Harbour in the vicinity of the main military base at Mount Pleasant.

The garrison on the islands numbers about 1,400 servicemen and civilian contractors who are based at Mount Pleasant Airport. This has resulted in several changes within the local infrastructure owing to the creation of what is in effect a small town at the airport, the most obvious of which are the road linking MPA with Stanley and the King Edward VII Memorial Hospital (known as KEMH) in Stanley (page 78) – a joint civilian and military venture.

Although wool production had been the economic mainstay of the islands from the middle of the 1800s, by the last years of the 20th century humanmade fibres had made it difficult to get a good price for Falklands' wool. Another major effect on the islands' economy came in 1987, with the introduction of the Falkland Islands Interim Conservation and Management Zone (FICZ) on 1 February, to protect stocks against overfishing. Vessels that wished to fish inside this zone, which extends for 200 nautical miles around the islands, had to obtain licences from Stanley (page 17). Today the revenue from these licences averages £30.5 million (2022) each year, which has been used to support the islands' health, education and welfare systems as well as improving transport links.

By the end of the 20th century the islands had become self-supporting except in matters of defence. Roads have been built between most of the major settlements and there is now a regular ferry between East and West Falkland, dramatically cutting travel times between farms. A telecommunication network was installed in 1989, linking all the islands, and there are now international satellite communications, with mobile-phone networks also available in many areas around the islands. Stanley has grown considerably since the war, and continues to do so. A secondary school for children aged 11 to 16 was opened by Lord Shackleton in 1992 using the

INTER-ISLAND TRAVEL

Travel on the Falklands was revolutionised in 1948 when the first planes were introduced for inter-island travel. The de Havilland Beaver Seaplanes ran until they were gradually phased out by the Britten-Norman Islander aircraft that are used today by the Falkland Islands Government Air Service (FIGAS) for passengers, mail or freight. The name Beaver Pond can still be found on many islands and refers to planes not animals.

monies created by the fishing licences scheme. This also includes the community swimming pool and library.

Mineral exploration has had a great impact on the islands. Early seismic surveys by the British Geological Survey indicated the location of substantial hydrocarbon reserves near the islands. This resulted in further surveying; low oil prices caused a cessation of work for many years, but plans are now being advanced for more exploration with a view to extraction. Investigation of the potential for extracting gold and diamonds from the islands has been undertaken, but so far very little to encourage further investment has been seen.

There have been significant changes in the islands' way of life since 1982 as a result of greater incomes from the fishing and tourism industries. This has paid for improved infrastructure enabling better access around the islands via the new roads and ferry as well as the use of modern technology, ranging from wind turbines for energy to the arrival of mobile phones and the internet, both now widely available across the archipelago. The future is now much rosier for those growing up on the islands today.

GOVERNMENT AND POLITICS

The Falkland Islands are a dependent territory of the United Kingdom, the executive authority being vested in His Majesty King Charles III, who is represented by the governor. The present Falkland Island constitution came into force in 1985, under the terms of which eight councillors are elected from Stanley and four from the *camp* (the countryside; see page 23) every four years. There are no political parties; all councillors are elected as independents. The Legislative Council, made up of ten members, is chaired by the governor and sits when called, usually about four times a year. The Chief Executive and the Financial Secretary also attend meetings. This Council holds its meetings in public and is responsible for passing laws for the government of the islands subject to approval of His Majesty the King through the Secretary of State for Foreign Affairs. Three of the legislative councillors are annually elected by their peers to serve on the Executive Council presided over by the governor. This Executive Council, which advises the governor, also includes the two ex-officio members, the Chief Executive and the Financial Secretary. These meetings are held monthly and may also be attended by the Commander of the British forces in the Falkland Islands and the Attorney General, who also attend the meeting of the Legislative Council. The defence of the Falkland Islands and foreign affairs relating to the islands are the responsibility of the British Government.

The flag of the Falkland Islands is blue with the Union Jack in the top left-hand corner and a white shield containing the coat of arms in the centre of the distal half. The coat of arms contains a white ram above the sailing ship *Desire* with the scroll at the bottom bearing the motto 'Desire The Right'; sheep and wool production being the mainstay of the islands' economy for many years (see opposite), and the *Desire* being the ship of John Davis, who sighted the islands in 1592 (page 6).

ECONOMY

The economy of the islands has changed more in the last 25 years than at any time in their history. For 150 years the export of wool was the main base for the economy until the introduction of the fishery zone in 1987. At various periods during the 18th, 19th and 20th centuries, seals, whales and penguins have been exploited until their numbers dropped below an economically viable level (page 10). In recent years the rise of tourism, particularly in the cruise-ship and squid-fishing industries, has resulted in a much higher standard of living.

AGRICULTURE Farming on the Falkland Islands is a monoculture of which the product is wool, which is generally exported to the United Kingdom. Farms on the islands were large; using ranch-style methods they carried approximately 700,000 sheep. Lord Shackleton's report on the islands' economy recommended subdividing the 36 large farms. Accordingly, there are now 84 owner-managed farms with an average farm size of 33,216 acres, although sizes do of course vary considerably. The Falkland Islands Government, by means of grants and loans made available to individual farmers, has aided this subdivision. Falkland Landholdings Limited was created in 1991 with the purchase of the four remaining farms owned by the Falkland Islands Company (page 9). These farms make up about 25% of the farmland on the islands. Further developments included the purchase of a national stud flock of sheep from Australia, with the aim of improving the quality of the islands' wool. The worldwide slump in wool prices has resulted in poor prices being achieved in the wool market.

The Department of Agriculture is involved in projects whose aim is to improve the quality of grasslands and livestock. The United Kingdom Falkland Islands Trust is a British-registered charity (w ukfit.org), which is working with the Department of Agriculture in various programmes of research in order to promote the sustainable growth of the islands' agricultural industry, such as studying the possible impact of climate change on the islands, projects to improve the pasture and studies concerning tussac grass planting and management.

At present several long-term projects are in progress: tree planting, using kelp as a fertiliser, marketing and an educational programme in local schools. The planting of trees on a large scale is not considered a feasible proposition on the islands but a need to shelter livestock, crops and gardens has been identified. Kelp has long been used as a fertiliser in other parts of the world, so it is a logical step to consider the effects of kelp on grasslands and tussac grass, as there are huge reserves of it growing around the islands. The Trust's consultants have assisted in the marketing of various agricultural projects and the Trust has contributed to various, educational, civic and cultural projects on the islands. It has also been involved in the creation of a database of scientific publications, enabling scientists and students to have better access to this information.

A large percentage of the goods for sale on the islands have been imported from Britain or Chile. The islands are self-sufficient in dairy products and many of the vegetables are grown locally. The hydroponics plant on the outskirts of Stanley supplies the town and some of the visiting cruise ships with fresh vegetables.

FISHING In the years following the 1982 war (page 13) the islands' infrastructure has undergone considerable expansion, especially after the introduction of the Falkland Islands Interim Conservation and Management Zone (FICZ) to protect fish stocks around the islands. This extends 200 nautical miles from the Falklands. Any vessel wishing to fish inside this zone now requires a licence from the Falkland Islands Government. Some 75% of the catch is squid. The annual revenue, averaging £30.5 million, far exceeds any other income to the islands. This money has been used to support local welfare and educational projects and has also helped to pay for the road-building scheme and the creation of the terminals at New Haven and Port Howard for the ferry link between East and West Falkland. These developments have resulted in most of the major settlements on the islands being linked by a hard-surface road. Some of this money has been reinvested in the form of fishery protection and research. The protection of this vital industry through conserving fish stocks has been achieved by gathering catch data and patrols of the closed areas and fishing zones. In the budget of 2023/2024 £2.3 million was earmarked for fishery research to maintain the sustainability of this industry.

PHILATELY Philately has been a successful source of income over the years, and first-day covers were especially popular after the war in 1982. Although stamps have been issued on the islands since 1878, it was another 100 years before sufficient demand justified the establishment of the Falkland Islands Philatelic Bureau. Prior to 1978 the post office staff dealt with the running of the philatelic department as part of the day-to-day running of the post office. Since 2014 a local company, Falklands Post Service Ltd (FPS Ltd), has been running the bureau and post office. The bureau is also responsible for the production and sale of stamps for the Government of South Georgia and South Sandwich Islands and is the sales agent for the British Antarctic Territory. The only period that stamps were not issued was during the occupation by Argentinian troops in 1982 (page 13). Stamps from the Falklands and the aforementioned regions are very popular among collectors, so the revenue from the sales of stamps remains a vital part of the islands' economy.

TOURISM Tourists to the islands were few and far between before the events of 1982. Since the construction of the airport at MPA and the regular flights from Britain and Chile, there has been a steady increase in the number of tourists making use of the growing variety of accommodation on the islands. The greatest increase in tourist numbers has been in the cruise-ship market, with over 20,000 visitors reaching the Falkland Islands this way in the summer of 1999/2000, a figure which had grown to 59,936 by 2022/2023. So many visitors landing on the islands imply

RESTARTING TOURISM ON THE ISLANDS POST-COVID: THE TRIP PROJECT

As there was no international tourist travel to the Falklands for the 2020–21 season, the Tourism Recovery Incentive Programme (TRIP) was created by the Falkland Islands Government to enable local tourist businesses to survive the lack of custom. This domestic travel incentive was open to all those usually resident in the Falkland Islands, with each adult receiving a digital voucher for £500 and children receiving £250 to be spent on accommodation, hospitality and other expenses while travelling and staying around the islands. Those stationed in the British Forces on the Falkland Islands also qualified to receive some financial assistance in the form of £100 per adult and £50 for each child. This project was administered by the International Tours and Travel Ltd, a travel agency based in Stanley, and proved to be very successful with over 95% of the population registering for this deal. A survey after the project, which ran from October 2020 to May 2021 found that 61% of those taking part said they would travel locally again even without help from TRIP. This project, now under the name TRIP2, was also operated in the 2021–22 season and no doubt enabled many businesses to stay in operation ready for the restart of international travel for the 2022–23 season.

obvious benefits for the economy, although Falklands Conservation has expressed concern over the negative effect of such a huge influx of visitors on wildlife and the environment. The publication of the Falklands Conservation countryside code (page 47) has helped to control any negative impacts and the Falkland Islands Government is now embarking on a new environmental strategy, part of which is to modernise the islands' wildlife protection and to improve biosecurity.

PEOPLE

The majority of the people who live on the Falkland Islands are of British descent, originating from the sheep farmers and other settlers who came to the islands of their own volition, and from seafarers who arrived and simply never left. Islanders are very friendly and approachable. Until the arrival of modern technology (television was only established in the 1990s), radio and telephone were the only means of communication. The result of this was that each settlement was isolated and developed its own community life. Of the total population of over 3,600, some 2,500 live in Stanley – the remainder live in *camp* (page 23). This figure does not include the military personnel and contractors at MPA, which would add about another 1,400 to the number of residents. The percentage of 'Kelpers', as the Falkland Islanders are called as a result of living on islands surrounded by bands of seaweed, living in Stanley has increased with many new houses being built to accommodate the needs of those now working in 'town' as the economic base moves from wool production to servicing the fishing and tourism industries.

Living in the **camp** was never easy; the islanders had to be very self-sufficient and able to turn their hand to almost anything. The only fuel for many years was peat, which had to be dug in the summer to dry out on the peat stack before it could be used. Each settlement had its own store and, if large enough, a small school. Living off the land in tune with the seasons was an important part of *camp* life. November was the time of year when 'egging' took place, the gathering of penguin and albatross eggs to supplement the locals' diet. Later in the summer edible berries were collected for making into preserves and pastries. The men were expected to look after the sheep and their dogs, to dig peat and to undertake all the maintenance, while the women did the cooking and managed the house and family.

The modernisation of **farm work** has changed the way of life for many. Vehicles such as Land Rovers and quad bikes along with motorbikes are now the preferred method of gathering the sheep and much of the shearing is done by roving 'gangs' of shearers who travel the world, so far fewer people are needed, thus reducing the amount of work needing to be done to manage the farms. The road system has meant each settlement is no longer many hours' drive from their nearest neighbours or any shop or even Stanley. Wind turbines now supplement the generators to provide electricity, which again has improved connectivity with other parts of the islands and the outside world via social media and the internet.

The population of the Falkland Islands is predominantly **Christian**, with several denominations being represented (see page 77 for information on places of worship).

LANGUAGE

Since the 1990s there has been a steady influx of workers from St Helena to join the British, and a small number of Chileans reside on the islands. There is no native language on the islands but there is an identifiable accent that has its origins in the West Country of England. Some words are pronounced differently from their English counterparts. Parts of horses' tack are still called by the names they were given by the gauchos from South America who lived on the islands in the 19th century (see above). This also applies to some of the place names on the islands and to fixtures such as cattle grids, which are sometimes known as *pasa libre*.

EDUCATION

Education is free and compulsory up to the age of 16. For those in Stanley there is a primary and a secondary school. The senior school was opened in Stanley in 1992 and has been regularly updated; it offers a range of subjects at GCSE level based on the English education system. There are primary schools out in *camp* at three of the larger settlements (Goose Green, North Arm and Fox Bay). Otherwise children in the smaller settlements are taught either over the phone (with online tuition being brought in) or by *camp* teachers who visit these farms on a regular basis.

Once children reach the age of ten or 11 they come to stay in Stanley, staying at the school boarding house in order to attend the primary school before moving up to the secondary school. For those wishing to continue their education, assuming certain grades have been met, the Falkland Islands Government will pay for two years of education in the UK at either Peter Symonds College in Winchester for A levels, or Chichester College for NVQs or National Diplomas. The government also offers grants for Higher Education courses, mostly with the UK. With the improvement of the local economy, a great many of these students return to the islands after their studies.

CULTURE AND SPORT

There are a variety of **clubs and societies** on the islands including a wide range of sports activities, with football and cricket being very popular, as well as everything from hockey to motocross plus drama and other arts. The majority of islanders keep in contact with what is happening on the islands by reading the weekly **newspaper**, the *Penguin News* (w penguin-news.com), and listening to the local **radio**, Falkland

Radio, available island-wide on 530 kHz and between 88.2 and 88.8, 96.5 and 101.0 MHz. The station also broadcasts some BBC World Service programmes during the night. There are also two British forces radio stations, BFBS Falklands (94.5, 101.6 and 106.2 to 106.8 MHz) and BFBS Radio 2 (97.2 to 97.8 and 91.1 to 100.4 MHz). The arrival of **television** in the 1990s had a major impact on island life as has the internet, with social media being a very popular way of keeping in touch with friends and relatives on the islands and abroad. Falkland Islands Televsion (FITV; w fitv.co.fk) now has a weekly community news programme among other shows. The expansion of the **mobile-phone network** around Stanley and to many areas in *camp* has also played its part in increasing connectivity.

The Falkland Islands are a very social place, and stopping for a chat is a way of life. The self-sufficient existence of the islanders has meant that some have turned their craftsmanship into **arts and crafts** such as spinning, weaving, felt-making and photography. The islands are also home to some very talented artists. These crafts can be seen displayed around the shops in Stanley (page 76). For more information on arts and entertainment, see page 62.

The islands are very British in character and have no major cultural differences from the UK. Living in a small community means there is a high level of respect for other people and their property. If visitors have a problem, the islanders will do their best to help them.

2

Natural History

The Falkland Islands have been described as one of the last wildernesses in the world. Whether it is the spectacular scenery, the throngs of penguins or the impressive elephant seals, there is much for the visitor to see.

FLORA

The flora of the islands can look rather uniform at times, but there are a great many attractive flowers hidden away out of the wind; some of the more noteworthy plants of the Falkland Islands are described below.

HABITATS The main influence on the environment is the almost barren soil covering the main islands, which is acidic and peaty, and is generally described as cold. This peat can be hard and dry when it is thinly spread over the underlying rock, or thicker and water-retentive in low-lying areas. These two types of habitat are described as hard and soft *camp*. (The word *camp* is derived from the Spanish word *campo*, meaning countryside.) The habitat of the islands can be classified into five major types, with several plant species occurring in more than one formation. **Feldmark** is most often found at higher elevations where the soil is thin and the vegetation is often eroded to expose areas of clay and thin shaly soil. Typical flora of this habitat includes cushion plants (page 27) such as balsam bog, *azorella* and the two common species of *blechnum* fern that occur on the Falklands, tall fern and small fern. This low-growing vegetation is often more coloured than the uniform hues of the lower slopes; the combination of the light and dark greens with the orange and browns of the ferns gives the higher elevations a distinctive appearance. Areas above 2,000ft (600m) show the best examples of feldmark formation, such as those found in the Wickham Heights and on many of the higher peaks in West Falkland. It is also found on some of the higher cliffs and rock stacks in the southwest and northwest of the islands.

Oceanic heath formation covers most of the Falkland Islands below the feldmark zone. There are two distinct types within this formation. Diddle-dee – a stumpy heather-like shrub – dominates the higher, well-drained slopes, forming a **dwarf-shrub heath**, where the peat is firmer over the rocky ridges or more fertile soil. Other species that grow alongside diddle-dee include the Christmas bush (page 28), mountain berry, balsam bog and almond flower, along with several others. White grass forms the **grass heaths** that cover almost half of the islands, making it the most common plant on the Falklands. In well-drained areas the white grass forms clumps of vegetation, while on wetter ground it forms a flat, lush surface that can be very difficult to traverse in a vehicle. Pigvine and berry-lobelia are two of the more easily located species that grow among it. A variety of other grasses, rushes and sedges are found in the damper habitats. The stone runs interrupt this oceanic heath formation, particularly in East Falkland, thus creating another type of habitat. Plants found in this unique environment include the endemic snake plant, vanilla daisy and the native strawberry.

Where the water table is on or very near the surface, the **bog formation** predominates. Large regions of East and West Falkland come into this vegetation category. This soft *camp* is home to many of the plant species found on the islands. White grass is still common but there are many wet marshy areas comprising short rushes and dense carpets of *astelia*. The peat below the vegetative horizon is deep and saturated with water. One of the more unusual plants in this habitat is the carnivorous sundew, capturing any unfortunate insect that comes its way, and there are also several species of short rushes. Close to the many small streams that are typical of this habitat it is also possible to find buttercups, blinks and pimpernel. It is very easy when walking across this soft *camp* to get a boot full of water, so try to avoid the streams and other such obviously saturated areas.

There are numerous small ponds on the islands that, along with the larger lakes and streams, support the **fresh-water formation**. Species seen in this habitat vary from the taller rushes to the low-growing arrow-leaved marigold, water milfoil and starwort.

Maritime tussock formation is confined to coastal areas below 650ft (200m) and is dominated by the tall tussac grass. A healthy specimen of tussac grass, growing in favourable conditions, can reach over 13ft (4m) tall and thrives in dense clumps around the coastline. Other species that can be found here include wild celery, cinnamon grass and native woodrush. This habitat was formerly much more extensive around the islands than it is today; overgrazing and fire have probably been the major causes in its decline, although pests and disease are also thought to have had some effect. When grazing ceases, the habitat has been shown to recover in some areas, but the associated erosion that often follows the removal of tussac grass means this is not always the case. It has been found to be a remarkably difficult plant to reintroduce, although some success is now being achieved: Falklands Conservation and others have started several replanting schemes with young tussac shoots being planted in fenced-off areas in various locations. One such scheme at Elephant Beach has been very successful, with new plants trebling in size in the first year, and similar success has also been had elsewhere, such as on Sea Lion Island. Tussac has also been planted in some of the newly cleared minefields near Stanley such as those in Surf Bay. This habitat is one of the most important on the islands, in particular when the numbers of breeding birds dependent on tussac grass are considered.

There is one other class of vegetation that can be found on the Falkland Islands, and that is **shrubs, bushes and trees**. The only two native species of bush are fachine and native boxwood, both thought to have been much more widespread prior to the introduction of grazing. The latter is a popular plant used in hedging around the settlements, often surviving long after the building it surrounded has been taken down. The other two most commonly found hedges are gorse, first brought in by the early settlers, and several species of pine tree, of which *macrocarpa* is the most apparent. A wide variety of other species have been tried in recent years. Woodland is not a term often used on Falkland; the only real exception to this is the 'forest' at Hill Cove on East Falkland where there is quite a stand of the *macrocarpa*. It would perhaps not be termed a wood anywhere else in the world, as it is only c100m long and c50m wide at its widest point, but it is the largest in the Falklands with trees reaching around 15–20m in height.

Over 177 species of plants and one hybrid have so far been identified as being native to the islands. Of these, 14 are regarded as endemic (such as the lady's slipper, coastal nassauvia, hairy daisy and Falkland rock cress), and two others are regarded as near endemic (the Falkland cudweed and shield fern). The native flora is much more diverse than that of any other of the South Atlantic islands. This is almost certainly due to the Falklands' proximity to South America, as the majority of the plants found here are also found in Tierra del Fuego. To date, 241 introduced species have been recorded, most originating from Europe. They tend to be concentrated around settlements, with 139 now regarded as naturalised. Many of these are usually considered as the common weeds of the northern hemisphere.

TUSSAC GRASS Tussac grass is the most easily identified plant on the islands. Although not as common as once was the case, it can be found in many areas. A visit to a tussac island such as Kidney Island (page 90) at the entrance of Berkeley Sound gives a much better appreciation of how the coast of the Falkland Islands must have appeared before the arrival of humans in the 16th century (page 6). Each plant sends out new leaves every year, the old leaves forming a robust pedestal strong enough to bear the weight of a sleeping sea lion. In the absence of any rodents, many of the islands' smaller seabirds can be found nesting in or under the tussac pedestals (see below). This environment is very fragile and can easily be destroyed in a few careless moments. Falklands Conservation (page 47) are involved in several successful reintroduction schemes, in particular at Elephant Beach on East Falkland where, after initial planting in 2005, the tussac has become robust enough to withstand some winter grazing as well as to protect the fragile peat. Other areas it has been reintroduced include the cleared minefields at Surf Bay near Stanley, and the local youth section of Falklands Conservation, the Watch Group, have planted some areas around Stanley as well as on some of the outer islands such as Bleaker.

TALL BUSHES Of the three tall bushes found on the Falkland Islands, the prickly leaves of the **gorse** (introduced from Europe), commonly seen forming hedges

THE IMPORTANCE OF TUSSAC GRASS

Tussac grass (*Poa flabellata*) is one of the most talked about plants on the islands, featuring as it does in many of the coastal photographs taken in the archipelago. Sadly, it is much reduced due to grazing pressure and fires, but there are many replanting programmes under way to return it to its former glory (see above). It is now thought to occupy some 20% of the area that it did in the past. This 3m-high plant, which can live for over 200 years, is home to a great variety of wildlife, in particular on the rat-free islands, where over half of the islands' bird species make a home in this vital habitat. The green part of the plant lives on a pedestal of dead leaves that eventually decays into a form of peat. It is here that the many birds nest, ranging from the endemic Cobb's wren to the much larger magellanic penguin. It also has an important job in greatly reducing erosion around the coastal fringes.

Where tussac has been protected from grazing animals, and on the smaller offshore islands, it can occur as dense stands stretching from the coastal edges to many metres inland. It is often so dense that it is the only plant around in some areas. On the occasional dead pedestals, various grasses and wild celery can be found clinging to a foothold amid this great swathe. Trying to navigate through a thick stand of tussac is an amazing experience, especially when trying to make sure one does not come across a sleeping sea lion.

around many of the older settlements, with its yellow flowers, is the easiest to identify. **Native boxwood**, originally from West Falkland, is now a common windbreak in Stanley; it has a heavily gnarled trunk and when in bloom the white flowers appear in dense crowds towards the tip of each branch. **Fachine** takes a little more searching to find, as it does not grow well in heavily grazed land; its daisy-like flowers bloom across the upper part of the bush, while the undersides of the pointed green leaves and the twigs are covered with thin white hairs, giving it a distinctive appearance. Probably the best location to see this plant in recent years has been on Saunders Island (page 156), especially near Port Egmont. Fachine and native boxwood are thought to be able to grow in more than one habitat, but are now reduced to surviving away from stock. Fachine usually prefers the wetter valleys where it can become the dominant plant, but has also been recorded on sand dunes close to beaches. This and the boxwood are two of the very few plants that can reach over 6ft (1.8m) in height. The boxwood is thought to be native to West Falkland and to have been introduced to East Falkland, being found, for example, growing in gardens around Stanley. In the wild it occurs on coastal cliffs and sandy slopes away from the attentions of grazing sheep.

BERRIED PLANTS Several of the berried plants of the islands produce edible fruit. By late summer the shiny red berries of the very common **diddle-dee** show up as coloured swathes across the drier landscape. The berry crop varies in quantity from year to year depending upon the weather at the time of flowering and rainfall levels as the berries grow; in a good year many species of bird can be seen feeding on this tiny red fruit with a distinctive, tart flavour. Local residents often pick these berries and turn them into jams, jellies and pies. This plant was popular with the early settlers, as its resinous wood was easy to set alight even on the wettest of days. **Tea berries** are less common, occurring as a low creeper in areas with a deep base of peat. The plant's insignificant four-petalled white flowers of spring are in the late summer transformed into dull pink berries, which are thought of as a delicacy on the islands, despite the difficulties involved in picking them. Its leaves were dried and used to make a type of tea by early settlers, hence its name.

Late summer and early autumn are the best times to go looking for the **native strawberry** in its favoured drier habitat. Resembling a small shiny raspberry, this distinctive fruit can be hard to find as the berries lie close to the ground and are partially obscured by leaves, but its sweet taste is well worth the effort. Sometimes confused with the native strawberry, the fruit of **pigvine** is not edible for humans but is a favoured food of upland geese. This very common plant can be found in most wet areas on the islands, particularly on the banks of streams. Flowering in November is followed by the formation of bright red berries growing on short stems that are just visible under the small rhubarb-like leaves. One of the prettiest flowers on the islands belongs to the **mountain berry**. Despite the name, this plant is widespread, its tiny white flowers hanging underneath wax-red sepals above small dark-green leaves, making a most distinctive plant. The fruit is comparatively large and is a dull pink to almost purple. ***Nertera granadensis*** – known as beadplant – is not unusual on the islands, especially in the wetter areas where it can form mats of vegetation. In autumn its dull, round orange/red berry stands out against a background of small, succulent-like leaves. The most striking feature of the **almond flower**, however, is the bloom not the berry. This cup-shaped white flower almost appears to grow straight from the earth as the stem and leaves are relatively inconspicuous. After flowering in midsummer a deep purple berry is formed, often around the bases of balsam bogs along with the mountain berry.

CUSHION PLANTS Some of the most unusual-looking flora on the islands are cushion plants. The largest and most intriguing is the **balsam bog**. Its densely packed rosettes of flowers form irregular mounds that can reach over 5ft (1.5m) in height and have a circumference in the region of 10ft (3m). These mounds are extremely hard and vary in colour from light to dark green, depending on their exposure to sunshine. A faint smell – hence the name balsam bog – exudes from the small globules of white gum that are secreted between the rosettes and eventually harden into small, brown lumps. This plant is usually found in dry, rocky ground from low coastal cliffs right up into the feldmark formation (page 23). **Coastal nassauvia** is one of the most attractive of the bog plants, forming low cushions or dense carpets of green on low rocks, or in the shrub heath close to the coast, occasionally well above sea level. Tiny, cream-white flowers can be seen throughout the summer and, when found in profusion, produce a sweet smell of nectar, which can be detected even on the windiest of days. This bog plant, along with **Moore's plantain** and **Falkland false plantain**, is one of the endemic flowers of the islands, and of these three endemic species is probably the most common. Two other bogs can easily be found on the islands. *Astelia* forms carpets of hard green leaves over very waterlogged peat, and it is the plant most often associated with the term soft *camp* (page 23) as it is widespread over the islands. The other bog family is *azorella*, of which four species are found in the Falklands. They form flat mats, hugging the ground or forming proper cushions, and are most often found in shrub heath on drier ground.

FLOWERS A wide range of brightly coloured flowers can be found on the Falkland Islands, many of which are small or are only in bloom for a short time each summer. Some of the most attractive flowers belong to the orchid family, of which four are found on the islands. The easiest to find, although this is by no means guaranteed, is the **dog orchid**. Its three white petals, often showing some purple tinges, are best looked for in the oceanic heath formation when in flower in November and December. Many of the endemic flowers escape detection, let alone identification by the casual botanist, while others are much more obvious.

The **snake plant**, part of the *nassauvia* family, is one of the strangest plants on the islands. It is typically found around the boulders in the stone runs, with long straggling stems reaching up to the light. Tough, almost-scaly leaves cover the stems, which end in club-like heads of densely packed white flowers creating a most unmistakable plant.

Two of the brightest coloured of the endemic flowers are the two species of ragwort. **Smooth ragwort** and **woolly ragwort** both have many bright yellow flowers sprouting from green stems and are found in heathlands intermixed with diddle-dee (see opposite) and grasslands around the coasts and inland up to 1,000ft (305m). Distinguishing between these two species is not as easy as their names would suggest, but careful examination of the structure as well as the appearance of the plant will result in correct identification.

Pale maiden, although now thought not to be an endemic species, is one of the most flamboyant flowers of the Falkland spring and is the national flower of the islands. The Falkland pale maiden is now considered to be a larger-flowered, wider-petalled form of a very widely distributed *sisyrinchium* in South America. Many grasslands and heathlands are still covered with the delicate, white, bell-shaped flowers in the early part of the summer, with some plants still in bloom in February, although they do not flourish in heavily grazed pasture.

Falkland lavender is one of the most attractive plants on the islands, but is only distantly related to the lavenders renowned for their aromatic oils. A low-growing shrub, which is not particularly noticeable for most of the year, it comes into its own when it blooms in midsummer and is covered with large, white, lilac or pale blue, daisy-like flowers. It is quite common around the islands, rarely found far from the sea on drier ground, and can appear to form a carpet of colour in certain areas.

Another plant that grows on coastal slopes with rather poor soil is the **lady's slipper**. This beautiful red and yellow flower, supposed to look – as the name suggests – like a lady's slipper, emerges from the centre of a rosette of some very hairy leaves in midsummer. It is often found in small colonies but is not thought to be common on the islands.

The unusually named **Christmas bush** gets its moniker from the fact that it is covered with off-white flowers from the end of December until January. The islanders used to pick the flowers for decorative purposes. This plant is common on the islands and is able to tolerate wet or dry ground and a wide range of soil types.

Very few of the plants on the Falkland Islands have been used medicinally, the main exception being **scurvy grass**. This member of the *oxalis* family has a singular appearance with large, pearl-white flowers, which are sometimes tinged with pink, resting upon thin, silvery grey leaves that radiate out from a central stem. The early sailors used this plant as a means of avoiding the disease scurvy and the first settlers on the islands made scurvy grass jam from this plant. Its name has continued to this day, even though in modern times only the plant stalks are used to make a drink. It is most often found near the coast and in the dwarf-shrub heath.

The other plant used for its anti-scorbutic properties was the **sea cabbage**. This very common plant occurs inland of the tide line on almost every sandy beach on the islands. Its thick, fleshy leaves, silvery grey in colour, form a pale line behind the flotsam and jetsam at the top of the beach. After Christmas, bright yellow flowers appear in bunches, making this one of the most memorable flowers in Falkland.

Of the plants that creep along the ground, one that stands out is the **berry-lobelia**, which catches the eye on account of the arrangement of its five petals. They are neatly arranged so as to leave a gap, as if something has eaten one side of each blossom. These flowers are usually white in colour, but a pale lilac form is also found. This plant occurs in thick mats on wet peaty ground on many islands.

The daisy family is well represented, although one of the first that the visitor finds is usually the introduced **European daisy**. Three other species are native, one of which – the **hairy daisy** – is endemic to the Falkland Islands. **Marsh daisy**, as the name suggests, likes the damper regions, while the **vanilla daisy** is one of the largest flowing plants of the heathlands, reaching up to 12 inches (30cm) tall.

Almost as tall is the only wild representative of the *primula* family, **dusty miller**. This plant flowers in the spring, although some are occasionally still in bloom in early January, in the dry open dwarf shrub heathland that extends from sea level to the highest mountain ranges on the islands. A thin round stalk supports a round head of pure-white, tubular flowers that each have a yellow centre. At a distance they can appear to look like a patch of small golf balls. Another plant that sends up a ball of flowers is **thrift**. This species is much taller and has deeper-pink flowers than the species found around European coasts. The thrift adorns the rocks and sand around many of the shores through the summer months. Dotted around the wet sand, a little way inland from the beach, are small patches of **pimpernel**. This low-growing plant forms small, pink, star-shaped flowers during January before setting seed and disappearing for another year.

One of the few plants used as food in the islands is **wild celery**, a close relative of the cultivated variety, which has the same familiar smell and the same white umbrellas of flower. It is usually found in close association with tussac grass (page 25).

Wetlands on the islands tend to be dominated by grasses and rushes. One of the few exceptions to this is the **arrow-leaved marigold**, which can be found in many wet habitats beside salt or fresh water. Its shiny, green, arrow-shaped leaves are mostly prostrate, but in some circumstances will form a more erect flower. Its off-white flowers appear in the centre of each stem in November and December.

The flora of the islands is still being investigated by Falklands Conservation (page 47) and they encourage visitors with an interest in botany to inform the charity of any unusual plants they see, complete with details of when and, most importantly, where the plant in question was sighted.

MARINE ALGAE

Kelp beds surrounding the islands are one of the features of the Falklands, damping down the waves even on the windiest of days. Various species of marine algae extend from the intertidal zone out to a depth of 100ft (30.5m), forming bands that can extend up to a mile (1.6km) offshore on all but the most exposed shores. Giant kelp can reach up to 200ft (61m) long, held up to the sun by many small air bladders, and constitutes the bulk of the kelp beds around the Falklands. Many other species occupy separate niches between the giant kelp and the top of the tidal zone, including the bright green leaves of the *ulva* family that are a major food source for kelp geese. A great many species rely on the kelp beds for food and shelter, thus making them one of the most important habitats on the islands.

FAUNA

LAND MAMMALS Endemic land mammals became extinct on the Falkland Islands when the last **warrah**, or Falkland fox, was shot in 1876. This relative of the Fuegian fox from South America was described by some of the first explorers to reach the islands towards the end of the 17th century. Different races existed on East and West Falkland, although the warrah was probably never very common. Like the fox in its bold, inquisitive behaviour, it was perceived as a threat by the escalating sheep-farming industry. A government bounty for each dead animal was the death knell for this species.

It is possible to see ten species of land mammal on the islands today, all introduced by humans. Some hitched a ride and have been present ever since people reached the islands, whereas others have been deliberately introduced. Rabbits, hares and cottontail rabbits have been found on the islands since the late 1800s. **Cottontail rabbits** are found only on New Island to the west of the archipelago, while **hares** are restricted to East Falkland, in particular the Port Louis area. The **rabbit** is more widespread, although not common. All three were introduced to supplement the diet of the original settlers.

Three other mammals have reached Falkland without humans' intentional help. **Brown rats**, **black rats** and the **house mouse** have been recorded in many locations around the islands and are thought to be responsible for the lack of breeding seabirds in some otherwise suitable habitats. The most destructive of the introduced species on the islands has been the **domestic cat**. Wherever this species is present, a dramatic decline in small birds has been noted. In contrast, on Carcass Island, which has remained cat free, small birds are abundant.

A visit to the southwest of the islands is necessary to see two of the other land mammals. **Guanacos** had been introduced in various locations over the years from South America but today can only be seen on Staats Island (page 182). This member of the llama family lives in small herds, which appear to have no predators, meaning food supply is the only limit on population numbers. The **Patagonian fox** was present on six islands in the southwest, although work is in progress to eradicate them from these areas. Where foxes are present, there are correspondingly low numbers of ground-nesting birds, including geese and other wildfowl.

The most intriguing of the introduced mammals is the **sea otter**, also known as the Fuegian marine otter. This animal, originally introduced to the islands in the 1930s, has managed to stay so well hidden that its present status on the islands is unknown. There is so much suitable habitat for this South American species that only brief sightings have been possible in the intervening years, usually in the southwest or southeast of the islands.

MARINE MAMMALS Watching some of the marine mammals that frequent the islands is one of the most memorable experiences on the Falkland Islands. Fur seal, southern sea lion and southern elephant seal all breed on the islands. The latter is the only 'true seal' – seals without external ears and whose main means of propulsion is their powerful rear quarters, unlike the 'eared seals' that have outer ears and use their large front flippers to walk on land and to swim. Hunting for **fur seals** in the 18th and 19th centuries drastically reduced the numbers of this animal (page 10), so much so that it almost became extinct on the islands before the first protective legislation was passed by the Falkland Islands Government in 1881, although poaching continued for a good many years until this species was totally safeguarded in 1921. There was an estimated population of 18,000–20,000 in 1992, spread over about ten sites such as on the tip of Volunteer Point and on New Island. A more recent survey (2021) found there to be 44,000 pups, indicating a healthy rise in numbers following the cessation of sealing activities. At sea identification can be difficult, as the pointed snout and heavy neck are not very visible when the fur seals are porpoising through the water. Males are larger and darker brown than the females with a much heavier neck and head. They reach about 6ft (1.9m) in length and can weigh up to 350lb (158kg). Rocky cliffs with accessible ledges near the water are the preferred breeding sites, most of which are found to the northwest and southwest of the islands. Breeding commences in early November when the bulls come ashore to claim their territories, followed by the females a few weeks later just before the pups are born. Colonies are rarely deserted during the year after the pups have departed, as different age groups and sexes are constantly present. The main prey consists of lobster krill, squid and some fish. New Island has the colonies most visited by tourists as elsewhere the seals keep to isolated rocky outcrops.

Southern sea lions also suffered heavily at the hands of the sealers. Formerly occurring in huge numbers, the southern sea lion population appears to have suffered a steady decline despite the cessation of sealing after World War II. A survey in 2021, funded by the Falklands Island Government, found a population of 5,375 pups at 70 breeding sites. The best known, and most often visited, sites are at Cape Dolphin on East Falkland and on Sea Lion Island.

An adult male is an impressive animal weighing up to 700lb (320kg) and reaching a length of about 8ft (2.6m). The name 'lion' stems from the heavy neck of the male that, when dry, looks similar to a lion's mane. They do not have the majestic appearance of the lion as they have a flat forehead and rather small eyes, giving them a somewhat mean look. The females are smaller, sleeker and are often a lighter brown in colour. Generally, they are shy animals who retreat when humans approach, but this cannot be guaranteed as they can move very rapidly; they also have a fearsome array of teeth. When hauled out on land, they can be seen resting upright with their head tilted slightly backwards; to all intents and purposes they seem to be fast asleep. Appearances are deceptive, as they are very aware of any nearby movement and react very quickly. If you come across a sea lion while on foot, it is a good idea to take an alternative route!

Southern sea lions breed later in the summer than the fur seal – the bulls setting up their territories in December and the females coming ashore to pup between the middle of December and the end of January. The colonies are at their most active during this time. Towards the end of the summer the males leave to feed up after fasting while protecting their harems, and after a few weeks the females and young also depart. Non-breeders can be seen at the fringes of the colonies during the summer and will come ashore after the males have gone back to sea. Away from the 60 or so colonies on the islands, small groups and lone seals can be encountered almost anywhere, even close to Stanley. Octopus, squid, lobster krill and fish make up a large proportion of their diet, although lone bulls can sometimes be seen hunting penguins near a rookery. This can involve a chase over the land for the more agile seal or a stealthy approach through the shallows to surprise the prey. Sea lions have also been known to take elephant seal young.

Seeing a bull **southern elephant seal** for the first time is a memorable experience. Initially, members of a group sprawled out on the sand seem to be doing very little except waiting for their old skin to moult and their new skin to grow. But this impression is soon shattered as they puff and blow, squabble over who lies where or just argue for the sake of it. Males are immense creatures reaching 18ft (5.5m) in length and attaining weights in the region of 4 tonnes (4.4 tons). The females are roughly half the size and only a quarter of the males' weight. An inflatable proboscis is the reason for this species' name, although it must be said that it does not greatly resemble that of an elephant. The proboscis of the male is inflated during territorial displays in the spring, when the elephant seals come ashore to lay claim to their preferred sites. It is quite usual to see large scars on the necks of the older males after many years of fighting over the best section of beach. By early October all the females will have arrived and are gathered into harems by the dominant males. Pups can be born from mid-September onwards, with the highest concentrations being noted in the first half of October. Just over three weeks later the single pup is weaned, during which period the female is mated, before both leave. The breeding bulls depart by mid-November, leaving the beaches for the non-breeding animals to come ashore to moult. Towards the end of the summer, once they have recovered their strength, it is the females' turn to come ashore, to be followed by the males in the early months of the winter. Most southern elephant seals stay at sea during the winter months, although on favoured beaches, such as those on Sea Lion Island (page 122), it is possible to find the occasional animal slumped on the sand. On land they are not the most elegant creatures, but they are sleek swimming machines in the water, well adapted for diving to great depths in search of squid and fish.

Early settlers found that a bull southern elephant seal could yield over 90 gallons of oil and was therefore a valuable export commodity (page 10). Within a hundred years of the first records of elephant seals on the islands they were almost extinct, and at the beginning of the 20th century only small breeding colonies were recorded. Over the years these colonies increased in number and size (despite a short period of hunting after World War II) until the 1950s, when there was an estimated annual production of 1,000 pups. Most colonies had seen a decline until recent years, when the population on Sea Lion Island increased slightly to nearly 600 breeding females (2019). Sea Lion Island is the premier site for this species in Falkland with 95% of the islands' population; Carcass Island and Saunders Island are also breeding sites. Moulting southern elephant seals can be encountered in a variety of locations, but are best seen on the aforementioned islands.

Other species of seal that have been recorded on the islands include the **leopard seal**, most often seen in the winter months, but visible at any time of year. Its large head, with an enormous mouth full of sharp teeth, make this an easy species to identify. It was formerly more common on the islands – there are records of small groups coming ashore on sandy beaches – but only single animals have been noted in recent years.

Apart from humans, these seals only have one major predator on the islands: the **killer whale** or orca. These elusive creatures can be an unforgettable sight. Small groups of shags, gulls and terns hovering over the surface on the outer reaches of the kelp are often the first clue given to the presence of killer whales, which appear in small groups or pods. These birds are waiting to feed on any titbits left over after the orca has finished with its prey. The huge, triangular, dorsal fin of the male shows up well when the whale is swimming parallel to the beach, but can be surprisingly difficult to discern as the whale moves towards or away from the observer. Females are not so easy to see, as their dorsal fin is much smaller. Pods of orca are a matriarchal society with the eldest female being the dominant figure, although at least one adult male will be present with a number of females of varying ages. The black-and-white patterning on the under body and flanks is only apparent if it rolls or, more rarely, leaps in the air. The small pale patch behind the dorsal fin is seldom visible. Killer whales are not common on the islands but are regularly sighted in certain areas, possibly in step with the breeding cycle of their main prey, the seals. On Sea Lion Island, one of the best locations to look for this species, they are repeatedly sighted when the elephant pups go out to sea for the first time, and also when the sea lion pups leave the breeding grounds. They can be seen at other times of year, but November and February are the preferred months.

Many other species of whale and dolphin have been recorded on the islands over the centuries. Nowadays the larger whales are few and far between, courtesy of the whaling industry. **Southern right whales** are more regularly seen in some of the deeper waters around the outlying islands, in particular near New Island and at the mouth of Berkeley Sound, as well as from Cape Dolphin at the north of Falkland Sound. Berkeley Sound is also a good site to look for **sei whales** late in the summer, especially from cruise ships as they enter Falkland waters. Falklands Conservation has been maintaining a catalogue of photographs of sei whale fins taken in this area. They request that any photos taken of this species that are of a reasonable size, good resolution and taken with a fast shutter speed be sent to e whales@conservation.org. fk. **Long-finned pilot whales** can be seen in small groups throughout the summer months, and strandings of this species have occurred around the islands in the past with the most recent being on Pebble Island in the early 1980s. Many other species of whale have been seen from the cruise ships that pass through Falkland waters, including the very rare **blue whale**.

Two of the smaller cetaceans are frequently observed in the islands: Commerson's dolphins and Peale's dolphins can be seen on most visits. **Commerson's dolphins** are smaller, about 6ft (1.8m) long, and prefer sheltered waters, often playing in the bow wave of boats entering the harbour. Port Howard and the Narrows in Stanley have been excellent places to see and photograph these attractive black-and-white dolphins as they speed alongside the boat. The origin of the local name 'puffing pig' can be heard as they gasp for air before diving back into the clear blue water. As soon as they see or hear an engine they make a beeline for the boat, their rounded dorsal fin hardly visible as they zoom through the water. **Peale's dolphins** are larger, up to 8ft (2.5m) long, and are generally much more lethargic swimmers, although they experience moments of frenzied activity, leaping out of the water and splashing around in the shallows. The taller dorsal fin, with its more pronounced curve towards the rear, is quite distinctive, as is the reduced amount of white visible on the upper parts when compared with Commerson's dolphins. They are habitually found moving along the edges of the kelp beds that surround the islands (page 29), appearing to have favourite haunts to which they regularly return. Carcass Island and West Point Island are both good locations to encounter this species.

BIRDS The visitor's general impression after a trip to the Falkland Islands is that it is full of birds of all shapes and sizes, and yet there are large areas with hardly any breeding birds. Those species that are able to live and breed on the islands have found their niches and have exploited them to the full, with little competition, and therefore seem to occur in disproportionately large numbers at certain locations. Predation by rats and cats has reduced the numbers of some land birds and smaller seabirds in many areas, but by visiting islands where such animals have not been introduced – such as Carcass and Sea Lion – it is possible to see most of the breeding birds of the Falkland Islands in one trip. Of the 59 species that habitually breed on the islands, most are water birds making use of the pools and lakes as well as the ample shoreline and good feeding offshore. There are two endemic species on the islands: the Falkland steamer duck, often seen cruising offshore in many locations across the islands, and Cobb's wren, found on rat-free islands.

Penguins
The penguin family are well represented on the islands, with five species nesting annually, plus the occasional vagrant from the Antarctic or sub-Antarctic islands. A visit to the **king penguin** colony at Volunteer Point on East Falkland is the highlight of many a trip (page 102). By far the largest breeding penguins on the Falklands, they can turn up on almost any island, sometimes mingling with gentoo penguins when they come ashore to moult. Small breeding groups are found on some of the other islands, but the sheer number of birds at Volunteer Point make it a truly memorable wildlife spectacle.

Gentoo penguins are much more widespread. Their preference for nesting on low ground means that their colonies are much more accessible than some of the other species of seabird. Some colonies do not conform to this rule by choosing hill-sites a long walk from the beach. The Falkland Islands shelter 30% of this species' global population with an average of over 100,000 breeding pairs on the Falklands in recent years, and the gentoo is one of the few penguins that stays around the islands in large numbers during the winter months. These are the most comical of the penguins, waddling to and from their rookeries, always using the same route. The gentoo is a tall, elegant penguin with a distinctive white blaze above and behind the eye and, as is the case with most of this family, a rather guttural call. Throughout the breeding season there is always some activity, whether it is the adult bird robbing bits of nesting material from its neighbour's nest in the early part of their season, or the young racing around the colony later in the summer, chasing their parents to persuade them to give up the meal that they have just caught out at sea. As they usually lay two eggs, there are often two juveniles begging for food by January and if food is plentiful they will make it to the end of the season.

The **rockhoppers** are the smallest of the islands' breeding penguins, yet they locate their rookeries on some of the most inhospitable coastline such as at Marble on Pebble Island, Kidney Island near Stanley (page 92) and near the settlement on Bleaker Island. Their climbing ability is second to none for a seabird, as they make their way up some of the steepest slopes to their cliff-top nesting site using only the sharp claws on their powerful feet to cling to the rock face. The colonies are noisy, smelly and marvellously photogenic. The vivid yellow tufts above each red eye contrast with their otherwise shining black-and-white plumage. Rockhoppers, unlike the other species of penguin breeding on the Falklands, can often be found in mixed colonies with other seabirds. Imperial or king shags and black-browed albatrosses are the most frequent cohabitants, along with the occasional macaroni penguin.

Macaroni penguins are at the northern limit of their range and breed in very small numbers, usually just a handful of pairs mixing in with the larger rockhopper penguin rookeries such as at Marble on Pebble Island, at White Rock, West Falkland and on Sea Lion Island with occasional hybrids occurring at some colonies such as on Saunders Island. It is a stockier, taller bird with fiery crests meeting on the forehead. Greater numbers of predators tend to be found on the perimeter of these mixed colonies. Turkey vultures, skuas and gulls are the most numerous, with snowy sheathbills appearing in large numbers around some of the more isolated colonies. Rockhopper penguins are the most pelagic of the penguins breeding on the islands; satellite tracking has found that they cover vast distances when out at sea, regularly reaching the South American coast.

Magellanic penguins are the first species of penguin encountered by most visitors to the islands. Their habit of breeding in burrows dug into the peaty soil results in rather more diffuse colonies than is true of other penguins. They are found on almost every coast with suitable nesting grounds and access to the sea, always avoiding cliffs and settlements. As with all the smaller local penguins, two eggs are laid at the start of the summer. By January the young are large enough to be exploring the environs of their burrows, dashing back for cover at the first sign of danger.

Grebes

Two species of grebe breed on the islands' freshwater pools, although they can occasionally be seen on freshwater streams near the sea and can also spend some time on coastal waters during the winter. The white-tufted grebe is slightly

AVIAN INFLUENZA

Avian influenza, or bird flu as it has also been called, has been hitting the headlines in recent years as it has been killing a great many wild birds around the world. This highly contagious disease has now spread from the northern hemisphere to South America. It has not only been killing a large number of boobies and pelicans in Chile, it has also transferred to mammals and has decimated the southern elephant seal population in Argentina. It appeared to initially have missed the Falklands, as it was discovered in South Georgia in late 2023, but later in that summer it was also found in the Falkland Islands. Species affected have included black-browed albatrosses, gentoo penguins and Antarctic skuas. The Falkland Islands Government responded quickly by closing some islands for a period until no further deaths were reported.

Therefore, any prospective traveller to the islands should look out for any announcements in case the disease should return. When on the islands, any sick-looking birds should be reported to your accommodation provider, who will take further action. Needless to say, these birds should not be handled, and instead be kept at distance and left to the authorities.

more widespread than the silvery grebe, although they can often be found on the same stretches of water. Slightly smaller than the white-tufted grebe, the **silvery grebe** is a delicate, paler-looking bird with a distinct black nape patch and attractive fan-shaped plumes on the ear coverts during the summer months. The **white-tufted grebe** in breeding plumage has an almost all-black head and neck, with a white patch on the rear of the face fanning out from behind the eye. In winter time the throat is a pale off-white colour, while the neck and crown are dull brown. Grebes are very active birds and are constantly diving, so their presence on a particular pool is not always immediately obvious, especially as they like to nest in pools with a healthy growth of aquatic vegetation, on which they build their nests.

Albatrosses The only species of albatross to nest on the islands is the black-browed albatross with 70% of the world's population breeding in the Falklands. However, other species have been seen from the islands at certain times of year. Late summer and early autumn are good periods to look for **royal albatross** from headlands such as Cape Pembroke on East Falkland or Tamar Head on Pebble Island. These huge birds can only be seen properly with a telescope, despite their enormous wingspan.

A visit to a **black-browed albatross** colony is an unforgettable experience, situated as they are along the tops of cliffs on some of the westernmost islands. Looking offshore from almost any vantage point on the Falklands one can observe black-browed albatrosses, but a visit to a colony is a must to see them at their best. West Point Island and New Island are home to two of the best-known colonies (pages 173 and 177), and subsequently these two islands are included in the itineraries of many of the Expedition cruise ships (page 54) that call into the islands during an austral summer. For the land-based visitor, Saunders Island is the most accessible and some cruise ships also call here.

These graceful birds return each year to their mud-pot nests situated high on the cliffs. One egg is laid in early October and the young are ready to leave in March and April. Once fledged these young will wander the southern oceans until they are ready to start breeding in their fifth season, having come to inspect prospective breeding sites for a few weeks in the previous two years. Concerns about the declining populations of this species, in the Falklands and elsewhere, have led to a campaign to raise awareness of the large numbers of these birds that are accidentally killed by the long-lining fishing industries in the South Atlantic. This is being run by the Agreement on the Conservation of Albatrosses and Petrels (known as ACAP; w acap. aq). Recent successful work to reduce this bycatch in the legal fisheries has resulted in an increase in the number of breeding pairs, with roughly 500,000 pairs thought to be breeding on the Falkland Islands – 72% of the world population. Numbers have remained relatively stable, although their productivity has reduced slightly.

Petrels Effortless, gliding flight is a characteristic shared with the **southern giant petrels**, which breed on the islands. These long-winged birds have a wingspan of about 80 inches (203cm) and a stocky, heavily built body. A heavy bill creates the impression of a massive head. The scavenging habits of this species gave rise to its local name of 'stinker', and this close association with humans can give the impression that there are more of these petrels around the islands than is actually the case. Older birds tend to show a pale head and forebody, while younger birds are more uniformly dark brown. Birds with almost white plumage, apart from a few single black feathers, are thought to originate from further south and are seen most years but do not join the breeding colonies. A single egg is laid on flat ground close to the shore, often near a slope to give them sufficient updraft to assist take off. These birds are very shy when nesting, so it is absolutely essential to give them a wide berth in order to avoid disturbing the colony. Maybe albatrosses are more elegant in flight, but giant petrels are nonetheless fantastic birds to watch gliding low over the water, with the merest twitch of a feather sending them in another direction.

Various other members of the petrel family can be seen from, or nest on, the islands. **Prions** are sometimes visible like grey and white spectres flitting between waves. They are best observed at sea around the west of the islands or from some of the exposed headlands in a strong gale. Nowadays they only nest on some of the outlying islands, but they do so in large numbers. Coming ashore at night, they are most often seen from ships around the islands. **Southern fulmars** and **pintado petrels** pass the islands during the spring and the autumn en route to and from their breeding grounds further south. These are probably the most common non-breeding species of petrel that can be seen from the shore.

Other nocturnally breeding seabirds include white-chinned petrels, sooty shearwaters and great shearwaters. All three fly low over the sea with outstretched wings shearing the surface of the water. Sooty shearwaters breed in large numbers on Kidney Island at the southern entrance to Berkeley Sound, and therefore big flocks can be seen in the vicinity. This tussac island is also prime habitat for white-chinned petrels and great shearwaters, although they are found in much lower numbers. **White-chinned petrels** and **sooty shearwaters** are an even, dark brown colour, with the exception of the silvery underwing of the sooty shearwaters. The latter are smaller birds flying in a very dynamic manner, unlike the more relaxed albatross-style flight of the white-chinned petrels. **Great shearwaters** have a warm brown colouring on the upper parts, apart from a dark cap and white bands over the nape and rump. The underbody is white apart from a dusky patch on the belly and a dark bar along the underwing. All three can be seen at sea around the islands but the entrance to Berkeley Sound is the most likely locality to see them.

Three species of **storm petrel** breed on the islands but the best way to see them, other than a lucky sighting at sea, is to visit a tussac island at night. Consequently, few visitors see black-bellied storm petrels, grey-backed storm petrels or Wilson's storm petrels, as these tiny seabirds are so elusive. Another very small seabird is the **common diving petrel**, which again breeds in some of the more inaccessible islands in the archipelago. This minute, black-and-white seabird has rarely been reported in large groups. It is only found on those very unusual, flat, calm days when something as small as these birds can be seen.

Shags

A walk along almost any shore on the islands will bring the visitor within binocular range of **rock shags**. Their cousins, the **imperial or king shags**, are not quite as numerous but can be found without too much difficulty. Both species are typical cormorants, with long thin necks often the only visible part of the bird when sitting on the sea. On land they can sometimes be seen roosting together on rocky outcrops, but tend to have differing requirements for choice of breeding site. Rock shags are found building nests on cliff sides or on other steep slopes, whereas the king shags prefer to nest on flat open ledges at the top of the cliffs, often in association with rockhopper penguins (page 33).

Herons

A widespread resident on the islands, the **black-crowned night heron** can be found feeding in fresh and salt water. When feeding, these herons are a solitary species, but they can be found roosting communally on old wrecks, jetties and on low rocky cliffs. Generally described as crepuscular, they can sometimes be seen by day feeding along the more isolated waterways. As with all herons they are very patient fishers, standing still for what seems an eternity before striking with lightning speed. Colonies of black-crowned night herons are most often found in reed beds, tussac grass and trees, or on low cliffs close to their feeding grounds. This normally silent bird lets out a harsh squawk when disturbed, hence its local name 'quark'. The name 'quark pond' often indicates the presence of this species. At the nest the young make such a wide range of hisses and guttural noises that it can sound as though several species are present. The dapper adults are in stark contrast to the brown, streaky plumage of the rather demonic-looking immature birds. The race of black-crowned night heron found on Falkland is endemic to the islands.

Waterfowl

Swans Usually only one species of swan, the black-necked swan, breeds on the islands. The coscoroba swan, although best regarded as a vagrant from South America, bred successfully on the islands in the 2000/2001 season, but has not done so since. Occasional single birds have appeared subsequently but have rarely stayed for long. **Black-necked swans** are the largest breeding bird on the islands but tend only to frequent a few favoured locations. Some of the largest counts have been obtained on Pebble Island, but the Hawk's Nest Ponds area on West Falkland and the Goose Green region on East Falkland are also good places to look for this shy species. The well-documented, shy behaviour of black-necked swans usually results in distant views of this elegant species. The rare good views reveal the red bill and the bump in front of the eye. When their cygnets are small, they sometimes get a free ride on their parents' back, so that all that can be seen is a tiny white head peeping out from beneath the adult's wings. Once the young are able to fly, all the birds leave the lakes and ponds to spend the winter months on tidal streams and estuaries, where they undergo their annual moult during the early autumn.

Geese Three breeding species of wild geese are represented on the islands. The term ubiquitous definitely applies to the **upland geese**. They have been recorded breeding on almost every acre in the islands. The white head, neck and breast of the male make them one of the first birds visitors identify on arrival, whereas the browner, more camouflaged plumage of the female and the young cause them to be less detectable. In the early 20th century the government classed them as a pest and introduced a bounty payment for goose beaks, as they were perceived to be in competition with the sheep for pastureland. Subsequently, it was found that the only problems occurred on greens and reseeded grasslands near fresh water, where ironically their presence was enriching the grass thanks to their frequent droppings! Upland geese have been a welcome addition to the local diet since the time of the early settlers, and their feathers have been used as brushes for sweeping and painting. Their presence on the islands has been better tolerated in recent years. It is possible to see them grazing beside the road in Stanley, often on Victory Green.

The other white goose on the islands is the male **kelp goose**. As the name suggests, this is a much more maritime species spending most of its time eating many of the algae that grow in the intertidal zone along the shore. Rarely seen more than a few yards from the coast, they will eat short grass a little way inland and in autumn will go in search of ripe diddle-dee berries (page 26), but otherwise only come above the beach to bathe and drink in fresh water. The white plumage of the male contrasts with the female's barred underparts and glossy black back, which renders her almost invisible on the beach. They remain in pairs throughout the year, usually staying on their territory, although small flocks are sometimes seen at the beginning and end of the breeding season.

The third species of wild goose, the **ruddy-headed goose**, is almost as numerous as the upland goose. Both male and female initially look rather like a female upland goose but are smaller birds that have much finer barring along the flanks, paler flight feathers and dull orange, not yellow, legs. Ruddy-headed geese have a much more upright gait and are generally noisier, especially when taking off. They do not range as far inland as upland geese, preferring to stay close to the coast. The numbers of ruddy-headed geese that breed on Falkland have become internationally important as a result of the species' population crash in South America. Since 1985 this species has been removed from the list of pest species that are legally hunted on the islands as a result of their increased global importance.

The larger **ashy-headed goose**, although superficially similar to the ruddy-headed goose, is the complete opposite in that it is a very rare bird on the Falkland Islands but is still common in South America. **Feral domestic geese** are included on any checklist of the birds of the Falkland Islands as they are considered to be wild birds. Since their introduction in the late 1700s they have maintained populations in settlements in East and West Falkland and some other outlying islands.

Ducks Nine species of annually breeding duck can be seen on the islands. Almost every bay or inlet on the islands has a pair or small group of **Falkland steamer duck** cruising around the shallows. This endemic species is one of two very similar species of steamer ducks that breed on the islands. It has been remarked that the only safe way to distinguish between the two is to wait until one takes off! **Flying steamer ducks** prefer large bodies of fresh water and are not commonly noted on the sea. Their longer wings, lighter body structure, especially around the head, and bill give them a much sleeker appearance than the stocky big-billed Falkland steamer duck. Adults of the latter species are often found in pairs or family groups spread over extensive kelp beds or spaced out along the shore, as they are extremely territorial. In late summer flocks of up to 200 immature birds may gather together in favoured feeding areas. The name 'steamer' originates from the 'steaming' action they use when escaping predators or chasing away other birds from their territory, as they race over the surface of the water with wings and feet sending up sheets of water. In windy conditions younger, and therefore lighter, birds are just about capable of flight, but only over short distances. A large percentage of their day is spent on the water diving for crabs and shellfish they pick up from the seabed. Flying steamer ducks are equally aggressive to their own kind, so it is unusual to see more than one pair on a particular lake, unless it has sufficient food supplies and is large enough to accommodate two pairs. This very shy species does not usually tolerate close approach by humans, whereas the Falkland steamer duck will quite often ignore the presence of anything other than another steamer duck. Observed at close range, it is possible to see the spurs on the forewing that the males use for defending their territory. Males of both species have an orange bill and are much paler on the head than the dull green/brown bill and darker head of the females.

Of the remaining species of duck, the **cinnamon teal** and the **red shoveler** are thought to be only sporadic breeders on the islands. The **speckled teal**, also sometimes known as the yellow-billed teal, is the smallest duck of the region and the most widespread. This neatly marked brown duck with a bright yellow bill in the male and a dull yellow bill in the female is most often encountered on fresh water, but can occasionally be seen on the sea. Typically, this bird is found in small groups, often heard before seen, and may allow close approach unless it accompanies its young.

Frequently confused with the yellow-billed teal, the **yellow-billed pintail** is superficially very similar in that it is a brown duck with a yellow bill. On closer inspection the long neck, more rounded head and longer tail, together with its larger size, should identify this species. It is also found on the region's rivers and lakes and has been reported from the sea in the winter months. It is the least common of the annually breeding ducks on the islands, but it is not confined to any particular site, having been regularly reported from East Falkland (especially Lafonia), Pebble Island and a few of the larger lakes on West Falkland.

By taking advantage of both fresh- and salt-water habitats, the **crested duck** is one of the most numerous on the islands. At first glance it appears a rather drab bird, but when seen in good light its plumage is an intricate pattern of browns and whites with a chestnut patch in the outstretched wing and a bright red eye. This elegant duck is a vocal species; small groups are constantly quacking and making a range of other noises among themselves.

The other two species of wildfowl that a visitor can expect to see on the islands are **Chiloé wigeon** and **silver teal**, the most attractive of the resident ducks. They have similar habitat requirements; the freshwater pools of Lafonia are the strongholds for both species. With a few exceptions, these two species are not easy to find on any of the islands to the west of Falkland Sound, although the Hawk's Nest Ponds on West Falkland and some of the pools on Pebble Island such as Long Pond and Bett's Pond, have been reliable locations in recent years. Chiloé wigeon can sometimes be found on the sea but are more easily seen on the freshwater lakes along with the silver teal. Neither species is very tolerant of humans and will soon move out to the centre of any lake. The head pattern on a silver teal is very distinctive: black crown, white cheek and blue bill, which has a splash of orange near the base. The rest of the body is neatly barred with black, brown and white. The Chiloé wigeon has an equally characteristic head pattern with a white crescent-shaped mark in front of the eye and a white patch behind the eye on an otherwise dark head. The orange flanks and white-edged black mantle feathers can be difficult to see at a distance. This is one of the larger species of duck on the freshwater pools, appearing to float higher on the water than most other ducks. On calm days the clear whistling calls of these charming birds echo across the water.

Birds of prey The only vulture to be found on the islands, the **turkey vulture**, can be seen around the whole archipelago, soaring high in the sky on calm days or hugging the contours in a howling gale. Their incredible mastery of the air is very different from their ungainly hop and waddle on the ground. The wrinkled head – red-coloured in adults and dirty-white in juveniles – and all-black plumage, along with its scavenging habits, do not make this one of the most popular birds on the islands. For many years they were thought to be killing the sheep they ate, hence the bounty paid for each of their rather ugly heads. Only in recent times have they been seen as scavengers rather than as predators, a vital role in an area with very little else occupying that niche; there are no members of the crow family here, for example.

Shrieking calls from oystercatchers are often the first hint that a peregrine is about to strike. **Cassin's falcon** is the local name for the race of peregrine falcon that breeds on the Falkland Islands. Waders such as oystercatchers and dotterel are among a wide range of prey taken by this sleek killing machine. The breeding range of the peregrine on Falkland is concentrated at the north and south of the islands, although wandering birds can turn up almost anywhere, as they sometimes have to travel for many miles to find food. Prions, caught several miles out to sea then brought back to a convenient sea cliff to be plucked, are a welcome supplement to their diet in the summer months.

Variable hawks are easy birds to see on the Falkland Islands, whether sat on a roadside telegraph pole or observed in the distance quartering the ground. This member of the buzzard family occurs in light and dark colour phases, the underparts ranging from a deep russet brown to white. The colour of the mantle is the best way to distinguish the sexes; the males have slate-grey feathers and the female's mantle is a bright, reddish brown. Variable hawks soon indicate if the visitor is too close to the nest by circling above the site and calling. Occasionally they have been known to try to dive bomb those who get too close. Introduced rats and mice have been a welcome addition to their diet, along with the usual prey of small birds, including the chicks of almost all the local waterfowl. They are very determined predators, seemingly able to shrug off the mobbing of a gull colony as they single out one chick before plucking it from the ground and carrying it off to eat in peace and quiet.

The only member of the bird of prey family to be represented by two species breeding on the islands is the caracara. The globally threatened striated caracara still maintains a foothold on the islands, as does the more widespread southern caracara. The Johnny Rook, as the **striated caracara** is known, is the rogue of the bird world. These long-legged creatures are very inquisitive, always the first to investigate anything new that just might be a source of food. Their habit of capturing interesting objects for a better look has resulted in many lost hats, gloves, lens caps, cameras, etc. This tameness, allied to a bloodthirsty attitude to anything smaller or less healthy than themselves, put them into conflict with the early sheep farmers. The outcome of this was a bounty paid for every beak, resulting in many hundreds of birds being killed until the act was annulled in 1920. The present-day population is concentrated around some of the outlying islands, with very few breeding records in close proximity to any settlement on East or West Falkland. This species has undergone a steady reduction of numbers in South America, so the small Falkland Island population of around 750–850 pairs is important for the survival of this species. The **southern caracara**, or *carancho*, has a wider distribution on the islands and in South America. The shy, timid nature of this bird has probably been its saviour as they are very difficult to approach, always managing to detect the presence of any intruder before the intruder sees them. Larger than the striated caracara, with a black crown highlighted by a pale face and large orange beak, it is an attractive species. In flight the broad black wings show a white roundel towards the wing tip, which aids identification from afar. A bounty, paid upon the production of their beaks, for their perceived predation of lambs, probably accounts for their timid behaviour.

Waders

Wading birds are found in most habitats on the Falkland Islands. Two species of oystercatchers can be seen around the shores. The startlingly black-and-white **magellanic oystercatchers** are the more common; the sooty-black **blackish oystercatchers** are a little more secretive and less obvious. Their preferred breeding and feeding habitats differ, as magellanic oystercatchers are usually found on open sandy beaches with low, grassy hills and the occasional freshwater pond nearby, while the blackish oystercatchers frequent rocky shores with good supplies of their staple food, mussels. These are not absolute requirements, as they can be found away from the typical habitat. They are a typically vocal species of oystercatcher and their high-pitched whistling call carried on the wind is one of the evocative sounds of the islands. The call of the blackish oystercatcher is very reminiscent of that made by the European oystercatcher, even though the magellanic oystercatcher is closer in appearance. Both species make their nest close to the top of the beach in a small scrape, which they sometimes line with small pieces of shell or lichen, and they are very vigorous in defending their eggs and their young from any marauding predators.

Magellanic snipe can be found in a wide range of habitats, from tussac islands to the open, white-grass plains, although their cryptic plumage conceals them well until they spring into the air from their hiding places. In the early part of the breeding season the drumming noise made by the tail feathers as they perform their display flights can be heard around the islands. Some birds seem oblivious to humans and can be watched, probing the ground with their long bills, from only a few feet away.

Soft, piping calls heard while walking over diddle-dee heathlands are often the first clue that the visitor is in the territory of a **rufous-chested dotterel**. This attractive bird is widespread throughout the islands on the drier heaths. Its reddish-brown breast, dark, horizontal breast line, and narrow, white eyebrows make this an easy species to identify. As soon as any intruder – human, sheep or cattle – enters the territory of a male dotterel, it starts calling and keeps a very wary eye on the progress of the unwelcome visitor. They have been known to try to drive off any livestock that get too close to the nest. This rather solitary species does gather into small flocks at the end of the breeding season. It is thought that some birds then leave the islands for the winter months before returning in August.

The **two-banded plover** is not quite as prevalent on the islands as the rufous-chested dotterel but can be encountered on most islands. Both species have a similar feeding technique in that they hunt by sight for the small invertebrates that make up a large proportion of their prey. A short run, stop and look, before another short run, can identify these two birds at great distance, as they look like clockwork toys running over the landscape. The male of this delicate plover, with its two black breast bands (the upper one usually incomplete) and its rufous nape and crown, is much easier to find than the duller-marked female. Two-banded plovers are a coastal species rarely found far from the shore, preferring sandy beaches to rocky coasts. The nest scrape can be situated anywhere from the top of the beach to the diddle-dee heaths a little way inland.

Several other species of wader have been recorded from the islands, most occurring as vagrants during the spring and autumn. The most numerous of these, and therefore the most likely to be seen on a visit to the islands, are the **white-rumped sandpipers** which breed in arctic North America and winter on the islands, forming large flocks in favoured locations such as around the pools on Pebble Island or the Canache near Stanley. These inconspicuous waders are best sought on open sand and mud flats, or short grassy turf. Their most distinctive feature is the white rump that is only visible during flight. White-rumped sandpipers have grey-brown upper parts and white underparts, making them rather drab birds in comparison with the resident waders.

Gulls The sea hen, as the **Falkland skua** is known, is a summer visitor to the islands that can be found harassing other birds (in particular, shags, gulls and terns) to obtain food. This large, brown, thickset seabird breeds in loose colonies on grassy headlands or hilltops not far from the sea around the coast of the Falkland Islands. They can be very aggressive in defending their nest sites, diving at any intruder and hitting them with their outstretched legs. They deliver painful blows, which are very effective in driving away human and beast. Not all are this ferocious; some well-known birds are so tame that they will allow themselves to be picked up, but discretion is much the better option when coming across breeding skuas.

Kelp gulls, dolphin gulls and brown-hooded gulls all breed on the Falklands, the last being the least populous. The ability of the **kelp gull** to extract food from a variety of sources has resulted in it being the most common gull on the islands, seen in every possible habitat, as happy to glide over the settlements as to follow fishing boats miles from land. These birds nest in large colonies sometimes mixed in with dolphin gulls. The black-and-white plumage of the kelp gull is very different from the mid-grey underparts, black mantle and wings of the **dolphin gull**. The latter also has a heavy, red bill and legs of a similar hue, making it one of the most attractive gulls in the world. It is by far the more aggressive of the two, finding food by harrying other birds, scavenging, or taking advantage of the rubbish provided by humans. It can also be very vigorous in defending its nest site and yet, where humans have trained it, it will take food offered from the hand. **Brown-hooded gulls** are the hardest of the three gulls to find away from the breeding grounds. They can often be found nesting on beaches or shingle bars in lakes in the company of South American terns and kelp gulls, but spend most of their time feeding over the kelp beds or over some of the islands' more active tide races. Small parties of gulls can sometimes be seen hovering low over the surface of the sea. The brown hood is only present when the bird is in breeding condition; some of the older birds develop a pink flush to the underparts in spring and early summer. When feeding over the kelp beds they can look rather similar to the South American tern but have a less fluid wing action and a white leading edge to the forewing in contrast to the almost uniformly grey-white thinner wing of the tern.

South American terns are absent from the islands during the winter months, reappearing in late September to breed on shingle and sandy beaches, or on rocky headlands. Some pairs will seek a similar habitat near the larger lakes on the islands. This graceful flier has a well-deserved reputation, similar to the skua's, for protecting its nest site against all comers. The first warning is a harsh cry coming from aloft as the adult bird positions itself above the nest. A swift retracing of footsteps would then be to the advantage of all parties, for continued disturbance can lead terns to desert their eggs, and they have been known to inflict a painful blow to those who ignore the warning cry.

Snowy sheathbills are one of those species whose whiter-than-white appearance is deceptive. A pure white, pigeon-like bird found around many of the big rockhopper penguin and king shag colonies, it is usually found feeding on anything from regurgitated food to dead chicks and stolen eggs, as befits a well-practised scavenger. Sheathbills can be found here throughout the year, but they are non-breeding, immature birds whose populations increase during the winter as birds arrive from their Antarctic breeding grounds.

Owls Finding either of the two species of owl that breed on the Falkland Islands takes some planning and a great deal of luck. **Barn owls** are very rare on the islands – a result of a lack of suitable breeding habitats. They are also hard to see due to their nocturnal behaviour. The chances of seeing barn owls are minimal, even though they patrol a very wide territory. **Short-eared owls** are more numerous but are still difficult to find, as they are most common on tussac islands, or in locations where the small-bird population has not been decimated by introduced ground predators. The island race of short-eared owl has adapted to the scarcity of land mammals and small birds by becoming mostly nocturnal, snatching storm petrels, diving petrels and large insects such as camel-crickets, which breed prolifically on these tussac islands.

Passerines The stretch of sea between mainland South America and the Falkland Islands means that very few small birds reach the islands. Some strong fliers, such as the **barn swallow** and the **Chilean swallow**, can be seen most years, but have not as yet been able to establish a breeding presence on the islands. Nine other immigrant species breed on a regular basis and exhibit characteristics of racial or specific endemism. One other, the **house sparrow**, has been introduced by humans and subsists around some of the larger settlements including Stanley. The introduction of cats, rats and mice many years ago has brought about a decline in the numbers of the **tussacbird**, but this species is still the most numerous of the small birds on the islands. It is now confined to tussac grass islands and to places such as Carcass Island where the aforementioned predators are absent. It is also now thought to be a separate species from the blackish cinclodes, which occurs in southern South America. The tussacbird is very tame and incredibly inquisitive, perching on visitors' shoes, investigating camera bags and generally inspecting anything that could conceivably hold a scrap of food. At first glance its dull black plumage, only enlivened by a dull yellow bill, does not make it the most attractive of birds, but its cheeky character soon endears it to all. Tussacbirds spend most of their time not far from the top of the beach, although on some of the smaller islands they can be found almost anywhere.

One species that appears to have benefited from humankind's arrival is the **dark-faced ground-tyrant**. This close relative of the flycatcher family, although still common around cliffs and other rocky outcrops, has learnt that there is a good supply of flies and other insect life around the settlement buildings. Its habit of perching on a good vantage point, to keep an eye out for prey, is thought to be one of the reasons that the species has not been decimated by the introduced cats and rats, as happened with the tussacbird, which is habitually a ground dweller. The grey-brown, dark-faced ground-tyrant is present over most of the islands and goes by the local name of 'news bird', as it often approaches any visitors to its territory, calling as if waiting to exchange gossip.

There are two species of wren breeding on the islands, the Falkland grass wren and **Cobb's wren**. The latter is an endemic species closely related to the house wren of South and North America. It is thought to have formerly existed in large numbers, but the presence of cats, rats and mice has restricted its range to those tussac grass islands upon which these predators have not been introduced. As a result, the wrens are very common along the upper shore on islands such as Sea Lion, Carcass and Kidney but are absent over much of the archipelago. Initially they can be difficult to see but soon give themselves away with their rattling 'chirr' call as they hop around the boulders at the top of the beach, disappearing under one rock and popping out from beneath another a few feet away. Cobb's wrens often adopt the typical wren pose of tail in the air when alarmed, and then vanish in the blink of an eye, their warm brown plumage matching the colour of the kelp strewn along the tideline.

Falkland grass wrens are much more widespread, inhabiting many of the white-grass plains, especially where the grass and reeds form clumps, as well as the bands of tussac grass. However, the difficulty in detecting the presence of this species after they have ceased singing makes any attempt at comparison of numbers with the more evident Cobb's wren unreliable. These streaky brown birds run about between clumps of vegetation like mice, rarely flying unless flushed. Despite being the smallest of the breeding birds on the islands, its song in springtime carries a long way over the grasslands or the reedbeds by some of the larger lakes where they breed.

The **Falkland pipit** is the best of the resident songbirds. Called the 'skylark' by early settlers, it sings as it soars, before parachuting to the ground, with its tail held up, emitting a series of whirring notes. As is the case with many good songsters, it is a well-camouflaged bird when on the ground, creeping around the grass stems in its preferred white-grass habitat. Visitors travelling across the open grasslands of the islands will regularly disturb Falkland pipits, whereas stopping to look for this secretive species will often prove futile.

The **Falkland thrush** can be found in a range of habitats from settlement gardens to tussac grass islands. Their loud song is a familiar sound in the Falkland spring as, perched on prominent song posts, they can be heard over the normal sounds of farm life. One of the largest land birds on the islands, they can be seen hopping around lawns or other areas of open grass as well as feeding under the fringes of mature tussac grass. The male shows a slightly darker head than that of the female, but both have rusty brown underparts with darker brown backs and tails. They are strong fliers, seeming to have no trouble in getting from one area to another even on the windiest of days. **Long-tailed meadowlarks**, on the other hand, are not such skilful fliers. The flailing of their wings keeps them airborne as they move from place to place in small flocks, but it is not uncommon to see one blown at great speed through the air on windy days. The bright red breast of the males has resulted in local names such as the 'robin' or 'military starling'. The drabber-looking females and young males are not as colourful. They are quite a vocal species, especially in spring, emitting a wide range of sharp notes.

The **white-bridled finch** (formerly called black-throated finch), the larger of the two finches on the islands, is the more widespread. Black-chinned siskins are rarely found far from the coast and prefer to nest in the hedges and bushes of many settlements. White-bridled finches have the appearance of a northern hemisphere bunting in that they are big-headed, long-tailed birds that feed by hopping along the ground with the body held in a horizontal posture. Found in a wide range of grassland and shrub habitats, including the perimeter of dense banks of tussac grass, the male and female black-throated finches were once thought to be two species as their appearance is so dissimilar. Males with their powder-blue/grey head, black eye and chin edged with white, with green in the wings, tail and belly, are a very different bird from the brown-streaked female. It is thought that this species was more common on the Falkland Islands before the introduction of cats, and the burning of white grass in spring, which, while encouraging new grass growth for the sheep, destroys nesting habitats. The island race of white-bridled finches has assumed increasing importance for the conservation of this species due to the decline in the southern South American race. The monotonous little ditty that is the song of the white-bridled finches is one of the sounds of spring.

Less frequently heard is the jangling song of the **black-chinned siskin** coming from the branches of a pine tree or echoing from deep within the tussac grass. The thin, piping call of the siskin is often the first clue that they are nearby, as they can be rather inconspicuous at times, despite the yellow and brown plumage of the male with his neat little black cap and chin. The female is a duller version of the male without any black on the head or chin.

House sparrows seem to fit in with the very Britishness of Stanley and the larger settlements, where they have settled since their initial arrival from Montevideo in 1919. It appears that they hitched a ride on four different boats and only took a few years to spread around the major settlements of the islands. They seem to be able to cope with the windy weather on the Falkland Islands, although they did decrease in number after the cold winter of 1995, but have since recovered in numbers.

They are still plentiful around Stanley and are occasionally seen elsewhere in East Falkland, but rarely far from habitation.

Migrants Various other species of bird have been noted as reaching the islands since records began. Some, such as **sanderlings** and **cattle egrets** are reported most years, but a great many others are only recorded as very rare vagrants. Broadly speaking, these vagrants can be put into three main categories. Firstly, there are an increasing number of records of long-range North American migrants, which have overshot the southern limit of their normal wintering range. The second group consists of species which undertake short-range migrations in South America and are then blown off course at a crucial moment during their flight. The third group includes the species, mostly seabirds, which breed well to the south of the islands, but which come back into Falkland waters at the onset of winter before returning south during the austral spring. **Pectoral sandpiper** and **Baird's sandpiper** are good examples of the first group; **white-crested elaenia** and **fire-eyed diucon** correspond to the second category, while **southern fulmar**, **pintado petrel** and **grey-headed albatross** fulfil the criteria of the third.

REPTILES AND AMPHIBIANS There are no reptiles or amphibians on the islands. The distance from mainland South America and the ambient temperature have stopped them colonising the archipelago.

INSECTS Insects are probably the least studied class of animal on the islands; many of those species that have been identified there are beyond the scope of this guide. Some insects are easily found and are identifiable by the layperson while others, more elusive, call for closer scrutiny. The **green spider** is one such species, which, despite its wide distribution throughout the islands, can often be hard to find. A search along a sheltered hedge or in a stand of *blechnum* fern in the lee of a rocky outcrop can usually bring to light a large-bodied spider with a bright green abdomen that has a pale, white, central stripe. Some may not be as brightly marked as others, but inspection of other webs will often yield a better-coloured specimen. One of the largest insects on the Falkland Islands, and prey for several species of bird, is the **camel cricket**. In common with many insects that have adapted to survive in windy environments, these are wingless and reach up to 1 inch (2.5cm) long with legs and antennae that are almost double the body length.

Moths and butterflies are by far the most common insects encountered by visitors to the Falkland Islands. Many species of moth, some of which have become flightless, are rather small and therefore difficult to find, but a number of the larger species are strong fliers, fluttering around lights at night or dwelling in the vegetation. Careful examination of each specimen is needed to confirm its identity. Butterflies are scarcer, with only four species recorded on the islands. One of these, a pale blue butterfly, has been observed on several occasions over the years, most often in the mountains, but never conclusively identified. The only species thought to breed on the islands is the **queen of Falklands fritillary**, which is a medium-sized, dull-orange butterfly with many small black marks forming a pattern towards the outer edge of each wing. This fast-flying butterfly is very difficult to approach or photograph, thus making it difficult to identify. In good years, when it is warm and dry, it is widely reported, but in wet, cold years very few are recorded. Westerly winds between midsummer and early autumn provide the right conditions for the arrival of the **southern painted lady**. Larger and more brightly marked than the fritillary, this fast-flying species is equally difficult to photograph. The third known species of butterfly seen on the Falkland Islands is the **Brazilian painted lady**, which was first reported in the summer of 1999–2000. This species is very similar to the southern painted lady and could possibly have been overlooked in the past as the more extensive black-and-white markings in the forewing and the size of the two 'eyes' on the upper surface of the hind wing are not easy to see on this very mobile insect. When perched, it can be seen that the underwing has a much more defined pattern with two large 'eyes' and a blue subterminal line, both features absent from the southern painted lady.

SEASHELLS AND CRUSTACEA A walk along the tideline will find a range of seashells thrown up by the last gale. The rough seas mean that many are broken up as they lie on the beach, but a careful search should find some complete shells. The best-represented family are the familiar limpet shells, of which the most numerous is the **common limpet** that can be found clinging to rocks in the intertidal zone or washed up on the strand line. Limpets are a favourite food of the blackish oystercatcher (page 40), which can often be found chiselling them off the rocks, either eating them on the spot or running the gauntlet of the marauding gulls to take them back to the nest for their young. One of the most attractive of the limpets is the rather delicately painted **keyhole limpet**, which is easily identified by the hole in the top of the shell and the reddish-orange lines that radiate to the edge.

In sheltered waters where the sand is relatively undisturbed, **clams** may be found. These rather thick shells are found below the surface protecting the animal's body, which is a rarely exploited food source on the islands.

Another species of bivalve that has been eaten by humans are mussels, the largest of which, the **blue mussel**, can reach up to 7 inches (17cm) long, growing on kelp strands or piers and jetties. This species is washed ashore in large numbers to form piles of bleached shells at the top of the beach. By searching through the piles of shells left at the top of some of the beaches, the presence of a gastropod can be detected even if the shell is not present. The **rough thorn drupe** is a whelk which can grow to 2½ inches (6cm) long and which preys on many species of bivalves. If a fresh shell is found, the spike on the lower edge of the shell may still be present. It uses this spike to force open the shells of bivalves such as clams and mussels; its other method is to use its radula, a rough 'tongue', to rasp a hole in its prey's shell. Any shell presenting a small round hole has been the prey of the drupe.

The complete shell of a **lobster krill** is rarely seen on the beach, and yet they leave their mark like no other creature. This ten-legged shrimp has the appearance of a small, red lobster and two of its legs are tipped with pincers, the largest reaching some 2½ inches (6cm) long. These crustaceans are very common around the islands, feeding on the nutrients brought by the northward-flowing Falkland Current. In turn they are the food for many of the birds and some of the animals that breed on the islands, especially towards summer's end, when they form vast swarms which sometimes tinge the sea with red. This red pigment takes quite some time to break down and can cause pink-coloured patches on the sand or stains in the droppings of seals and penguins.

CONSERVATION

The wildlife of the Falkland Islands attracts many tourists to the islands. The teeming seabird colonies and huge sea mammals that are found in magnificent scenery make the Falkland Islands an outstanding location. However, this special place is in need of special protection. The first law designed to protect the wildlife was the Wild Animals and Birds Protection Ordinance, which became law in 1913 and only applied to a few species. The complete banning of hunting of any fur seals followed this in 1921. Very little changed over the next 40 years until 1964, when the Bird Protection Ordinance was revised and nature reserves were established. The Nature Reserves Ordinance made it possible for the flora and fauna of certain habitats to be preserved. Wildlife reserves are sites with total protection where no farming is allowed, while the wildlife sanctuaries are on private land where wildlife is protected and farming allowed to continue. Probably the best-known wildlife reserves are the Jason Islands (page 170), New Island (page 173) and Kidney Island (page 90). The steady acquisition of small islands resulted in a total of over 50 wildlife reserves, some owned by the government, some owned by private individuals. There are 22 Important Bird Areas and 16 Important Plant Areas – places of international significance for the conservation of birds or flora. Examples include Kidney Island, Sea Lion Island and Pebble Island.

In 1980 a new conservation body, the Falkland Islands Foundation, was formed. It has since merged with the Falkland Islands Trust to form **Falklands Conservation** (UK office: The Lodge, Potton Road, Sandy, Bedfordshire SG19 2DL; Stanley office: Jubilee Villas, Ross Rd FIQQ 1ZZ; w falklandsconservation.com). The late Sir Peter Scott conceived the idea of a conservation charity after a visit he and other conservationists made to the islands in 1979. Falklands Conservation is a charitable organisation concerned with protecting the unique wildlife of the Falkland Islands.

FALKLAND ISLANDS COUNTRYSIDE CODE

1 Always ask permission before entering private land.
2 Keep to paths wherever possible. Leave gates open or shut as you find them.
3 Be aware of the high fire risk throughout the islands. Be extra careful if smoking. Take cigarette butts away with you.
4 * Do not drop litter. Take your rubbish home with you.
5 Do not disfigure rocks or buildings.
6 * Do not touch, handle, injure or kill any wild bird or other animal.
7 Never feed wild animals.
8 Always give animals the right of way. Remember not to block the routes of seabirds and seals coming ashore in their colonies.
9 Try to prevent any undue disturbance to wild animals. Stay on the outside of bird and seal colonies. Remain at least 6m (20ft) away. When taking photographs or filming stay low to the ground. Move slowly and quietly. Do not startle or chase wildlife from resting or breeding areas.
10 * Some plants are protected and should not be picked. Wildflowers are there for all to enjoy and they should be left where they are found.
11 * Whalebones, skulls, eggs or other such items may not be exported from the Falkland Islands. They should be left where they are found.

* Such actions (with few special exceptions) may constitute an offence in the Falkland Islands and could result in fines up to £3,000.

Adopted for the Falkland Islands from guidelines adopted by members of IAATO, South Georgia Management Plan, Galápagos Rules for Preservation and the Code of Conduct for visitors to the Antarctic.

It belongs to the global organisation BirdLife International (w birdlife.org), which is working to protect birds and their habitats, and to the World Conservation Union (IUCN).

Research projects on seabirds, including penguins, are looking at breeding populations, with regular survey work taking place as well as studies looking at winter distribution of the crested penguins including rockhopper. This work is being undertaken to learn more about ecological factors and distribution, and also to monitor any threats to their populations. The charity is also involved with many other projects varying from surveys of the marine debris that gets washed up along the shores to the sei whale project studying this species in Berkeley Sound. It is also involved in habitat restoration in several locations around the islands such as that at Spring Point and Dunbar farms and at Cape Dolphin Farm, where a seed bank of local plants known as the Native Seed Hub has been created. Based on its findings, Falklands Conservation advises the Falkland Islands Government on a wide range of issues affecting wildlife. This includes environmental assessments and how to protect any wildlife from potentially harmful developments. It is also involved in direct action such as organising beach cleans, rescuing oiled seabirds, planting tussac grass and rat-eradication programmes. The office on Ross Road has items for sale, welcomes all callers and is interested in any wildlife sightings of note. By joining the charity, visitors are helping to protect the islands' wildlife and aiding the wide range of research work that is being undertaken.

Members of Falklands Conservation receive a journal, *Falkland Islands Wildlife Conservation* which gives updates on their work and information about the organisation. There is a youth section, which is part of the 'Wildlife Watch' run by the Wildlife Trusts in the United Kingdom. Children between the ages of eight and 16 get involved with projects such as tussac planting and have opportunities to visit some of the more remote locations, sometimes camping, on the islands. The 1964 ordinances were replaced in 1999 by the Conservation of Wildlife and Nature Bill, which sought to ensure that the Falkland Islands Government met its international obligations under the Bonn, Ramsar or Biodiversity conventions. Additional legal protection for black-browed albatross, southern giant petrel and white-chinned petrel was agreed in 2004 when the 'Agreement for the Conservation of Albatrosses and Petrels' was signed. This recognised that these species are some of the most threatened in the world and sought to co-ordinate efforts to protect them.

New Island, one of the best-known wildlife refuges on the islands, was originally divided into two: New Island North and New Island South. In 2006, the **New Island Conservation Trust** (w newislandtrust.com) was able to purchase the northern half of the island, bringing the whole island under one management. This registered charity aimed to conserve the unique habitat on New Island and to encourage research into wildlife on the island by providing facilities for long-term field studies. In 2020, it merged with Falklands Conservation.

A national park, potentially named the 'Hill Cove Mountains' is being proposed by the Falkland Islands Government. A draft policy statement was published in early 2024; at the time of writing, this was out for public comment and will hopefully come into being in the near future. The park had originally been proposed in 2001 but had been on the back burner until recently. This area of nearly 30,000 acres lies on West Falkland near the settlement of Hill Cove and contains 109 native plants, of which nine are endemic, and ranges from 100m to 700m in height, including the peaks of Mount Adam, Mount Robinson, Rat Castle and Mount Donald.

3

Practical Information

WHEN TO VISIT

To see the islands at their best it is advisable to plan a visit during the austral summer, **October to April**, when the tourist industry is geared up to ensure that visitors truly appreciate the archipelago, its wildlife and its way of life. The long summer evenings of December and January offer a welcome respite from winter in the northern hemisphere. It is possible to visit the islands at any time of year; however, some of the accommodation (page 59) closes out of season.

The reproductive cycles of the local **wildlife** may dictate when a visit to the Falklands is scheduled. Penguins are a major attraction (page 33) and they, in common with many other breeding seabirds, are at their most vocal when displaying in the early months of the summer. Chicks abound in midsummer. Southern elephant seals (page 31) and southern sea lions (page 30) can be seen throughout the tourist season, as can the scarce fur seal. The greatest concentrations of these impressive beasts are to be found during the pupping seasons in spring and midsummer. Killer whales, although far from common, are best observed when the pups start leaving the beaches.

As is to be expected, the flora is much more impressive in springtime when the majority of plants are in bloom; however, there are always some late spring and summer flowers, and several species produce attractive berries in the early autumn. For more information on the islands' flora, see page 23.

It is possible to come to the islands **to fish** for sea trout from 1 September to 30 April, although September and October and mid-February to mid-April are thought to be the optimal times for this species. Falkland mullet are not so seasonally variable and can be caught throughout the fishing season.

HIGHLIGHTS AND SUGGESTED ITINERARIES

It is not possible to do justice to the islands in a short stay – a **minimum of two weeks** is recommended in order to properly experience the way of life on the archipelago. It is possible to see something of the islands in a brief visit, but that would only provide a frustratingly superficial glimpse of what they have to offer. Keep in mind that away from Stanley, accommodation options are few and far between so be sure to book in advance to avoid the disappointment of missing any of these wonderful islands.

For many, the chance to see penguins and albatrosses is one of the major draws. For others, it's the opportunity to see a range of birds that are hard to see elsewhere such as striated caracara and tussacbird, plus the two endemics, Cobb's wren and Falkland steamer duck. The clear blue skies and wonderful scenery plus the photogenic wildlife mean the islands are very popular with photographers.

Travelling around the islands gives many photographic opportunities, ranging from watching the sheep shearing to viewing the isolated shepherds' houses set in spectacular scenery, as well as a chance to experience *camp* life. History buffs come to the islands to see some of the wrecks of the days of sail such as the *Lady Elizabeth* at the end of Stanley Harbour, or to visit the sites made famous in the 1982 war.

Any itinerary for a visit to the Falkland Islands should include a few days in **Stanley** (page 68), exploring the town, its environs and the Historic Dockyard Museum. The islands' tourist industry makes Stanley the focal point of any tour and, while there are places to stay within easy reach of the main airport at Mount Pleasant, the relatively wide range of accommodation available in Stanley plus the activities and entertainments on offer make it the ideal place to begin and end a visit.

Recommended day trips by road from Stanley include **Gypsy Cove** (page 85) for a first glimpse of penguins, and **Volunteer Point** (page 95) for the majestic king penguin colony (page 103). For the latter, allow a full day; for the former a few hours should suffice owing to its relative proximity to the town.

As an introduction to the outer islands or a conclusion to a tour of the Falklands, **Sea Lion Island** (page 122) is always enthralling. It's possible to observe abundant wildlife from right outside the door of the island's lodge. The short flight from Stanley takes less than 30 minutes before landing at the airstrip very close to the accommodation – tussacbirds may come to inspect your baggage and gentoo penguins can be heard in the near distance. Magellanic penguins can be heard calling to each other in the quiet of the night. A short walk in any direction from the lodge will bring visitors in contact with elephant seals, sea lions, penguins and a range of other seabirds. It is possible to walk the whole island in a day, but a more leisurely approach would reveal so much more. Try to allow at least two nights, but ideally three to make the most of it.

A 15-minute flight from Sea Lion Island is the settlement of **Port Howard** (page 129) on West Falkland, where it is possible to discover what living in *camp* is all about during a stay at Port Howard Lodge (page 133). This working farm, set in some magnificent scenery, is one of the best centres for fishing on the Falkland Islands and constitutes the ideal base to explore the wide expanses of West Falkland. The small museum next to the lodge (page 134) gives another dimension to this settlement as there are lots of photographs and artefacts from the Argentine occupation in 1982.

Vast areas of West Falkland are now accessible from Port Howard thanks to the road system and, as such, it is possible to be based here for several days while exploring the surrounding area. Recommended excursions include a day trip south to **Fox Bay** through some spectacular scenery to the eponymous settlement and the local penguin colonies. This tour usually incorporates a variety of stops en route, including some of the crashed aircraft from 1982 and the Hawk's Nest Ponds, before a reasonably direct drive back in the late afternoon. To the northwest of the island, visitors can take a day trip to the settlement of **Hill Cove** with its 'forest' before passing back through Turkey Rocks with sufficient time and the appropriate permissions to enter the farmland. A jut of quartzite, Turkey Rocks are popular with the local turkey vultures (hence the name…), but also give super views out over the rolling white-grass landscape. A further full-day drive by 4x4 out on the *camp* tracks to the northern coast of West Falkland at **White Rock** is another must for penguin fans. Its rugged coastline is a photographer's delight with penguin colonies situated where the diddle-dee heath and white-grass slopes meet the quartzite cliffs. Port Howard is a rather underestimated location as far as viewing wildlife is concerned, as there is only a limited selection of species close to the settlement, but the trips out from here access some of the best wildlife sites on the islands.

Another short flight from Port Howard to the northwest brings you to **Pebble Island** (page 145), where the various habitats shelter many of the bird species that breed on the Falkland Islands. The large pools on the eastern side are home to huge concentrations of waterfowl and the penguin rookeries are among the largest colonies seen on the islands. In the late 1990s and early 2000s the presence of two rare species of penguin, the erect-crested penguin and the macaroni penguin, meant that it became one of the very few places in the world where six species of penguin could be observed in one day. In more recent times, it has remained a reliable site for sightings of the macaroni penguin in the Falkland Islands, but the erect-crested has not been seen here for many years. It is possible to spend a minimum of three days on Pebble Island without returning to any of the wildlife sites, but a week would be preferable for those on a longer stay in the islands. This abundance of wildlife set in spectacular scenery, all within a short drive from a very relaxing lodge (page 147), makes this island a desirably integral part of any tour of the Falkland Islands.

These three locations combined with those that can be reached from Stanley make up the bare minimum of a trip to the islands. With longer, other suggestions include at least two days on the fabulous **Carcass Island** (page 165), with its throngs of small birds and day trips to **West Point Island** (page 171) for its wonderful albatross colonies, and **Saunders Island** (page 156), home to the magnificent black-browed albatross colony. There is a variety of accommodation on Saunders Island (page 158), enabling visitors – particularly photographers – to spend more than one day at the various colonies.

For passengers aboard one of the cruise ships which frequent the islands (page 54), any itinerary that includes Stanley, West Point Island and New Island is going to provide an excellent introduction to the Falkland Islands. The smaller Expedition cruise ships will typically make one or two stops at islands to the west or south of the archipelago (depending upon where they are coming from) on their first day and then a whole or part day in Stanley before sailing on. The larger ships usually only visit Stanley for the day or half day.

TOUR OPERATORS

Many tour operators advertise trips to the Falkland Islands, of which the majority visit most of the wildlife sites as part of their itinerary. Some companies have a great deal more Falklands experience than others, which should be kept in mind when making enquiries, and some only visit the islands occasionally (ie: not annually). For tourist information and local tour operators, see below and page 72; and for cruise-ship operators, page 54. Alternatively, **w TravelLocal.com** is a reputable UK-based website where you can book direct with selected local travel companies, allowing you to communicate with a ground operator without having to go through a third-party travel operator or agent.

LOCAL TOUR OPERATORS
There are 2 main travel agents based in Stanley. They will be happy to create a costed itinerary for a visit to the islands, including airport transfers, accommodation, local transport & excursions. One other, Penguin Travel, mainly deals with cruise ships & their passengers.

Falkland Islands Holidays [69 H4] PO Box 117; ☎22622; e info@falklandislandsholidays.com; w falklandislandsholidays.com.
International Tours & Travel [69 E2] 1 Dean St, FIQQ 1ZZ; ☎22041; e db.itt@horizon.co.fk; w falklandislands.travel
Penguin Travel [69 E1] Crozier Pl, West Store Complex, FIQQ 1ZZ; ☎27632; e penguin.travel@fic.co.uk; w penguintravelfic.com

UK *(national code +44)*
Abercrombie & Kent ☎01242 547 701;
w abercrombiekent.co.uk
Aqua-Firma Worldwide Ltd ☎01428 62001;
w aqua-firma.com
Audley Travel ☎01993 838000;
w audleytravel.com
Birdquest ☎01254 826317;
w birdquest-tours.com
Discover the World ☎01737 214250;
e travel@discover-the-world.com;
w discover-the-world.com
G Adventures ☎0344 272 2060;
w gadventures.com
Geodyssey ☎020 7281 7788;
w geodyssey.co.uk
Journey Latin America ☎020 31317308;
w journeylatinamerica.com
Last Frontiers ☎01296 653000; e info@
lastfrontiers.com; w lastfrontiers.com
Natures Images ☎01952 411436;
w natures-images.co.uk
Naturetrek ☎01962 733051; e info@naturetrek.
co.uk; w naturetrek.co.uk
Rainbow Tours ☎020 31312024; e info@
rainbowtours.co.uk; w rainbowtours.co.uk
Responsible Travel ☎01273 823700;
e rosy@responsibletravel.com;
w responsibletravel.com
Wildfoot Travel ☎0800 195 3385;
w wildfoottravel.co.uk
Wildlife Worldwide ☎01962 302086;
e reservations@wildlifeworldwide.com;
w wildlifeworldwide.com
Windows on the Wild ☎020 8742
1556; e info@windowsonthewild.com;
w windowsonthewild.com

EUROPE
Abenteuer Team Germany; ☎+49 201 8515
2452; w abenteuerteam.de

Auf Kurs! Inselreisen Germany; ☎+49 40 5712
965; w aufkursinselreisen.de
Duma Naturreisen Germany; ☎+49 00711
8386580; e duma@naturstudienreisen.de;
w duma-naturreisen.de
Experience Travel Netherlands; ☎+073
5482060; e info@experiencetravel.nl;
w experiencetravel.nl
Objectif Nature France; ☎+33 1 53 44 74 30;
w objectif-nature.fr
Tour 2000 Italy; ☎+39 712 803 752;
w tour2000.it

USA AND CANADA *(national code +1)*
Adventure Life ☎406 541 2677;
w adventure-life.com
Cheeseman's Ecology Safari's ☎0800 527
5330, (toll free in US) 408 741 5330; e info@
cheesemans.com; w cheesemans.com
David Hemmings Photo Tours ☎604 629 9577;
w hemmingsphototours.com
Goway Travel ☎877 417 7186; e info@goway.
com; w goway.com
Joseph Van Os Photo Safaris ☎206 463 5383;
e info@photosafaris.com; w photosafaris.com
Ladatco Tours ☎305 854 8422; e tailor@
ladatco.com; w ladatco.com
McDonald Wildlife Photography Inc ☎717 543
6423; e info@hoothollow.com; w hoothollow.com
Naturescapes ☎+1 410 239 8025;
w naturescapes.net
Vent ☎+1 512 328 5221; w ventbird.com

AUSTRALIA *(national code +61)*
**African Wildlife Safaris & Natural Focus
Safaris** ☎1300 363302; e info@awsnfs.com;
w africanwildlifesafaris.com

NEW ZEALAND
Exploring Kiwis e hello@exploringkiwis.com;
w exploringkiwis.com

RED TAPE

The Falkland Islands are relatively free of red tape apart from the usual entry formalities. All travellers arriving on the islands should have a valid passport, a visa if required (see w falklands.gov.fk/visitors/visiting-the-falkland-islands for more information) and return air tickets or evidence of prepaid onward travel arrangements. The visa requirements are broadly the same as those for the UK. Visitors must also have sufficient funds to cover their stay on the islands and have pre-booked accommodation.

A Falkland Islands Departure Tax will be levied on the islands for those visitors who have not paid this in advance through their tour operator. At present the tax is £25 only payable in cash (pounds sterling, US dollars or euros).

One further restriction that visitors should be aware of is that, as all the land on the Falkland Islands is privately owned, permission should be granted from the owner before crossing land for whatever reason.

EMBASSIES

The Falkland Islands' status as an overseas territory belonging to Britain means that all diplomatic business is dealt with in London and as such the islands have no overseas embassies. The British Government is represented on the islands by a governor who is based at Government House [74 B1](Ross Rd, Stanley FIQQ 1ZZ; ☏ +500 28200; e gov.house@horizon.co.fk; w gov.uk/world/organisations/governors-office-stanley; ⊕ 08.00–noon & 13.15–16.30 Mon–Fri).

The Falkland Islands Government have an office in London (Falkland Hse, 14 Broadway, SW1H 0BH; ☏ +44 (0)20 7222 2542; e reception@falklands.gov.fk; w falklands.gov.fk/londonoffice) that deals with raising awareness of the islands as well as giving the views of the local government and the islands' residents to officialdom and the general public in the UK. It is also the point of contact for civilians trying to book on the Ministry of Defence flights from the UK to the Falklands.

GETTING THERE AND AWAY

BY AIR There are two air routes to the Falkland Islands: from RAF Brize Norton in Oxfordshire, England or via commercial airlines to Santiago, Chile, then connecting with the **LATAM Chile** (w latam.com) flights via Punta Arenas to Mount Pleasant Airport. The LATAM Chile flights operate every Saturday. Travelling from **England**, the Royal Air Force flights are now operated for the Ministry of Defence (MOD) by a company called Air Tanker. These flights leave the UK twice weekly, but are sometimes subjected to delays if adverse weather conditions are prevailing on the islands; a comprehensive travel insurance package is advised. Typically, this means leaving the UK on Sunday and Wednesday evenings and returning on the corresponding Tuesdays and Fridays. This schedule may change during bank holiday periods. The RAF baggage allowance is 28kg, with any excess regarded as freight, only carried if there is space, and charged at £10/kg. The RAF flight takes 18 hours including a stopover of 90 mins to 2 hours on Ascension Island in the South Atlantic Ocean, during which time the plane is refuelled and stocks of food are replenished. Four meals are provided during the flight, two during each leg of the journey.

Travellers using the RAF flight are advised that, as this is not a commercial flight, it can be delayed or diverted. An overnight bag should be taken as hand luggage and any onward travel should take possible delays into consideration. On disembarking at Ascension Island all passengers are directed to a NAAFI lounge/compound where toilet facilities can be found and drinks are available from a small duty-free shop. No access is permitted to the plane until the call for boarding is relayed over the public-address system.

If planning to travel independently on the RAF flight you must deal directly with the travel co-ordinator at the Falkland Islands Government office (see above), where full information and a travel form can be obtained.

An alternative is to travel via **Chile**. Tourists can board the LATAM Chile flight in Santiago, via Punta Arenas to the Falkland Islands. There is also a monthly flight via **Argentina** which calls at Río Gallegos on the second Saturday of the month on its way to the islands, returning one week later. From Río Gallegos, it is possible to fly to Buenos Aires and other destinations in Argentina as well as Punta Arenas in Chile. Connecting with the LATAM Chile service is a Falkland Islands Government Air Service (FIGAS; w falklands.gov.fk/aviationservice) flight from Mount Pleasant to Port Howard on West Falkland, and on to Pebble Island. This flight is designed to give short-stay visitors the maximum time with wildlife, and must be pre-booked with FIGAS or with one of the local tour operators (page 73).

Flights from Sao Paulo to Mount Pleasant had started in November 2019 but were suspended during Covid and have yet to be restarted due to the Argentine Government revoking permission for the flight.

Airport transfer Transfers between Mount Pleasant and Stanley connecting with the RAF and LATAM Chile flights are available from **Falkland Islands Tours and Travel** (⌕ 21775; e admin@fitt.co.fk; w falklandtravel.com) or **Penguin Travel** (⌕ 27632; e penguin.travel@fic.co.uk; w penguintravelfic.com). Transfers are best booked in advance and take the best part of an hour, costing roughly £20. **Taxi** firms operating out of Stanley can also be booked for this journey; see page 72.

BY SEA An increasing number of visitors are reaching the islands on board **cruise ships** that call in on their way to South Georgia and to the Antarctic, with just over 59,936 passengers visiting this way in the 2022/2023 summer season. The sheer size of the larger ships restricts their visits to Stanley. They typically anchor out in Port William and then use their tenders to come through Stanley Narrows to land at the public jetty in front of the visitor centre. These visits range from a few hours to a full day depending upon their itineraries. The smaller ships, usually termed Expedition cruise ships, can land at a variety of sites. They most often stay around the islands for one day on an outer island followed by another day or half day in Stanley. The weather plays a major role in how successful these landings are with some cancelled because of strong winds. Some of the more popular destinations away from Stanley include West Point Island, New Island, Saunders Island and Carcass Island to the west of the archipelago, and Bleaker Island in the southeast of the Falklands.

It is also possible to **sail** to the islands on a private yacht, but it is essential to contact the Customs and Immigration Department (e admin@customs.gov.fk) and the Harbour Authorities (The Marine Officer, Fisheries Dep, PO Box 598, Stanley; e fishops@fisheries.gov.co.uk) at least 24 hours before arrival as well as seeking clearance by customs and immigration in Stanley before continuing elsewhere in the islands. For those arriving from South America, the islands are typically more than one day's sail from ports such as Ushuaia in Argentina.

Cruises calling at the Falklands can be arranged through the following operators among others:

Abercrombie & Kent International Inc USA: ⌕ +1 800 323 7308, +1 630 954 2944; e info@abercrombie.com; UK: ⌕0845 070 0601; e info@abercrombiekent.co.uk; w abercrombie.com
Exodus UK: ⌕0203 553 9398; w exodus.co.uk

Hurtigruten w hurtigruten.co.uk
Lindblad Expeditions ⌕+1 212 261 9000; w world.expeditions.com
Quark Expeditions w quarkexpeditions.com
Rockjumper w rockjumperbirding.com

Scenic	w scenic.co.uk
Seabourn	w seabourn.com
Silversea	w silversea.com

Wildwings ℡0117 965 8333; e tours@
wildwings.co.uk; w wildwings.co.uk

No vaccinations are mandatory to enter the Falklands. Visitors travelling to the islands via South America should consult their doctor or travel clinic as to which vaccines they may require. It makes sense to be up to date with routine vaccinations in your home country such as measles, mumps, rubella, diphtheria, tetanus, polio and (for higher-risk groups) COVID-19 and influenza. The islands' water supply is safe to drink.

Prolonged immobility on long-haul flights can result in deep-vein thrombosis (DVT), which can be dangerous if the clot travels to the lungs to cause a pulmonary embolus. The risk increases with age, and is higher in obese or pregnant travellers, heavy smokers, those taller than 6ft (1.8m), and anybody with a history of blood clotting disorders, recent major operation or varicose vein surgery, cancer, a stroke or heart disease. If any of these criteria apply, consult a doctor before you travel.

TRAVEL CLINICS AND HEALTH INFORMATION A full list of current travel clinic websites worldwide is available on w istm.org. For other journey preparation information, consult w travelhealthpro.org.uk (UK) or w wwwnc.cdc.gov/travel (USA). All advice found online should be used in conjunction with expert advice received prior to or during travel.

HEALTHCARE The islands have one well-equipped hospital in Stanley (page 76) which has doctors, dentists and other medical staff to cope with any health concerns. UK citizens can access free medical care through a reciprocal healthcare agreement. Travellers with complex medical problems may need to be medically evacuated to Chile or Uruguay. This is costly and not covered by the health agreement with the UK, so it is important to have comprehensive travel insurance. Mountain rescue is provided by local defence forces.

WALKING AND HIKING The climate in the Falklands is relatively cool and temperate but conditions can change rapidly. Walkers should wear a brimmed hat and high-factor sunscreen (SPF 30+) during the spring and summer. Carry sufficient food and water to account for emergencies and prolonged time periods outdoors. It is also sensible to bring a basic first aid kit. The last remaining landmines were cleared in 2020.

Hypothermia occurs when the body loses heat faster than it can be generated, and the commonest cause is a combination of wet or inadequate clothing, and cold wind. It's easily avoided by making sure you always have a waterproof, a sweater or fleece, and a survival bag with you – even if you're hiking with only a daypack. If one of your group shows signs of hypothermia – uncomfortable shivering, followed by drowsiness or confusion – it's essential that they are warmed up immediately. Wrap them in warm clothing, or even better a sleeping bag, then increase blood-sugar levels with food and hot, sweet drinks.

SAFETY

The Falkland Islands must be one of the safest places for travellers to visit. Crime is relatively unknown; muggings and pickpockets belong to another world. For

Practical Information SAFETY

3

those travelling on their own, the Falklands are one of the best places in the world to visit, as everyone is welcome and if help is needed there is always someone who can assist, no matter the issue. The friendly islanders will often go out of their way to help visitors, and if an **emergency** does arise, phoning 999 will alert the emergency services. The one question often asked about the islands concerns minefields and any other military activity. Apart from a few vehicles in Stanley, and occasional planes and helicopters, the military presence is more-or-less confined to the area around Mount Pleasant. Life on the islands carries on pretty much as it always has done. The image of the Falkland Islands and **minefields** is unfortunately engraved on public consciousness outside the islands even though the mine clearance was completed in 2020 and is thus no longer an issue. That said, it's still sensible not to touch any unidentified metal objects.

Driving on the islands is a unique experience whether it is over the *camp* or along the modern road network (page 58). There have been accidents along the road between Mount Pleasant Airport and Stanley, mostly due to excessive speed when there was more of a loose surface. Driving along this road, with its deep roadside ditches, demands a great deal of concentration in windy conditions. The well-concealed boggy areas have trapped many a vehicle passing over the *camp*, and local knowledge can save a lot of hard digging. If driving away from the made-up roads, a 4x4 is essential as the ground can be very soft in places, even in the summer months.

TRAVELLING WITH CHILDREN

There is very little set up specifically for children, but they will be made welcome. As the wildlife is so tame, youngsters will be able to really appreciate what is there – no staring at dots in the distance! However, the appropriate distance from the wildlife must be kept at all times. There are obvious safety precautions to bear in mind, such as making sure they are wearing seatbelts when flying between the islands, avoiding steep cliff edges and respecting the sea; as ever, a common sense approach is best.

WHAT TO TAKE

To experience what the Falkland Islands have to offer means spending a lot of time outdoors. The weather changes rapidly (page 5), making a waterproof coat, a hat or hood, and several layers of clothing essential. The wind dominates during the summer, which must be kept in mind when preparing clothes for the trip. A good pair of shoes or walking boots is very necessary, as the ground can be uneven and slippery in some locations. A lightweight pair of waterproof trousers is a useful inclusion. Away from Stanley it is customary to have a light pair of shoes to wear indoors, leaving the outdoor shoes by the door.

The strong sunshine on the islands can very quickly burn unprotected skin, so a high-factor suncream and lip balm should be packed. All personal medical supplies and toiletries should be brought with you, as supplies may well be limited on the islands. As it is impossible to take too many photographs of penguins let alone the other wildlife and super scenery, it is worth bringing sufficient memory cards. There is limited availability of these in Stanley only, and both memory cards and batteries can sometimes be difficult to obtain, especially after a cruise ship has called in, so you are advised to bring all you require.

Electrical supply is the same as in the UK, ie: 240v, 50Hz and uses the standard three-pin plug.

While most of the wildlife is habituated and tolerates close approach, binoculars do make a tremendous difference in getting the best views. Many of the hotels and lodges have a limited supply of reading material so it's worth making sure you have enough for when not out and about.

MONEY AND BUDGETING

The Falkland Islands pound is equivalent to one pound sterling. The notes and coins are similar to those used in the UK but each has its own design. Although the UK has changed to polymer notes, there are no plans to change the Falkland currency as yet, but a new £1 coin was launched in 2023. And as of 1 January 2025, 1p and 2p coins are being withdrawn from circulation. It is possible to use British money on the islands, as the two currencies are interchangeable. Exchange facilities are available at the only bank on the islands, The Standard Chartered Bank on Ross Road, Stanley. Mastercard and Visa can be used at a number of outlets on the islands. It is important to bear in mind that there is no cash machine, although the bank will give cash against credit cards with proof of identification. US dollars are widely accepted on the islands, with euros accepted in Stanley and in the most popular lodges away from town. Falkland Island currency is not readily exchangeable outside the islands; it is therefore a good idea to make sure you are not still in possession of any when you leave.

BUDGETING The wide range of accommodation on the islands means it's possible to spend from £20 to £260 per night per person, depending upon quality and level of comfort. The lodges on the outer islands are comparable in price with the hotels and bigger accommodations in Stanley, but the self-catering properties are much cheaper. If self-catering, food and basic provisions are slightly more expensive than in the UK with fruits such as bananas or melons being much more costly. Food prices do not vary greatly around the islands but there may well be limited availability of some items so it's best to check when booking any self-catering away from Stanley. Drink prices in hotels will be typically more than those in the shops in Stanley, but owing to the lack of UK duty, prices are still very comparable with the UK.

GETTING AROUND

BY AIR Travelling around the islands is much easier than it was prior to the early 1980s. The quickest way to get between the islands and settlements is by air on the **Falkland Islands Government Air Service (FIGAS)**. These planes operate from their base at Stanley Airport (Flight bookings: ✆ 27219; e reservations@figas.gov. fk; w falklands.gov.fk/aviationservice) and can take up to eight passengers plus pilot, although many airstrips are only capable of accepting planes with a reduced number of passengers. Luggage is limited to 44lb (20kg) per passenger with a charge of £1.55/kg for any extra luggage if space and weight restrictions permit carrying excess baggage. Schedules are organised on a day-to-day basis depending upon demand. Once all requests for flights have been made, a schedule is drawn up for the following day's flights. There are usually at least two flight times, or three if it's a particularly busy day in the summer, departing from Stanley at 08.00 and then again in mid-morning, using three of the five planes they operate. The flights vary considerably in itinerary as they will be trying to carry as many passengers as possible on the lowest number of flights. It may be that one goes direct from one island to another or it may be via various other airstrips or even via Stanley. The flight schedules are announced on the radio on the evening before and can be found by following FIGAS on Facebook. Your accommodation provider will be checking flights each day; they are also emailed to all destinations the evening before. Sample fares for non-residents, at the time of writing, are Stanley to Sea Lion Island for £109.14 and Stanley to Pebble Island for £118.17.

BY SEA The *Concordia Bay* ferry between New Haven on East Falkland and Port Howard on West Falkland has opened up travel opportunities between these two islands (page 133). For those hiring vehicles in Stanley (see opposite), this is an alternative to flying between the two main islands, but note that it is advisable to check before hiring that the car-hire company allows its vehicles to be taken to West Falkland. The journey takes 1 hour 45 minutes and the schedule is regularly updated as the ferry also delivers cargo to all inhabited islands; go to w workboat.co.fk or email e admin@workboat.co.fk for the latest information. It is advisable to book ahead as it can be very busy in holiday periods, such as around Christmas and New Year, as well as at weekends. Tickets are sold as returns with the fare for one adult being £22.80 and a car of less than 6m £56.90.

BY LAND The road network has been improved so that it now links all of the major settlements on the islands; all others can be reached by traditional routes over the *camp* on the rough, rather difficult-to-drive tracks that can only be driven using a 4x4. Local knowledge is essential in finding the correct route. Although the distances between settlements are not great, driving over *camp* is slow going with average speeds of 5 to 10 miles an hour typical, so it is a good idea to allow plenty of time if doing such a journey. Owing to the loose surface of the unmetalled roads, driving in high winds can be difficult and thus keeping a reduced speed is advisable. When passing approaching vehicles it is a good practice to reduce speed to try and avoid flicking up any road chippings; many vehicles on the islands have a cracked windscreen from these loose stones. Sheep are often to be found grazing beside the roads and can sometimes dash in front of vehicles so keep a watchful eye on livestock and slow down, especially if they have lambs, which will often do the unexpected. Generally there is only one made-up 'road' between each of the settlements, so roads are easy to follow. There are also signposts at every junction. Driving off-road over *camp* is a very different matter. As self-driving beyond the main islands isn't an option, visitors to Carcass Island, Pebble Island, Sea Lion Island and Weddell Island can be transported by the lodges' 4x4 vehicles.

Car hire It is possible to hire self-drive 4x4s for driving in *camp* and 2WD vehicles for use on the metalled roads around Stanley from the companies listed below. Drivers over 18 with a current valid driving licence issued by any competent authority are allowed to drive for up to 12 months on the islands. As in the UK, it is the law to wear a seat belt and drink drive laws are enforced. The speed limit around Stanley is 25mph with a limit of 40mph elsewhere in the islands. The police occasionally do speed checks, particularly on the road to Mount Pleasant and along the Stanley bypass that runs along the south side of the town. Prices for car hire start from around £65 per day – usually for a three-day minimum hire. Demand does vary during the year so if you are thinking about hiring a car, it is best to check availability in advance. The roads in Stanley are mostly on a grid system so navigation around the town is quite easy. The roads that run up and down the hill, ie: north and south, have priority over those running east–west.

Falklands 4x4 27663; e reception.
falklands4x4@fic.co.fk; w falklands4x4.com
MAAZ Tours & Travel m 53006; w maaztours-
falklandislands.com
Mercado Vehicle Hire m 52946;
w mercado.co.fk/car-rental

Moody Enterprises Vehicle Hire 22444;
contact Roger Spink; e rkspink@hotmail.com
**1 Stanley Services Limited Vehicle
Hire** 22622; e office@stanley-services.co.uk;
w stanley-services.co.fk

Taxis Taxis are generally used around Stanley or to go out to the airport, and are sometimes used by those wanting a quick visit to sites close to Stanley that do not require a 4x4, such as Gypsy Cove. See page 72 for a list of taxi numbers.

MAPS The first big map of all the islands aimed at tourists was the 1:250,000 map entitled *Falkland Islands with Visitor Information*, which was last issued in 1995 and is no longer available. This covered all the islands in reasonable detail including many of the *camp* tracks. The most recent *Falkland Island Explorer* 1:365,000 scale map published in 2007 has a less detailed map on one side, but does have some information about the geography, history and wildlife of the islands on the reverse. It has a more detailed map of Stanley, but because of the rate of change around the town in recent years it is out of date.

ACCOMMODATION

The accommodation of the islands varies from hotels and guesthouses to self-catering and camping. The rates charged vary according to season, so each establishment should be contacted to confirm charges at the proposed time of travel. Popular destinations such as Sea Lion Island, Saunders Island, Pebble Island and Carcass Island can get booked up very early so it is a good idea for independent travellers

ACCOMMODATION PRICE CODES

Prices are based on the cost of a double room per night including breakfast:

££££	Expensive	£120+
£££	Moderately expensive	£80–120
££	Moderate	£30–80
£	Inexpensive	< £30

to get these key accommodations booked in first and arrange other stops around those dates. The local agents (page 73) are very good at getting this jigsaw puzzle of accommodation to work, but it can mean flying back and forth across the archipelago.

As can be expected, Stanley has the greatest range of accommodation: from the largest hotel, the Malvina House Hotel (page 73), to the small B&Bs that also allow camping in their gardens. Some of the latter are recently refurbished and so have a more modern style of décor while others are more traditional, very much like the older-style B&Bs still found in the UK.

In *camp* there is usually only one place to stay in any given location. These vary from purpose-built, fully catered lodges such as that on Sea Lion Island and fully catered, converted farm manager's houses, such as can be found at Port Howard or Pebble Island, through to smaller self-catering places, typically in some of the smaller settlements on West and East Falkland. These smaller properties have become more popular in recent years since the advent of roads connecting all major settlements. They are usually less expensive and less busy, except during holiday periods and in peak summer, and are ideal for independent travellers with their own transport as well as being popular with the Falkland Islanders looking for a few days' break.

One thing to bear in mind while staying in *camp* is that you will be expected to take off your outdoor shoes and leave them by the door to prevent goose and sheep droppings being walked in. This rule no longer applies to the majority of accommodation in Stanley, but it is best to check before entering, especially into private houses.

Typically, the larger establishments will be fully catered, offering a packed lunch for those out for the day whereas the smaller places in Stanley will only offer breakfast. Some of the larger hotels in Stanley are popular places for evening meals so have a very high standard of cuisine. Elsewhere, the food is a slightly simpler style, reflecting its generally British origin, but again is very good value for money and very welcome after a day out watching wildlife. Most accommodation around the islands has 24-hour power, but it is worth checking on arrival and timing the charging of electrical devices accordingly.

There are no official **campsites** on the Falkland Islands. Camping is permitted in certain areas but only with the owner's permission, which is best sought by phone when on the islands. Some areas of a farm may well be out of bounds during the spring lambing season (September/October). Campers are usually required to be completely self-sufficient. Certain guidelines should be obeyed (see below), as well as any further requests by the owners. Four farms owned by **Falkland Landholdings Ltd** (Fitzroy, Goose Green, North Arm and Walker Creek) allow camping. As above, permission must be granted by the manager.

CAMPING GUIDELINES

- No fires should be lit for any reason.
- Cooking should be on a paraffin or gas cooker and never be left unsupervised when lit. Fire can be very destructive in the dry grasslands and can burn for many years in peat.
- Gates are always to be left as they are found.
- Farm animals must never be approached or disturbed in any way.
- All litter must be removed upon leaving the site.
- Vehicles should not leave the track without permission.
- Information on destination and length of trip should be given before departure.

RESTAURANT PRICE CODES

Prices are based on the cost of a main course, per person exclusive of drinks:

££££	Expensive	£20+
£££	Moderately expensive	£15–20
££	Moderate	£10–15
£	Inexpensive	< £10

EATING AND DRINKING

The food on the islands is very British in character, with much use made of homegrown vegetables, local lamb, mutton, beef and fish. Portions are habitually on the generous side, with *smoko* – homemade cakes and biscuits with tea or coffee – being enjoyed in the gaps between meals. Diddle-dee jam and teaberry jam can sometimes be found, the latter being more seasonal and the former often sold in the shops in Stanley. Homemade soup with fresh homemade bread is a common meal at lunchtime and is often welcome after a morning spent wildlife watching. For those looking for something a little different, upland goose pâté is available as a starter in some restaurants, while toothfish (Patagonian sea bass) is a popular choice for a main course. Other fish options can include locally caught trout and mullet. Outside of Stanley there is nowhere to eat out other than the lodges and the larger guesthouses, and then only by prior arrangement. The range of places to go out for a meal in Stanley is changing all the time, from à la carte through to fish and chips and bar lunches.

All lodges across the islands are licensed and stock a good range of beers, wines and spirits. The same can be said for the hotels in Stanley. There are also six pubs in Stanley, which are open between 10.00 and 23.00 on Monday to Thursday, between 10.00 and 23.30 on Friday and Saturday and between noon and 14.00, and again between 18.00 and 22.30, on Sundays. Most alcohol is imported into the islands and, despite the transport costs, drinks are not as expensive as might be expected owing to the differing tax levy between the islands and the UK, the main source of the imported drink. Draught beer is now brewed on the islands again by Falkland Beerworks (w falklandbeerworks.com), after a short-lived brewery in the late 1980s. This Stanley-based brewery opened in 2012, starting with four beers: 'Rock Hopper', a natural blonde at 4.2% ABV; 'Longdon Pride', a best bitter at 4.2% ABV; 'Peat Cutter', an oatmeal stout that is a little stronger at 5.5% ABV; and 'Black Tarn', a dark mild at 3.4% ABV. More recently, they have added 'Iron Lady', an IPA (India pale ale) at 5% ABV, and 'Cape Pembroke', a pale ale at 4.5% ABV, to their list. Some of these are available on draught in the Victory Bar and at the Malvina House Hotel in Stanley, with bottled beers available at the Waterfront Hotel and also in the Kelper Store. Stocks can run low after visits from the larger cruise ships to Stanley.

PUBLIC HOLIDAYS AND EVENTS

Liberation Day on 14 June commemorates the liberation of the islands after the invasion by Argentina in 1982, and is marked by a service in Christ Church Cathedral followed by a parade to a wreath-laying ceremony at the Liberation Monument, a short distance along Ross Road. There is usually a large military representation for this. **Battle Day** on 8 December is to commemorate the battle between the British

1 January	New Year's Day	25 December	Christmas Day
March/April	Good Friday	26 December	Boxing Day
21 April	Queen's Birthday	27 December	Additional day's
14 June	Liberation Day		holiday after
First Monday	Peat Cutting Day		Christmas for
in October			Stanley Races
8 December	Battle Day		

Navy and the German South Atlantic Squadron in 1914, which resulted in the loss of most of the German squadron. There is a parade to the 1914 memorial on the headland to the west of Government House followed by a service and a fly-by from the RAF. **Peat Cutting Day** was reinstated as a public holiday on the first Monday in October in 2002 to mark the traditional start of the peat-cutting season. There is relatively little peat cut these days as most islanders use oil or electricity for heating, but the day off work in some hopefully spring-like weather is enjoyed all the same.

The major sporting event in the Falkland Islands' calendar is the **Stanley Races** over 26 and 27 December. This takes place at the race course at the eastern end of Stanley and involves a variety of horse races of up to a mile in length. There are also junior races as well as many others over this popular two-day event. A similar event, the **West Falkland Sports**, takes place around the end of the shearing season, the location moving to a different settlement on West Falkland each year.

SHOPPING

As would be expected for such a small community, the opportunities for shopping are not as highly developed as in more heavily populated areas. There is, however, a wide range of goods aimed at the tourist market on sale in Stanley (page 76). They range from the expected postcards, T-shirts, baseball hats and other clothing, through a variety of cuddly toys (mainly penguins), to jewellery, paintings, drawings, leatherwork and other mementoes. There is now a wide range of high-class locally made items, including wool and felt products, soaps and lip balm, a diverse range of jewellery made from materials such as pewter, enamel, silver, and much more. Many, of course, feature the ever-popular penguins, but others carry images of other aspects of the Falklands and its wildlife that make ideal gifts. Most of the larger lodges have a range of postcards, T-shirts and other articles for sale. Falkland stamps (page 18) are a popular item with their associated first-day cover and other philatelic items.

Basic provisions can be bought in the larger food stores in Stanley or in the stores in the larger settlements.

ARTS AND ENTERTAINMENT

There is a wide variety of **art** available on the islands, some of which can be seen in the local shops in Stanley. The most obvious art shop is **Studio 52** owned by Julie Halliday, which is also her studio and is situated along Ross Road, a short walk from the Christ Church Cathedral. An **annual craft fair** (f FalklandCraftExhibition) is held in the Falkland Islands Defence Force Hall in September, outside of the usual tourist season. As expected, wool products are very prominent, but felting is also increasing in popularity, as are various types of jewellery, woodwork, leatherwork and some wonderful photography and painting. The other annual display is the **horticultural show** (◼ Falkland Islands Horticultural Society), which takes place in Stanley at the end of February or in early March. Entertainment on the islands is typical of that of a small British town with a variety of clubs and organisations covering many aspects of community life, especially those with sporting connections, but there is also the **Falkland Islands Operatic and Drama Association**. The closure of the **cinema** in Stanley in the 1970s meant that until recently the only way to see a film was to make the drive down to Mount Pleasant Airport to the Phoenix Cinema in the military base – the schedule for the forthcoming week was published in the *Penguin News* every Friday. However, there is now a new cinema in Stanley called the Harbour Lights Cinema, which opened in 2019 and is situated within the Malvina House Hotel. The space is also used for lectures and meetings, etc.

Live music in public is not a common event on the Falklands, but there are occasionally musical events where bands play, with folk/country and rock music being popular. **Balls** are still very popular on the islands; the May Ball and Winter Ball result in many weeks of practice in the run up. There is also the Conservation Ball, which is a big charity fundraiser for Falklands Conservation and takes place in October each year in the Town Hall in Stanley.

The **golf course** in Stanley lies to the east of town and is an enjoyable 12-green, 18-tee course. On a windy day it can be more than challenging and even on a rare

PHOTOGRAPHY

The light on the Falkland Islands can be a photographer's dream, illuminating the clear blue skies, the deep blue sea and the abundant, extremely photogenic wildlife. Not every day is like that of course, but there are plenty of photographic opportunities – professional photographers visiting the islands often comment that they are glad they brought plenty of memory cards. When taking photographs, it is important to admire the wildlife from a respectful distance; the Countryside Code guidelines suggested by Falklands Conservation (page 47) are to be obeyed at all times.

Spare batteries can sometimes be bought on the islands but cannot be guaranteed, and the same is true for SD cards, lens caps, filters, etc. Very long lenses are not really necessary for most of the local wildlife, as it is so tame, although they can have their uses for taking close-ups of seabirds. Wide-angle lenses are very useful, as there are many magnificent panoramas that would make superb photographs. A good lens cloth and a dusting brush are essential on the islands: as you're rarely far from the sea, salt spray can be a problem.

Visitors will have just as much to **film**, whether it be on a mobile phone or a dedicated camera. Much of the wildlife is very lively, with squabbling elephant seals, baby penguins or just the sea crashing on the shore providing dramatic subjects. Wind noise can be a problem at times, but does add to the atmosphere of the video. As with photography, remember to keep a respectful distance from wildlife and don't interfere with their normal behaviour – in such a photogenic place, it is possible to get good footage with almost any device when the sun is out.

Photography tours can be organised with Design in Nature (ⓦ designinnature.com).

calm day it can easily catch you out. It is maintained by the hard work of the resident golfers and there are competitions each weekend with a high standard of play. The rest of the week it is usually unmanned. Contact Sharon Jaffray (e shazken@ horizon.co.fk); at present the green fee is £10.

MEDIA AND COMMUNICATIONS

NEWSPAPERS AND BROADCASTING The weekly **newspaper**, the *Penguin News* (w penguin-news.com), comes out every Friday. It is eagerly awaited as it covers everything from local news, jobs and items for sale, to stories about Falkland Islanders abroad, as well as local TV and radio listings. **Falklands Radio** [74 D2] (w radio. co.fk), based in Stanley, operates 24 hours a day, and coverage includes world and local news, music and sports programmes. The daily flight times for the Falkland Islands Government Air Service planes are announced twice a day at 18.15 and 20.30. It is broadcast island-wide on 530 kHz and between 88.2–88.8, 96.5 and 101.0 MHz, depending on location. There are also two **British Forces Broadcasting Service** radio stations: BFBS Radio Falklands and BFBS Radio 2; the latter is broadcast at GMT (ie: –3 hours to Falklands time). These operate between 97.2 and 101.6 MHz. The television channels are provided by BFBS Radio Television and include two BBC channels (1 and 2) and one ITV channel, plus BFBS extra. There is also KTV (w KTV. co.fk) that offers a wide range of channels via subscription. Falkland Island Television (FITV; w fitv.co.fk) carries local news stories and a magazine programme.

TELEPHONES The telephone system on the islands is maintained by Sure (w sure. co.fk), which also provides direct dialling worldwide via satellite linkage. Mobile-phone coverage, again provided by Sure, was initially based around Stanley but is now much more widespread. Those with a contract phone with roaming enabled can sometimes use their own phone, but owing to limited broadband width on the islands, connection speeds for those wishing to use mobile data are slow and expensive. It is worth checking with your provider before you go that your phone will work on the islands, as very few providers actually do work outside of the local ones. There is also the option of buying a pay-as-you-go service for which you will need an unlocked SIM-free phone.

The 2m VHF network, which operates in a similar way to CB radio, is still occasionally used in *camp*. A licence, available from the post office, is required to operate this equipment.

INTERNET Internet is provided by Sure South Atlantic and the majority of the larger businesses and accommodation now use email. Internet is now available at many of the larger hotels and guesthouses, with internet cards a popular way of providing a connection. It is slower than many other parts of the world, but will easily deal with emails and other low uses of bandwidth. There are also many 'SURE Wi-Fi hotspots' around the islands. These can easily be found by looking for the signs on the windows of hotels, shops, restaurants, etc. These hotspots and some other shops sell internet cards in £5 and £10 denominations – it is important to log out each time to avoid wasting your card's credit.

CULTURAL ETIQUETTE

Those living on the Falklands are very welcoming, but it is always best to let them reveal anything about themselves and their family rather than being too inquisitive about their lives. Many are proud of their island roots and will talk about them, but it is always better to leave it to them to start that conversation.

TRAVELLING POSITIVELY

Many of the souvenirs on the islands are made elsewhere and do of course support those selling them, but it is always a good idea to search for those items that are made locally. There are many to be found, including artwork, photographs, pottery, knitwear, and more.

For those looking to support a local organisation, Falklands Conservation (w falklandsconservation.com) is always a good option, as this internationally recognised conservation organisation runs many admirable projects around the islands.

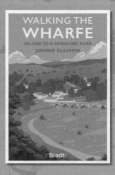
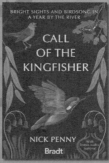

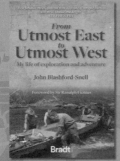

Part Two

THE GUIDE

4

Stanley

Stanley is probably the smallest and most remote capital city in the world. The official existence of Port Stanley began in July 1845, when the islands' capital was moved from Port Louis to an area originally called Jackson's Harbour. It was situated on a north-facing slope in order to face the sun throughout the year. It grew dramatically during the Californian Gold Rush in the mid 1800s, with this boom lasting until the 1890s. Subsequently, Stanley has continued to be the commercial centre of the islands and the main port of access. There was heavy fighting in and around Stanley during the 1982 war (page 13); the memorials are now the only evidence of this period of conflict. Since the war the capital city has established a squid-fishing industry and has dramatically increased in size in direct proportion to the revenue derived from this.

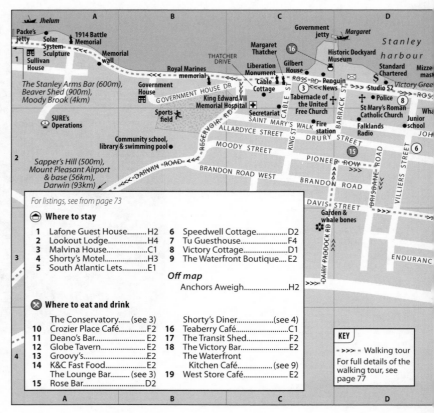

For listings, see from page 73

Where to stay
1	Lafone Guest House..........H2	6	Speedwell Cottage................D2
2	Lookout Lodge....................H4	7	Tu Guesthouse.....................F4
3	Malvina House....................C1	8	Victory Cottage....................D1
4	Shorty's Motel.....................H3	9	The Waterfront Boutique....E2
5	South Atlantic Lets.............E1		

Off map
Anchors Aweigh......................H2

Where to eat and drink
	The Conservatory......(see 3)		Shorty's Diner...................(see 4)
10	Crozier Place Café.............F2	16	Teaberry Café.........................C1
11	Deano's Bar........................E2	17	The Transit Shed...................F2
12	Globe Tavern......................E2	18	The Victory Bar.....................E2
13	Groovy's.............................E2		The Waterfront
14	K&C Fast Food....................E2		Kitchen Café.................(see 9)
	The Lounge Bar...........(see 3)	19	West Store Café.....................E2
15	Rose Bar.............................D2		

KEY
= >>> = Walking tour
For full details of the walking tour, see page 77

The early history of Stanley is perhaps best illustrated by the shipwrecks that are dotted along the seafront (page 77). These date from a time before the Panama Canal, when all shipping had to sail around Cape Horn and many ships needed some repair after being damaged by bad weather. Stanley became a major repair centre and the most badly damaged were condemned – these are the remains you see today.

A wide range of architectural styles prevails in the city, ranging from the magnificent brick-built Christ Church Cathedral, to Jubilee Villas (both page 80) – an imposing terrace of four tall, red-brick houses with large bay windows – to the hospital and school with their colourful roofs and white-clad exterior. Upland geese and Falkland steamer ducks frequent the waterfront, while turkey vultures and kelp gulls glide overhead. It is also one of the few places on the islands where house sparrows, introduced during the 19th century, have remained plentiful. Stanley is where many Falkland holidays start and finish, and therefore it has a good selection of accommodation and tour operators able to cater to visitors' tastes and interests.

HISTORY

Port Stanley originates from the 1841 instruction of Lord Stanley, the British Secretary of State, to Governor Moody at Port Louis, to investigate the potential of Port William as the location of a new town. Captain Ross of the Ross Expedition

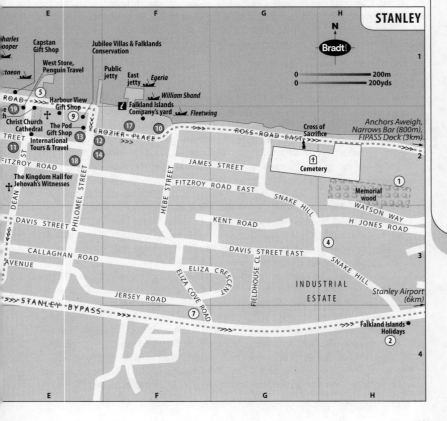

made a comprehensive survey of the area and informed Governor Moody that Port William had a good deep-water harbour, which would easily be accessible to the Royal Navy fleet. The sheltered waters of Jackson's Harbour were deemed suitable for the new port. Work was initiated in July 1843 and was finally completed on 18 July 1845. At Governor Moody's suggestion, the capital was renamed in honour of the Secretary of State, and so Port Stanley came into being. Local opinion was not completely in favour of this choice – one contemporary quote described the area as 'the most miserable bog hole' in the islands. By 1849 the population had risen to 200. The early residents became increasingly affluent on account of the high prices they could charge for repairing ships that had been damaged on the fierce Cape Horn route, thanks to Port Stanley being the nearest port with facilities to repair large vessels. During the Californian Gold Rush, and also the ensuing Australian Gold Rush, business boomed as many unseaworthy ships were forced to take shelter in the islands. Provisioning of these boats was another facet of the growing prosperity of the port. Among these general merchantmen were Welsh barques who had taken coal to South America and were then returning to Swansea or Cardiff laden with copper ore. Port Stanley was one of the busiest ports in the South Atlantic at this time. By the 1890s, however, the number of sailing vessels calling into the harbour began to decrease with the introduction of the more reliable, stronger-built steamships. This was compounded by the completion of the Panama Canal in the early 1900s, which reduced the amount of traffic that had to round Cape Horn, thereby drastically reducing the numbers that needed to call in for repair. Instead, whaling and sealing activities around the islands and in adjacent seas meant a different type of vessel used the harbour around the turn of the century. Around the same time, worldwide high wool prices led to a demand for

LANDSLIDES IN STANLEY

After its formation in 1845, the capital expanded on land in step with the escalation of traffic in the harbour. Population growth entailed the need for more fuel and as such peat was cut in progressively greater quantities from the hillside behind the town. A severe winter in 1879 covered the ground with snow between May and August. The citizens awoke around midnight on 29 November to find that thawing snow had flooded the peatbogs, causing a moving mass of peat, 4ft (1.2m) in depth, to gush through the town. The avalanche of peat swept away everything in its path from its genesis to the east of the town down to the sea. Miraculously, nobody was killed. All communications between east and west Stanley were severed. The only means of contact was by boat. It took a week to dig a trench at the back of the hill in order to drain the water from the peat workings. Water retention in this area remained a problem for some years.

On 2 June 1886 a second landslide occurred. As with the first slip, a large mass of saturated peat broke off from a ridge above the town and made its uncontrollable descent, demolishing all buildings or filling them with turf before pouring into the harbour. Remarkably, despite the fact that this second slip was also at night, only two lives were lost. The most notable building to be washed away was the Exchange Building, which had been used as a school and a church. Christ Church Cathedral, consecrated in 1892 and completed in 1903, now occupies the site of that building. Fortunately, landslides are no longer a concern as water does not gather in the old peat workings in modern times.

fleeces from the Falkland Islands. These were brought in from the outlying farms before being sent to their final destination from Stanley.

Port Stanley was still the city's official name during World War II, but in 1956 the officer administering the islands for the Government of the Falkland Islands suggested that as the common usage was Stanley, this should be adopted as the official name. The name 'Port Stanley' was still widely used in the media during the Falklands War in 1982, but Stanley seems to be the accepted form nowadays.

The port experienced a large number of ship movements during and after the Argentinian invasion in 1982. The floating hotels known as 'coastels', used by the military to accommodate their forces after the war, prior to the construction of the new base at Mount Pleasant, ensured there was plenty of activity in the port. On 1 February 1987, the Falkland Islands Interim Conservation and Management Zone (FICZ), which extends for 200 nautical miles around the islands, was introduced. This fishery protection area has resulted in many more ship movements in Port Stanley because vessels have to visit the islands to collect local fishing licences, fetch provisions, visit agents and land some of their catch. The licensing of survey work investigating hydrocarbon deposits near the islands in the early 2000s also led to an increase in shipping activity around Stanley.

The growth of the tourism industry, seen particularly in the numbers of cruise-ship passengers during the late 1990s and 2000s, has resulted in an increase in the size and number of shops in Stanley, especially near the public jetty. There is now also much more accommodation in the capital with the Malvina House Hotel (page 73), for example, being twice the size it was 30 years ago. In addition to the tourism industry, the squid-fishing industry now employs many more people than it did in previous years. The recent advent of a fledgling oil industry has also created more work (although it is still in stasis at the time of writing, waiting for an increase in the price of oil to make such exploration work financially viable). Stanley's booming economy and this increase in job prospects has led to many people moving from *camp* to the capital. As a result, Stanley has continued to expand, with new estates being built around the margins of the town.

In recognition of these changes, Stanley was granted city status on Friday 20 May 2022 as part of the late Queen Elizabeth II's Platinum Jubilee celebrations. It was one of eight successful applications out of the 39 that entered, and marked the first time that one of the British Overseas Territories and Crown dependencies had been granted this honour. The application had to show the town's strong royal links and their cultural heritage, as well as a distinct local identity.

GETTING THERE AND AWAY

Stanley can be reached by land, sea or air. The majority of visitors who reach the capital do so via the **cruise ships** that call in at the islands (page 54). Smaller vessels can pass through the Narrows and anchor in the harbour using their Zodiacs to come ashore or they can come alongside the floating dock known as FIPASS [map, page 84] (Falkland Interim Port and Storage System) before being shuttled into town. Larger ships must anchor out in Port William and visitors are then ferried ashore from Port William to the public jetty midway along the seafront. Visitors sailing their own boats must follow the arrival procedure described on page 54.

Although there are various **overland** routes to Stanley, most traffic uses the all-weather road, which leaves the town to the south and leads on around the slopes of Sapper's Hill. This is the route used to reach the military base and international airport at Mount Pleasant (MPA) and all other destinations on East Falkland.

The drive from Stanley to the airport takes an hour through typical Falkland habitat of diddle-dee- and white-grass-covered slopes.

Visitors landing on the islands from overseas airports can only do so at Mount Pleasant. The **airport** at Stanley is used for **internal flights** by the Falkland Islands Government Air Service (FIGAS) (**w** falklands.gov.fk/aviationservice). This service is used to transport people and goods all over the Falklands, and is therefore the only practical way for visitors to travel around the islands. The Islander aircraft have a capacity of eight passengers with a luggage limit of 20kg per passenger. Stanley Airport has a hard surface, but other landing strips may be on grass, gravel or on the beach, thus requiring a reduced payload. Consequently, tourists travelling in groups around the islands may well travel in different planes. The airport is a 5-minute drive to the east of the town; visitors can hire a taxi for this journey (see below).

The daily flight schedules are now available on Facebook (search for FIGAS.air. service) and are issued the afternoon before the flights concerned.

GETTING AROUND

Stanley occupies such a small area that it is possible to walk the length and breadth of the town in one day and still have time to explore – the grid-like layout of the town means that it is difficult to get lost for long. Note that the traffic going up and down the hill has priority, so care must be taken at any crossroads. It is possible to **hire vehicles**, including 4x4s, in Stanley, but they are usually limited to travel on surfaced roads and are not generally for *camp* driving; details of hire-car companies are listed on page 59. There are **taxi** companies who offer airport runs as well as services within town as listed below; a short trip in Stanley costs around £6, while trips to Mount Pleasant Airport cost in the region of £20–25.

Bonner's Taxi Service m 51126
Letty Taxis m 56427

Stanley Cabs m 51001;
e stanleycabsdiscovery1@gmail.com
Town Taxis m 52900

TOURIST INFORMATION AND LOCAL TOUR OPERATORS

TOURIST INFORMATION The **Jetty Visitor Centre** [75 F2] (The Jetty Centre, Stanley, Falkland Islands FIQQ 1ZZ; ☏ +500 22215; **w** falklandislands.com) is situated adjacent to the public jetty at the end of Ross Road in Stanley. Here visitors can get information about local tours and things to do from the helpful staff, as well as pick up leaflets and maps of the local attractions of Stanley. There is also a selection of local gifts on sale. This spacious building is only a few yards from the main jetty used by most of the cruise ships so can be very busy when a big ship calls. On such days it has extended opening hours to match the times the passengers are on shore. Otherwise, the centre is open in the summer months from 10.00 to noon and 13.00 to 16.00 on weekdays, 09.00 to 17.00 on Saturdays and 10.00 to 14.00 on Sundays. The seats outside the building are a good place to rest and watch all the comings and goings. Wi-Fi is also available for those with an internet card (page 64) and, for those who have friends arriving by ship, there is a webcam on the roof looking at the jetty so you can watch them arrive!

The large car park beside the centre (and toilets) is the start point for many of the bus tours that operate from Stanley for those not being picked up at their accommodation. The **local tourism office** has its administrative base upstairs in the Jetty Visitor Centre.

LOCAL TOUR OPERATORS

The tour operators listed here offer individual tours to many of the popular wildlife & historical sites & will also assist with accommodation booking.

Falkland Islands Holidays [69 H4] PO Box 117; ✆22622; e info@falklandislandsholidays.com; w falklandislandsholidays.com

International Tours & Travel [69 E2] 1 Dean St, FIQQ 1ZZ; ✆22041; e db.itt@horizon.co.fk; w falklandislands.travel

Penguin Travel [69 E1] Crozier Pl, West Store Complex, FIQQ 1ZZ; ✆27632; e penguin.travel@fic.co.uk; w penguintravelfic.com

DAY EXCURSIONS

Several tour operators based in Stanley or in nearby settlements offer motorised guided tours for the day, whether to explore the town or to make excursions around East Falkland. All visit the most popular sites & are led by experienced off-road, *camp* drivers, which is essential in reaching many of the locations mentioned in this guide. Owners of many of the smaller companies fit in touring around other jobs so it's a case of ringing them up & seeing when they are free or, if you are looking for ideas, you can see where they recommend going. Each driver has their own history on the islands & will cheerfully relate this to you, along with many other facets of island life.

Adventure Falklands ✆21383; e shaun@adventurefalklands.com; contact Shaun Jaffray

Bluff Cove Falkland Penguins Tours Bluff Cove, East Falkland; ✆21720; e bluffcove@horizon.co.fk; w falklandpenguins.com. This company works exclusively with cruise-ship passengers & can only be booked through the cruise ship.

Carrot Tours m 52323

Derek's Tours ✆32000. Tours at Volunteer Point.

Discovery Falklands 33A Davis St; ✆21027; m 51027; e discovery@horizon.co.fk; w discoveryfalklands.net; contact Tony Smith. General, wildlife, battlefield tours & filming tours.

Estancia Excursions m 52400; w estancia-excursions.com; contact Nyree Heathman

Falklands Nature m 54433 w falklandsnature.com

Falklands Outdoors m 55030 w falklandsoutdoors.com. Various outdoor activities for small groups.

Kidney Cove Tours ✆31001; m 54665; e allowe@horizon.co.fk; w kidneycovetours.com; contact Adrian & Lisa Lowe

Lachlan Neil Ross ✆21935

Lucky Private Tour m 55643; w luckyprivatetour.com

MAAZ Tours & Travel m 53006; w maaztours-falklandislands.com

Owl Tours & Crafts m 52428; e c.e.davies@horizon.co.fk

Port Louis Tours m 51082; w portlouistours.com. Based at Port Louis.

Wild Falklands Design in Nature Studio, 12 Fitzroy Rd East; ✆21186; e georginastrange@gmail.com; w designinnature.com; contact Georgina Strange. A photo-tour specialist.

WHERE TO STAY *Map, page 68*

Accommodation in Stanley ranges from large, well-appointed hotels, through large B&Bs, to smaller guesthouses. As Stanley is so small it is possible to walk from your accommodation to highlights such as the whalebone arch in less than 10 minutes. The accommodation along Ross Road does have the advantage of some rooms facing the sea, but as Stanley is built on a slope, so do many of the other places to stay.

HOTELS AND MOTELS

Malvina House Hotel [68 C1] (72 rooms) 3 Ross Rd; ✆21355; e info@malvinahousehotel.com; w malvinahousehotel.com. The largest place to stay in Stanley, with uninterrupted views over Stanley Harbour. The hotel is named after Malvina Felton, the daughter of John James Felton who built the property in 1881. The hotel was completely rebuilt in 1968 & has since been enlarged & upgraded several times to cope with the increased visitors to the islands. The hotel's Conservatory Restaurant (page 75) overlooks the harbour & is a popular place for celebratory meals & as such is often busy. Those not staying at the hotel should book in advance; those staying at the hotel have priority. The Lounge Bar (page 75) is also part of the same establishment. The hotel welcomes non-resident patrons. It is also home to the Harbour Lights cinema (page 76) which opened in 2019. Major credit cards accepted. ££££

The Waterfront Boutique Hotel [69 E2] (8 rooms) 36 Ross Rd; ☎ 21462; w waterfronthotel.co.fk. Located nearer the public jetty, this building incorporates the Waterfront Kitchen Café (see opposite), which is a popular place with locals & visitors alike & also has super views over the harbour. It is a great place for people & boat watching. A Full English b/fast is included in the room rate & lunch & dinner can be taken in the café. Luxury rooms & junior suites are available, all are light & airy & local artworks decorate the walls. £££

Lookout Lodge [69 H4] (60 rooms) Kiel Canal Rd; ☎ 22834; e reception@lookoutlodge.co.fk; w lookoutlodge.co.fk. This newish hotel, situated in the south of Stanley a short walk from Ross Rd, is reminiscent of an American motel with a large, canteen-style dining room. It has a wider variety of accommodation options than most of the other hotels in Stanley, offering FB premium rooms, various permutations of room & catering options & room-only options with shared washing facilities. ££–£££

Shorty's Motel [69 H3] (6 rooms) West Hillside; ☎ 22861. A short walk away from central Stanley, this motel has 4 twin & 2 dbl en-suite rooms & is situated next door to Shorty's Diner (see opposite) for meals. It has a classic motel design, spread across a single storey, with all the rooms accessible via a walkway that runs around the side. The rooms are not large & are popular for short stays with those working in Stanley & with some of the military having a break from their base at Mount Pleasant Airport. ££

GUESTHOUSES AND B&BS

Lafone Guest House [69 H2] (5 rooms) Ross Rd; ☎ 22891; e arlette@horizon.co.fk; f; contact Arlette Betts. This large house is set back from the road just to the east of the main town centre & has

been refurbished to a high, modern standard. It has a large sun lounge that looks out over Stanley Harbour towards the Narrows & there is a smaller upstairs lounge for those wanting a bit of me time. Continental b/fast is included & dinners can sometimes be provided by talking to the owner. It also has the 'BBQ Hut' which can be rented for a minimum of 10 people with all you need for a BBQ except food & drink. £££

Tu Guesthouse [69 E4] (3 rooms) 21 Jersey Rd; m 54517; w tuguesthouse.com. This newly renovated guesthouse takes 6 guests in 3 en-suite rooms that can be super king size or twin bedded. B&B is the most popular option, but extra meals such as packed lunches & evening meals can sometimes be arranged. It has a guest lounge & dining room. ££

SELF-CATERING ACCOMMODATION

Victory Cottage [68 D1] (2 rooms) 7 Marmot Rd; m 56170; w victorycottage.com. This 2 bedroom self-catering cottage on Ross Rd, opposite Victory Green on the waterfront, is ideally situated in central Stanley. The rooms are 1 king & 1 twin with 2 sgl beds that can also be joined. There is a 3-night minimum stay in this property. ££££

Anchors Aweigh [69 H2] (1 room) 7a Pitaluga Pl; m 52948; e mf@horizon.co.fk. This new studio apartment to the east of Stanley has 1 king-size bed (with a pull-out bed for a child or extra person) & a fold-away kitchenette. There is also a decked patio with BBQ & the rental of 2 e-bikes can be arranged. £££

South Atlantic Lets [69 E1] (4 rooms) The Boathouse, Ross Rd; m 52131; f. 2 apartments, 'The Charles Cooper' & 'The Lady Elizabeth', which opened in 2019. Each has a twin & a dbl room and is situated close to the Capstan Gift Shop with views out over the harbour. £££

Speedwell Cottage [68 D2] (1 room) 2 Villiers St; m 51104; contact Jeannie McKay. This 3-room property has a lounge that doubles up as a bedroom, a shower, toilet & wash room, & a dining room with a connecting kitchen. All the major amenities & sites in Stanley are only a few mins' walk away. ££

✕ WHERE TO EAT AND DRINK   *Map, page 68*

There are a range of places to eat in Stanley to suit every pocket, whether one is looking to sample *smoko* (page 61) or something a little stronger, such as one of the locally brewed beers (page 61).

RESTAURANTS

The Conservatory Restaurant [68 C1] Located at the Malvina House Hotel (page 73). This restaurant is the top dining place on the islands & serves à la carte menus at lunch & dinner. It's situated over 3 levels, so guests can look across the harbour while dining. As expected, the food is of a high standard & uses local produce including squid, lamb & fish such as seabass & toothfish. ££££

Groovy's [69 E2] Philomel St; ✆ 23375; ⏰ lunchtimes & evenings Mon–Sat. Situated a short walk up from the public jetty this recently opened restaurant combines music, drinks (including cocktails) & food, & has become very popular with the locals. It serves a mixture of food, from full meals such as fish & chips & curries to sandwiches & tapas. £££

K&C Fast Food [69 E2] Philomel St; ✆ 22922; ⏰ 11.00–14.00 & 17.00–21.00 Mon–Thu, 11.00–14.00 & 17.00–00.30 Fri–Sat, 09.00–15.00 Sun. A typical fast food menu including pizza, burgers, kebabs, etc. Delivery also available – phone for details. ££

The Lounge Bar [68 C1] Also located at the Malvina House Hotel (page 73). Formerly known as the Beagle Bar, the spacious Lounge Bar has views out over the harbour & serves bar food including steaks, burgers & fish & chips. It can be very busy on w/ends & cruise-ship days. ££

Shorty's Diner [69 H3] West Hillside; ✆ 22855; f; ⏰ 08.30–20.30 daily. Serving a variety of fast food-style meals including burgers, short ribs & fish & chips, etc. This diner is popular with local families, particularly on w/ends. ££

The Waterfront Kitchen Café [69 E2] Located in the Waterfront Boutique Hotel (see opposite); ⏰ 07.00–22.00 daily. Situated a few mins' walk from the public jetty, with super views over the harbour, this establishment serves a range of food – from light snacks through to full meals – & makes use of local meat such as lamb, beef & mutton. It can be very busy on cruise-ship days as, owing to its slightly elevated position, it's a great place for people watching. The w/ end brunch is popular with locals. ££

Crozier Place Café [69 F2] Crozier Pl; ⏰ 09.30–16.00 Tue–Fri & 10.00–16.00 cruise-ship days. This traditional, British-style café serves everything from tea & homemade cakes to meals cooked in house. Dishes range from classic British fare such as fish & chips, to Falkland specials including lamb dishes. £

The Transit Shed [69 F2] Crozier Pl; ⏰ 10.00–16.00 on cruise-ship days. Selling a mixture of local arts & crafts as well as cream teas, along with drinks & other cakes & snacks. Opening is advertised on The Falkland Islands Company Facebook page a few days in advance of a ships visit. £

CAFÉS

Teaberry Café [68 C1] Historic Dockyard Museum site; ✆ 22462; e teaberrycafe@horizon.co.fk; w teaberrycafe.com; ⏰ 07.30–16.00 Mon–Fri, 14.00–17.00 Sat–Sun, extended hours on cruise-ship days, winter 07.30–15.30 Mon–Fri. This small café is part of the Historic Dockyard Museum complex, but is open to all & on w/ days is open longer hours than the museum. It offers a wide variety of coffees & teas as well as sandwiches, rolls & soups that can be eaten in or taken away. £

West Store Café [69 E2] Ross Rd; ✆ 27664; ⏰ 08.30–17.30 Mon–Fri, 09.00–17.00 Fri, 09.00–16.00 Sun. This typical British self-serve café is situated on the corner of the West Store supermarket (page 76), overlooking the junction of Ross Rd & Dean St. It provides hot & cold drinks including milkshakes, & homemade sandwiches, soups & a variety of cakes. £

PUBS

There are 6 pubs in Stanley &, while the emphasis is on drinking, most also serve classic bar food (fish & chips, burgers) during summer lunchtimes & evenings. Opening hours vary between establishments, but most are generally open from late morning until 23.00 (22.30 on Sun). Those near the public jetty, such as the Globe Tavern & The Victory Bar can be busy on cruise-ship days; the others, a few mins' walk away, are less crowded. The Victory Bar (& the Lounge Bar in the Malvina House Hotel; page 73), serves some of the local Falkland beers; all other beers are imported in cans or bottles from the UK.

Deano's Bar [69 E2] 40 John St; ✆ 21296. £
Globe Tavern [69 E2] Crozier Pl; ✆ 22703. £
Narrows Bar [map, page 84] Ross Rd East; ✆ 22267. £
Rose Bar [68 D2] 1 Brisbane Rd; ✆ 22066. £
The Stanley Arms Bar [map, page 84] Jeremy Moore Av; ✆ 21790. £
The Victory Bar [69 E2] 14 Philomel St. £

ENTERTAINMENT AND NIGHTLIFE

The Malvina House Hotel [68 C1] (page 73) opened a 55-seat **cinema**, the Harbour Lights, in 2019 (adult tickets £8.50/child £6.50). Otherwise, the only other cinema option is the Phoenix Cinema at Mount Pleasant Airport (w ssvc.com/cinema). The weekly programme is advertised in the local newspaper, the *Penguin News*, which is published every Friday. See page 62 for more on arts and entertainment.

SHOPPING

When shopping for **food and provisions** in Stanley it usually means visiting the main supermarket, the **West Store** [69 E1] (⊕ 08.00–20.00 Mon–Fri, 09.00–18.00 Sat, 09.00–17.00 Sun), situated on the junction of Dean Street and Ross Road, or one of the other shops along Ross Road, not far from the public jetty. Other than the West Store, these are mostly gift shops with a wide range of Falkland- and Antarctica-themed items. Each shop has a mix of locally produced items, such as jewellery, knitwear, calendars and coasters, as well as some mass-produced T-shirts, sweatshirts and other items. As expected, there is also a wide range of knitwear available, ranging from sweaters to unique hats and scarves. Closer to the public jetty, Ross Road's largest store, the **Capstan Gift Shop** [69 E1], stocks soft furnishings, jewellery and birthday cards as well as a selection of the usual tourist gifts. It also has a good selection of books about the islands and further south. Almost opposite is the **Harbour View Gift Shop** [69 E2], which is more aimed at the tourist market. If you're looking for that quirky gift from the islands (one of many fridge magnets, a logoed baseball hat or a penguin-themed souvenir), this would be the place to go. **The Pod Gift Shop** [69 E2], a short walk from the public jetty up Philomel Street, is a spacious building and stocks a wide range of T-shirts, sweatshirts and hats, plus coasters and tablemats emblazoned with local photographs. Stanley's shops are open from 09.00 to 17.00 Monday to Saturday and are open Sundays on busy cruise-ship days, although there will be seasonal variations. Some items can be in short supply after a visit from some of the larger cruise ships. It is therefore worth checking when such large vessels are due so as to beat the crowds.

OTHER PRACTICALITIES

Facilities are remarkably good considering the size of population, with all one's basic needs catered for, from medical to banking, etc. There is also now widespread internet availability.

The King Edward VII Hospital is where the main healthcare facilities are situated, including a small accident and emergency unit as well as more long-term care for those more seriously ill. There is a dedicated outpatient suite, and pharmacy and dental services are also located here. For medical emergencies away from Stanley, consultation is initially by phone to the 'on call' doctor in Stanley.

GENERAL FACILITIES
King Edward VII Memorial Hospital [68 C1] St Mary's Walk; ☎28000 (reception), 28052 (out of hours); ⊕ 08.30–17.00 Mon–Fri
Library [68 B2] Community School, Reservoir Rd; ☎27147; ⊕ 09.00–noon & 13.30–16.30 Mon–Fri & 13.45–17.00 Sat

Post Office [68 D1] Town Hall, Ross Rd; ☎27181; ⊕ 08.00–17.00 Mon–Fri
Standard Chartered Bank [68 D1] Ross Rd; ☎22220; ⊕ 08.30–15.00 Mon, Tue, Thu & Fri, 09.00–15.00 Wed
Swimming Pool [68 B2] Community School, Reservoir Rd; ☎27291; e receptionist.leisure@

sec.gov.fk; w falklands.gov.fk/leisurecentre;
⊕ 06.00–21.00 Mon, Tue & Thu, 06.00–20.00
Wed, 08.00–18.00 Sat & Sun. Not all sessions
are open to the public; see their website for
weekly updates.

PLACES OF WORSHIP

Christ Church Cathedral [69 E2] Ross Rd;
⊕ 08.00 & 17.00 daily. Anglican services are
held here every Sun. Holy Communion is at
08.00, Family service/Communion & the Sun
School is at 10.00. Evensong is at 19.00.

Kingdom Hall for Jehovah's Witnesses
[69 E2] Dean St; ☎21267
St Mary's [68 D1] Ross Rd. The Roman Catholic
church is the white building with the red roof
opposite the Post Office on Ross Rd. W/day services
are held at 09.00 & those on Sun are held at 10.00.
Tabernacle of the United Free Church [68
C1] Barrack St. This blue & white church is a short
walk up the hill from the western end of the post
office. Services are held on the 1st & 2nd Sun of
each month at 10.00, & at 19.00 on the 3rd &
4th Sun.

WHAT TO SEE AND DO

CITY WALK ALONG ROSS ROAD This walking tour takes in the oldest and most interesting parts of town, along the seafront with views out to some of the town's shipwrecks, and the first few streets behind Ross Road, which itself runs along the water's edge. A stroll along the seafront gives a good snapshot of most of the major events to have occurred on the Falkland Islands, but those who wish to know more can follow the self-guided **maritime history trail** using the free illustrated booklet available from the tourist information office and some other local shops. There are also information posts dotted along the side of Ross Road, near the wrecks themselves.

The Historic Dockyard Museum and around A good place to start your walk is at the **Historic Dockyard Museum** [68 C1] (⊕ 10.00–16.00 Tue–Fri, 13.00–17.00 Sat & Sun, on cruise-ship days also open Mon & for extended hours; £5, free for cruise-ship visitors with ID cards) situated in the old dockyard on Ross Road. The perfect starting point for a history lesson about Stanley, the museum houses information ranging from the first settlers up to the present day. Exhibits cover every aspect of life in the Falklands including the Falklands War and other conflicts, *camp* life, shipwrecks and natural history. There is a very poignant video playing in one room, showcasing interviews with islanders about their experiences during the war. To see it all takes the best part of 2 hours, with some visitors coming back for more than one visit.

The main museum building is situated in a former store, one of the oldest buildings in Stanley, which dates back to 1843. The site beyond once included storerooms, workshops, a jail, a magazine (used for storing munitions) and a smithy, and many of these buildings have been restored to their former glory as part of the museum's exhibits. For those seeking refreshment, the Teaberry Café (page 76) is on site.

The support to the outer end of the government jetty comes from the remains of the *Margaret*. This vessel, built in 1836, reached Stanley in 1850 on its way from Liverpool to Valparaíso. It was leaking, damaged and dangerously overloaded when it reached the islands. The boat was condemned, although remained in the harbour for some years before being cut down, filled with rubble and used for the base of the end of the jetty.

Leaving the historic dockyard, on the right is **Gilbert House**. Not part of the museum, this building was originally used as a staging post for newly arrived settlers to the islands – this was their home until permanent accommodation could be found. It then became a small hospital before being partially destroyed by fire in 1984. It now houses the councillors' office and the government archivist.

4

Walking west along Ross Road The memorial just opposite the Historic Dockyard Museum is the **Liberation Monument** [68 C1]. Paid for by public subscription and erected by volunteers, it was officially unveiled on 14 June 1984. The military personnel who gave their lives to liberate the islands are remembered on the surrounding wall. Liberation Day, 14 June, is marked in the islands each year by a public holiday. Some 50yds away is the **bust of Margaret Thatcher** [68 C1], prime minister at the time of the Argentine invasion, and largely held responsible for the decision to send the task force to regain control of the islands. The **Secretariat** [68 C1], just behind these memorials, houses the islands' administrative offices and treasury buildings. Adjacent to these buildings is **Cable Cottage** [68 C1], the Attorney General's Chambers, which housed the Stanley end of the telegraph cable that linked the islands to Montevideo in the early 1900s.

A hundred yards west along Ross Road, cross Reservoir Road where there is a sports field. (A new all-weather sports field was opened on the Stanley Bypass in 2023, which will be part of a sports complex when finished.) The large building behind this is the **community school** [68 B2], which was opened in August 1992. This impressive structure provides the islanders with a swimming pool, library (both page 76) and a wide range of leisure and sports facilities which are available for all to use when they're not being used by the school. The large blue-roofed building on the opposite side of the road is the **King Edward VII Memorial Hospital** [68 C2], which is a joint civilian and military hospital. The smaller properties along Thatcher Drive, in front of the hospital, provide sheltered accommodation.

Back on Ross Road, continue past the junction of Reservoir Road to the **memorial to the Royal Marines** [68 B1], which was unveiled in January 2008. The memorial commemorates the long relationship between the Falklands and the Royal Marines, which was established in 1765.

Just below the school playing field is a long-angled driveway that leads up to **Government House** [68 B1]. Originally built in 1845, this building has been regularly extended, improved or just generally altered over the years. Every governor and his wife seem to have added their own touch to the building. Each spring, when the gorse hedges are in bloom, this is a very picturesque situation in the lee of the *macrocarpa* trees. The conservatory at the front of the house is home to one of the most prolific grapevines on the islands. The house itself, though not open to visitors, is full of all manner of memorabilia from throughout the ages. Outside the west entrance are a pair of brass guns cast in 1807, and elsewhere there is a harpoon gun that was presented by a South Georgia Whaling Station and a shell that is supposed to have come from the German cruiser *Leipzig*. The bullet holes still visible in the walls mark the most dramatic period in the history of this building, which suffered during the invasion and subsequent recapture of Stanley from the Argentinians. The large trees are a good place to look for some of the smaller birds such as black-chinned siskins and the occasional swallow blown in from South America.

Just past Government House is a track leading up to the satellite dishes that bear witness to SURE's operations on the islands [68 A2]. Beyond this is the very visible **1914 Battle Memorial** [68 A1]. This monument commemorates the Battle of the Falklands fought on 8 December 1914, in which a British Squadron under the command of Vice Admiral Sturdee destroyed a German Squadron under Vice Admiral Graf Von Spee. A public holiday on the Falklands was declared on this date and every year there is a parade and a ceremony, which includes a display by the Royal Air Force and the Royal Navy. The memorial was paid for by public subscription and was first unveiled on 26 February 1927. Between

SURE's headquarters and the memorial is a **memorial wall** [68 A1] built in 2014 to commemorate the centenary of the two battles at sea in World War I. There are three plaques on the wall, detailing information about the two battles and the people involved. There are also a couple of benches and a pretty flower garden – this is a quiet place to sit in the sun out of the wind.

A nearby artistic creation, situated on the seaward side of the 1914 Battle Memorial, is the **Solar System Sculpture** [68 A1] created by sculptor Rob Yssel. This 1:1 billion scale model is made of recycled material. Most visitors don't get further than the sun sculpture near the memorial, but the more intrepid looking for a longer walk (and to put our place in the solar system in perspective) can continue west, towards the hills that overlook the town, to see the whole artwork. This walk is a good few miles and, as there is no obvious trail to follow, some of the outer planets are hard to find. The sun sculpture is visible (with binoculars) from every planet as they are in line of sight.

The slight headland at this point is a good place to look for crested ducks and Falkland steamer ducks, which are often found feeding along the tide line on either side of this promontory. The omnipresent southern giant petrels seem to delight in flying as close to the sea wall as they can, just lifting a wing to drift out to sea before returning whence they came.

The wreck of the *Jhelum* [68 A1], roughly 100yds further west, is one of the largest hulks still visible in Stanley but is now very much reduced as some of the structure was removed when it started to break up and become a danger to other shipping in the early 2000s. The ship lies at the end of a very rickety walkway known as **Packe's Jetty** opposite Sullivan House. This three-masted barque, built in 1849 in Liverpool, spent most of its working life plying between Europe and South America, carrying general cargo out to the latter and bringing guano, nitrates or copper back to the former. It set sail for Europe, laden to the gunwales, on 13 July 1870, and just managed to round Cape Horn before reaching the islands in a very poor condition. The crew refused to sail any further. The ship was surveyed, then condemned and scuttled in its present position.

The large shed on the waterfront, half a mile further west along Ross Road, was used by the Beaver float planes between 1953 and the early 1980s, when they were phased out. It is still known as the **Beaver Shed** [map, page 84]. Lying just offshore from here, in the shallow water at the western end of town are the remains of the *Capricorn* [map, page 84]. This Welsh barque, built in 1859, was carrying coal from Swansea to the west coast of South America when its cargo caught fire. It was scuttled in shallow water with the aim of extinguishing the fire before putting in to Falkland to carry out repairs. Having been condemned as unseaworthy, the ship was then used as a lighter in Stanley Harbour, then for storage, before being scuttled in its present position. During World War II the *Capricorn* was used as the head of a small jetty. Most of its hull was stripped for use as firewood in the late 1940s.

Those looking for a longer walk can continue on to Moody Brook (page 81).

East from the Historic Dockyard Museum

The Malvina House Hotel [68 C1] (page 73) is opposite the entrance to the Historic Dockyard Museum (page 77). Continuing east along Ross Road, the next collection of buildings on the north side of the road [68 D1] includes the **post office**, which houses the philatelic bureau, the **Town Hall** and the justice department with the police station on the opposite side of the road. The colourful building further down the road is **St Mary's Roman Catholic Church** [68 D1]. This church was built in 1899 while the adjoining earlier church (a much smaller building) was built in 1886 and is now used as the church hall. The only bank on the islands is the Standard Chartered, which has its offices just beyond the Town Hall. The old offices are now the mineral department on the other side of the road.

The grassy lawn a few yards further along Ross Road is known as **Victory Green** [68 D1–75 E1]. The mast displayed in the middle of the green is the mizzen-mast of the SS *Great Britain*, which lay for many years in the outer harbour at Sparrow Cove (page 88) before being transported to Britain in the 1970s. The four old cannons spaced out along the green originated from Port Louis, the original capital of the islands. The other guns are 19th-century Hotchkiss guns, which are fired on celebration days and to salute visiting ships. From this vantage point it is possible to look over the water to the northern banks of the harbour and see the names of four ships spelt out in white stones on the dark vegetation. These names are *Beagle, Barracuda, Protector* and *Endurance*. The *Beagle* and the *Barracuda* were naval cruisers on protection duty around the islands at the end of the 1800s. They were also involved in keeping law and order among the whalers and sealers that were in the area at the time, and to keep poachers from the islands. HMS *Protector* was an Antarctic ice patrol-ship that patrolled Falkland and Antarctic waters from 1955 until it was replaced by HMS *Endurance* in 1968. *Endurance* entered the world headlines in 1982 when it participated in the retaking of South Georgia by the British forces. Previously, it had been due to withdraw from service, but continued after the war until replaced by the new *Endurance* in 1991.

The hulk of the ***Charles Cooper*** [69 E1] lies a short distance offshore opposite the West Store, the largest shop on the islands. The *Charles Cooper* was an American ship, dated 1856, which arrived in Stanley on 25 September 1866 leaking badly on passage from Philadelphia to San Francisco with a cargo of coal. The cost of repair proved too great and it was sold on the islands. This is one of the best preserved of the hulks in Stanley Harbour, thanks to its alloy roof, but little of the main deck remains. The carved transom is now in the museum. In 1968 it was bought by the South Street Seaport Museum in New York, as one of the last examples of a North Atlantic packet ship. It is also popular with the local birdlife as rock shags, gulls and turkey vultures favour it as a roosting site. Another wreck lies just inshore of the *Charles Cooper*, the ***Actaeon*** [69 E1], or what remains of it. This ship was built in New Brunswick in 1838 and put in to Stanley on 27 January 1853, on its way from Liverpool to San Francisco with a cargo of coal. It had been beaten back while trying to round Cape Horn and had put into the islands for repair but was scuttled after a survey found it was unseaworthy. Very little remains above water, and the outline of the vessel is best seen from the air when flying over the harbour.

Christ Church Cathedral [69 E2] and its whalebone arch, on the opposite side of the road, must be one of the best-known, most-photographed buildings in the islands. It is the southernmost cathedral in the world and for part of its history was the main cathedral for the missionary diocese of South America. Consecrated in 1892 and finished in 1903, it has remained in use to this day. The whalebone arch, situated next to the cathedral and made from the jawbones of two blue whales, was presented to the islanders in 1933 by whalers from South Georgia. The arch and the cathedral were renovated in 1991.

About 300yds further on, at the head of the public jetty in front of **Jubilee Villas**, among the oldest buildings in Port Stanley, is a small plaque commemorating the visit of HRH Prince Alfred, Duke of Edinburgh in 1871, the first royal visit, and the visit of the late Duke of Edinburgh in 1957. The easternmost building is now the offices of **Falklands Conservation**, a non-governmental environmental charity (page 47), which is involved with a wide range of research and advisory roles concerning the islands' wildlife. The Falkland Conservation garden contains examples of some of the Falklands' flora for all to appreciate. The ruins of the *William Shand* [69 F1] are best seen from the public jetty looking towards the East jetty. This barque, built in Greenock in 1839, visited Stanley on the outward journey from Liverpool to Valparaíso in February 1859, and returned to the islands after a severe battering as it tried to round Cape Horn two months later. It was condemned and ended its days in Stanley.

Ross Road ends at the junction with **Philomel Street**, to the right. By following Crozier Place up around the Falkland Islands Company's yard [69 F2], it is possible to continue along the waterfront along Ross Road East. From here, a backwards look at the East jetty reveals two more casualties of the rough seas around Cape Horn. The wreck of the *Egeria* [69 F1] has been roofed with corrugated metal and used as a storage area for wool and other cargoes. It was a barque from New Brunswick, built in 1859, and reached Stanley in 1872 on its way from London to Callao, Peru with a cargo of cement. Like so many ships before, it was thwarted by the Cape Horn weather and put into the islands damaged and leaking. It was condemned and scuttled adjacent to the *William Shand*. The last wreck visible on this walk is the *Fleetwing* [69 F2], which lies on the foreshore opposite the offices of the Falkland Islands Company. Built in South Wales in 1874 it spent most of its life carrying phosphates. It reached the islands in October 1911 with a cargo of coal, destined never to leave.

In the not so distant past, the **cemetery** [69 G/H2] marked the eastern end of town; however, there are now several new housing estates built further east of the cemetery, meaning you can walk along Ross Road East for nearly a mile before leaving the built-up area of Stanley. Facing the harbour, in front of the cemetery, is a war memorial known as the **Cross of Sacrifice**, which lists the roll of honour of the 43 Falkland Islanders who died in active service during the two world wars. The cemetery has been in use since the 1840s and the headstones narrate the events of the last 180 years. The oldest headstones are situated towards the western edge of the grounds. Victims of the Battle of the Falklands in 1914 and of the Battle of the River Plate in 1939 are buried here. On the slopes behind the graveyard is the **memorial wood** [69 H2], which has been planted as a living shrine to those who lost their lives in the events of 1982.

Just before Ross Road East continues uphill, there is a walk along the waterfront that takes you past the Stanley Growers fields before ending up at the road that leads out to the FIPASS dock. Turning right here takes you up to the Airport Road. Ross Road East itself continues to the south, becoming Rowlands Rise, and eventually joining Airport Road, which becomes the Stanley Bypass nearer to town. You can walk either way to complete a circular walk (taking care to avoid traffic as there are no pavements on the bypass road), but the coastal route is much nicer.

LONGER WALKS IN AND AROUND STANLEY *Map, page 84*

For those who like to get their hiking boots on and fancy more of a walk, there are several options. **Moody Brook** at the west end of Stanley Harbour is about 2 miles from the centre of town, following Ross Road. There isn't a mass of abundant wildlife or historic sites along the route, but it makes for a pleasant stroll on a sunny day. Once past the Beaver Shed (page 79), you'll soon reach the **golf course** (page 63) 100yds further on at the end of the main part of town.

The estates just beyond the golf course, built as Stanley has continued to expand, are now overlooked by newer estates on the hill above. After another half mile or so you will reach Moody Brook, which was named after Richard Moody, the first Governor of the Falkland Islands. There is a plaque on the north bank of the stream to commemorate the site where the first and last shots of the Falklands War were

4

fired in 1982. On a clear day it is possible to see the length of Stanley Harbour from here, even as far as the wreck of the *Lady Elizabeth* in the eastern end of the harbour.

Another superb view over Stanley can be had from **Sapper's Hill**, which overlooks the town from the west. From here you can see Stanley laid out before you, over the harbour to Port William, and out over the South Atlantic Ocean to the south. This viewpoint is reached by heading west towards Government House from the Historic Dockyard Museum, but turning south down Darwin Road, following it to the Stanley–Mount Pleasant Airport Road for half a mile and then turning on to the track that leads up the hill for a few hundred yards. On the way back, you can take a different route by following the Stanley Bypass and turning left into Dairy Paddock Road before soon reaching one of the most unusual **gardens** in Stanley. In it, next to the 'say no to whaling' sign, are the impressive skulls of killer and sperm whales along with a metal sculpture of a whale and a harpoon gun from the whaling days.

By continuing down Dairy Paddock Road for another 100yds, you come to **Pioneer Row**, where some of Stanley's best-preserved older houses can be found. In 1849, 30 prefabricated cottages were brought out and erected by 30 married pensioners from Chelsea and Greenwich in London. They were to form a garrison and be part of the colonisation of the islands that was being encouraged at that time. Stanley must be one of the most colourful capital cities in the world, with its brightly painted wood and metal. There are very few stone or brick-built houses: the local stone is not suitable for use in construction and the cost of importing bricks is too high to use them in general building work. Wood and galvanised tin are much cheaper and seem capable of withstanding the Falklands weather. The corrugated iron sheets used in roofing and for walls are known locally as 'wriggly tin'. Many houses were brought down in kit form and assembled on the spot. While Stanley has expanded considerably over the years, most of the housing is still being constructed from timber with tin commonly used for cladding, with many modern houses still being imported in kit form and assembled on site.

From Pioneer Row, turn east on to Brisbane Road and then south, continuing until you meet Davis Street which runs from west to east. By heading east, you will reach Dean Street where you can turn south uphill to reach the Stanley Bypass. This 5–10 minute walk leads you to the **peat diggings**, once used as a source of fuel in town, which are especially prevalent behind Airport Road. Prior to the 1982 war a household would annually use about 120yd^3 for heating and cooking. The convenience of gas, oil and electricity has resulted in a decline in the amount of peat cut, so that many of the peat banks are no longer being used. Subsequently, most of the peat diggings have grown over but any still being used clearly demonstrate the depth of cut needed to get one full turf.

Those wanting a longer walk can continue on to the sites made famous during 1982, such as Tumbledown, Two Sisters, Wireless Ridge and Mount Longdon.

For a walk in this direction, follow the route to Moody Brook (page 81) and then continue north, climbing uphill to **Mount Longdon** (about 4 miles from Stanley). From here, you can walk in a loop southwestwards to **Two Sisters** and then curve back towards Stanley, where you reach **Tumbledown Mountain**, adding at least another 2 miles to your route. From here, head for **Sapper's Hill**, half a mile away, and from there return back into Stanley along the road. The remains of foxholes, dug for shelter by the forces stationed here, are still visible when walking over this area, although some have filled with water and vegetation. It does not take much imagination to see how exposed this site was and to realise that any shelter was very valuable in those days of war in 1982. Depending upon your walking speed and interest in the area, this walk can be done as a strenuous half-day hike or as part of a full-day walk in the hills. As with anywhere on the Falkland Islands, the very changeable nature of the weather means that waterproofs are an essential part of your equipment: even though you might be within sight of Stanley, you are still exposed to the elements and can get wet and cold. You are also advised to make sure that someone knows where you are going and when you expect to return as the walking is over rock and diddle-dee heath with very few obvious paths. Although the area is safe to walk, it's advisable not to touch any metal objects and report anything that you think could be unexploded ordnance.

Gypsy Cove, Cape Pembroke and Surf Bay are all easily accessible from the centre of Stanley for those on a tour or with their own transport. See pages 85, 88 and 90 respectively.

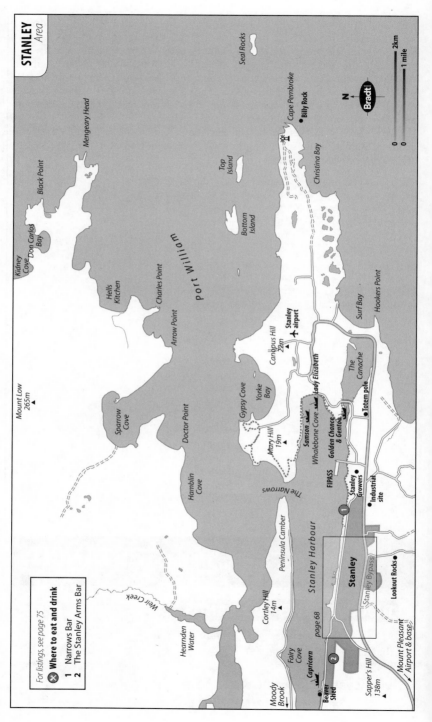

STANLEY Area

For listings, see page 75

⊗ **Where to eat and drink**
1 Narrows Bar
2 The Stanley Arms Bar

N

Bradt

0 _____ 2km
0 _____ 1 mile

Seal Rocks

Cape Pembroke
● Billy Rock

Christina Bay

Top
Island

Bottom
Island

Mengeary Head

Black Point

Kidney
Cove Don Carlos
Bay

Hells
Kitchen

Charles Point

Arrow Point

p o r t   W i l l i a m

Mount Low
265m ▲

Sparrow
Cove

Doctor Point

Hamblin
Cove

Canopus Hill
29m ▲

Stanley airport ✈

Surf Bay

Hookers Point

Gypsy Cove

Yorke
Bay

Mary Hill
19m ▲

Samson ⚓

Whalebone Cove **Lady Elizabeth** ⚓

Golden Chance ⚓
& Gentoo

● Totem pole

The
Canache

Peninsula Camber

FIPASS

Stanley
Growers ●
● Industrial
site

The Narrows

Stanley Harbour

page 68

Cortley Hill
14m ▲

Weir Creek

Hearnden
Water

Fairy
Cove

Moody
Brook

Capricorn ●
Beaver
Shed ●

Sapper's Hill
138m ▲

Mount Pleasant
Airport & base

Stanley Bypass

Stanley

● Lookout Rocks

5

East Falkland

Once Stanley has been explored, there are many sites on East Falkland that can be reached on a day trip from the islands' capital. Any part of the islands away from Stanley is referred to as *camp*, a term originating from the Spanish word '*campo*', meaning countryside. In some cases (such as at Volunteer Point, Cape Dolphin, San Carlos and Port San Carlos), there are places to stay in the more outlying *camp* settlements, which can save travel time to-ing and fro-ing from Stanley. The road network on East Falkland reaches most of the settlements north of the Goose Green/Darwin area as well as south over Lafonia to North Arm. The majority of East Falkland's sights are within a 3-hour drive of Stanley; some require a full day to get there and back, with enough time to look around, while others can be visited in a few hours, including travel time. It is also possible to use Darwin (page 110) as a base from which to explore the surrounding countryside rather than Stanley.

Although some of the most famous wildlife sites are on the outer islands, there is plenty to see on East Falkland itself, with the Volunteer Point king penguin colony being the highlight of many visitors' trips to the islands. The sites closer to Stanley, such as Gypsy Cove and Surf Bay, are popular trips for those staying in the capital.

For those interested in the Falklands war, taking trips to Goose Green and to the areas around 'bomb alley' (as San Carlos Water was briefly known) is recommended. The minefields that were found in many locations on the Falkland Islands, and in particular on East Falkland, have now all been cleared.

GYPSY COVE, CAPE PEMBROKE AND SURF BAY – A DRIVING TOUR FROM STANLEY

Lying to the east of Stanley, these three sites are only a few miles apart and, if time allows, all three can be visited in a single day trip from the capital. For those who like a very long walk, it is also possible to hike between all three of these sites. Although Gypsy Cove, popular for its penguin colony, is closest to town as the crow flies, the road to reach it takes you to the south of the airport, past Surf Bay and its white-sand beach. Cape Pembroke is a good spot to look for passing seabirds such as albatross and to visit the remains of dwellings of the area's earlier settlers. At its tip, it is about 5 miles in a straight line from Stanley, but as much of the distance travelled is over rough tracks, allow enough time to get there and back.

GYPSY COVE AND AROUND Gypsy Cove is within easy reach of Stanley, as it is only a 15-minute drive from the hotels or the public jetty. It is a popular first stop for many first-time visitors to Falkland, providing an introduction to the islands' penguin species as magellanic penguins breed here. Gypsy Cove can get very busy during holiday periods and when large cruise ships call into Stanley Harbour. On these days there may well be a warden on site. The wardens will give visitors information and instructions about the wildlife of the area. All visitors are asked to follow the wardens' advice in order to ensure that the wildlife is not disturbed. There are helpful signs explaining what wildlife can be found in the area and reminding visitors to keep a respectful distance. There is also a walkway to ensure that everyone keeps the appropriate distances when the wardens are not present; see opposite for further details.

Getting there and away About 5 minutes from Stanley, along the airport road, you pass a **totem pole** which was first erected by the British troops and decorated with signs mentioning the name of their hometown and the intervening distance. This has been added to over the years so that most of the cities of the world are mentioned, plus nearly every locality in the UK. The pole is located outside the industrial site, beyond the hydroponics garden (Stanley Growers), almost as far as the Canache. Many of the vegetables consumed on Falkland are cultivated in these greenhouses.

The road from Stanley to the airport becomes more built up every year in step with the city's expansion. The first turn-off on the left leads to the floating dock known as **FIPASS** (the initials stand for Floating Interim Port and Storage System), the unloading point for all the larger cargo vessels that call in to the Falklands. Proposals to replace this port are in an advanced stage, but a final plan has yet to be agreed as this book goes to print. The tarmac road continues towards the airport past **the Canache**, a shallow lagoon where sailing ships used to come for repair and to have their hulls scraped, a process known as careenage. The name 'Canache' is a corruption of careenage. At low tide during the summer white-rumped sandpipers can be found along the shore in the company of the resident two-banded plovers.

From the Canache, it is possible to continue via the airport road, bypassing the airport around the western perimeter before joining the main track, overlooking Yorke Bay, which leads to the car park at Gypsy Cove. The small pond near the airport can be a good site for wildfowl during the summer months. **Yorke Bay** used to be a very popular beach for the inhabitants of Stanley to visit on fine summer days but was out of bounds for many years due to the minefields laid in 1982. Happily, these have now all been cleared and the beach is once again open for all to enjoy.

The latter part of the track beyond the airport is a gravel road, but is passable without a 4x4. The drive to Gypsy Cove via this route takes 10 minutes or so.

An **alternative route** to Gypsy Cove crosses the narrow bridge at the Stanley end of the Canache. The two ships sunk in the mud beside this narrow bridge were originally used for fishing before being converted to carry cargo around the islands. The *Golden Chance* lies well up the beach while the *Gentoo* is in deep water. The latter was brought into the islands in 1927 and based at Pebble Island until 1965. It was then used for a variety of cargoes until being moved to the Canache, where it sank during the Argentinian occupation of 1982.

The gravel track continues around the edge of Canopus Hill to **Whalebone Cove**, where the wrecks of the *Lady Elizabeth* and the steam tug *Samson* can be clearly seen (see opposite); it is worth stopping for a photo opportunity at the small layby closest to the *Lady Liz*. The grasslands at the head of Whalebone Cove are full of pale maiden. These delicate, yellow-centred, white flower blooms can be seen in profusion around here in springtime. From the track, looking out over the *Lady Elizabeth,* it is possible to see along the southern edge of Stanley Harbour, and past Stanley out to Mount Tumbledown, the Two Sisters and Mount Harriet.

From here, the track continues on as it winds around the rocky outcrops until it joins the track from the airport that leads to Gypsy Cove and its car park. A gate to

The most impressive shipwreck still visible on the islands, the **Lady Elizabeth**, known locally as *Lady Liz*, is stranded in the middle of the beach at Whalebone Cove with the steam tug *Samson* on the northern shore. The *Lady Elizabeth* was built of iron in 1879 in Sunderland, with a length of 223ft (68m) and a weight of 1,096 tonnes (1,208 tons). It had visited the islands on several occasions before its final trip. On one of these visits it was carrying the bricks and cement for the new cathedral being built in Stanley. The ship's last voyage began in December 1912, carrying wood from Vancouver to Mozambique. It hit severe gales off Cape Horn, where deck cargo and four men were washed overboard, before putting into Berkeley Sound to the northeast of Stanley on 12 March 1913. On entering the sound, *Lady Liz* hit Uranie Rock, causing it to hole and lose a section of keel. It was towed into Stanley by the tug *Samson*, where its owner's intention was to repair the hull so that the ship could continue its voyage. This was not to be its destiny, as it was later condemned and sold to the Falkland Islands Company for £3,350. The sails were used as covers for calf-pens at Darwin. The hull was used as a floating timber warehouse alongside the East jetty in Stanley for three years before being moved further out into the harbour and used for general storage. *Lady Liz* broke free from these moorings on 17 February 1936 and drifted ashore to its present position. The masts still standing high in the sky give the impression that it is just waiting for the weather to change before setting out on the high seas again. Gales in the early 2010s broke the bowsprit, however, so on closer inspection it no longer looks quite as intact.

The **Samson** joined the *Lady Liz* ashore in Whalebone Cove in 1945, after gale-force winds caused its moorings to break. It had been built in Hull in 1888 and reached Falkland in 1900. The Falkland Islands Company brought it to the islands because a powerful tug was needed in the islands. The *Samson* was involved in saving several vessels and their crews, which had hit the treacherous Billy Rock at the entrance to Stanley Harbour. It was in use as a lighter from 1924 onwards, until it broke adrift and ended up at its present location.

the east leads along an obvious track, overlooking the western end of Yorke Bay, to Gypsy Cove itself.

What to see and do Gypsy Cove is on the northeast part of the peninsula, which ends at Cape Pembroke. This area is internationally recognised as a Wild Animal and Bird Sanctuary because of the variety of wildlife seen here. Walking down from the car park, the higher section of the bank is covered with diddle-dee, which leads on to tussac grass on the steeper slopes and, eventually, sea cabbage growing in the loose sand by the beach. The main attraction here is the small colony of **magellanic penguins** that have located their burrows in the sloping banks of the cove. The penguins are present at this site between October and March, and they lay two eggs during November, hatching them during late December and early January. Those birds not actively engaged at the nest can be seen gathered in small groups on the sand or bathing in the shallows. It is important that these birds do not waste energy moving away from curious wildlife-watchers, therefore Falklands Conservation guidelines recommend that visitors maintain a distance of at least 7.5m from the birds, adding the proviso that if they look nervous then you should retreat further.

The other guidelines issued by the charity (applicable everywhere on Falkland, not only at this site) are that visitors should proceed carefully in the vicinity of the burrows and should not obstruct the birds' passage between their burrows and the sea. At Gypsy Cove, the soft, peaty earth is ideal for penguins to burrow in, but also means that it is all too easy to inadvertently crush the burrows underfoot. Stick to the well-made path and lookout points to view the wildlife without disturbing either it or its fragile habitat. Falklands Conservation also advises not to walk through the tussac grass, an easily damaged habitat where many birds nest. Finally, visitors are warned to move slowly, avoiding sudden movements when near the wildlife.

Other birds seen in the Gypsy Cove area include Falkland steamer duck, which often gather in sizeable flocks on the end of the long sandy beach in **Yorke Bay**, just a few yards away. The rocky outcrops on the outer edge of the cove are used as a nesting site by a small group of rock shags and have also been home to nesting black-crowned night herons in the past. In springtime, the song of white-bridled finches and grass wrens can be heard on calm days as they sing from the tussac clumps that dot this area. A leaflet about Gypsy Cove and its wildlife can be obtained from Falklands Conservation or the Falkland Islands Tourist Board, at the offices in Stanley or online (**w** falklandislands.com/dbimgs/Gypsy%20Cove.pdf). The view northwards from here out across Port William towards Mengeary Point is superb on a sunny day, as the white-grass- and diddle-dee-clad hills glow in the sunshine. Almost directly opposite Gypsy Cove, less than 2 miles away across Port William, is **Sparrow Cove**, which for many years was the home to the SS *Great Britain* before it was taken back to the UK. On windy days black-browed albatross can be seen gliding low over the water along with a scattering of feeding penguins and terns.

CAPE PEMBROKE One of the most exposed parts of the coast near Stanley, Cape Pembroke is a great place to blow away the cobwebs. As well as opportunities for birdwatching, the area has historical connections with both the Falklands War and early life on the archipelago.

Getting there and away The most easterly point of the Falklands, Cape Pembroke is situated 7 miles from Stanley. In order to reach the Cape itself, drive from Stanley along the airport road towards the airport, then head out to the east on to the track that leads towards the lighthouse. Once past the initial section of gravel, there are many different routes along the headland. Some of these can get very boggy and are therefore very difficult to drive through, so a 4x4 is a good idea, although I have seen 2WDs out near the lighthouse. The best routes across this terrain will depend on how wet the ground is and how many vehicles have churned up the tracks before you. Local knowledge is a major advantage in finding the correct route, so it's advisable to go with a local driver (page 73) rather than head out on your own for the first time. The drive straight out to the lighthouse will usually take less than half an hour but that does not allow time for any photo stops.

What to see and do There are some shallow pools in the peat on the southern side of this headland, usually inhabited by an interesting selection of wildfowl. Silver teal have been known to breed on these ponds in the past. Concealed among the more common plants are some of the island's more unusual flora, such as dusty miller, pimpernel and dog orchid. The last flowers before Christmas; consequently the basal leaves are all that is visible for most of the summer. The shallow pools found close to the track, not far from the turn-off from the main road, can occasionally be temporary homes to Baird's sandpiper, a rare visitor from North America during the

A welcoming sign and colourful buildings greet cruise-ship visitors as they land at Stanley's public jetty PAGE 71

top
(JR/S)

Government House on Stanley's Ross Road is a riot of colour in mid-summer when lupins and red hot pokers are in full bloom PAGE 78

above left
(BI/S)

Rob Yssel's Solar System Sculpture is a new artistic creation made from recycled materials PAGE 79

above right
(SH/S)

Stanley's Historic Dockyard Museum contains a wonderful collection of artefacts with exhibits covering many aspects of island life, from historic shipwrecks to the modern day PAGE 77

below
(JR/S)

above
(SS)

The site of a frenzy of activity during 1982, the British War Cemetery at San Carlos is now a place of quiet reflection PAGE 108

left
(SA/D)

The top of the 1914 Battle Memorial on Ross Road in Stanley, which was erected in 1927 to commemorate the Battle of the Falklands between British and German fleets on 8 December 1914 PAGE 78

below
(WW)

The SS *Great Britain*, one of the islands' most famous shipwrecks, is remembered by its mizzen-mast which is displayed on Stanley's Victory Green PAGE 80

Bodie Creek Suspension Bridge was built in 1924–25 and is a must-see for those spending time in the Darwin and Goose Green area PAGE 114 above (B/A)

Pilot whale bones can be found on Pebble Island's Elephant Beach PAGE 152 above right (SS)

A bust of Margaret Thatcher, prime minister at the time of the Argentine invasion, can be found in Stanley PAGE 78 right (WW)

The wreck of the *Lady Elizabeth*, stranded at the eastern end of Stanley Harbour, serves as a poignant reminder of the dangers of sailing the South Atlantic in years gone by PAGE 87 below (B/S)

THEY ARE FEW IN NUMBER BUT THEY HAVE THE RIGHT TO LIVE IN PEACE, TO CHOOSE THEIR OWN WAY OF LIFE AND TO DETERMINE THEIR OWN ALLEGIANCE.

– MARGARET THATCHER, APRIL, JULY 1982.

above
(JR/S)

With adults toing and froing and the young begging for food, imperial shag colonies are constantly active and make for a lively spectacle PAGE 36

below
(SS)

Getting up close to a black-browed albatross colony, such as the one found on Saunders Island, is an unmissable experience PAGE 160

Rockhopper penguins are full of character and can be seen arguing among themselves as they travel in groups to and from their colonies PAGE 33

above
(JR/S)

Magellanic penguins often greet each other with a mutual braying song, which is at its loudest at sundown as they return to shore PAGE 34

top right
(DP/FITB)

A white flash over the eye is the easiest way to identify a gentoo penguin PAGE 33

bottom right
(AI/S)

Macaroni penguins are the rarest of the five species that breed on the islands PAGE 34

below
(WW)

above right
(WW)

The Johnny Rook, as the striated caracara is known, can be found only on the outer islands and is often inquisitive of anything new PAGE 40

above left
(G/S)

Juvenile Falkland thrush can be seen around many settlements and tussac islands, where their parents' song rings out in spring PAGE 44

middle left
(WW)

The striking black-and-white magellanic oystercatcher can be seen, and usually heard, on many of the islands' sandy beaches PAGE 40

bottom left
(WW)

The smallest of the islands' endemic birds, Cobb's wrens are found only on rat-free islands PAGE 43

below
(NG/FITB)

A female upland goose leading her very new young along a typical Falkland Island beach PAGE 37

Sitting at Elephant Corner and being entertained by southern elephant seals is a highlight of any visit to Sea Lion Island PAGE 126

above
(OP/S)

Bleaker Island's southern sea lions are best seen from the cliffs above their haul-out site PAGE 118

right
(WW)

Peale's dolphins can sometimes be seen surfing through the breaking waves in places such as Bertha's Beach on Saunders Island and many other locations PAGE 119

below
(DP/FITB)

above
(H/D)

Hiking between the landing site and bird colonies on New Island, one of the many great walks on the islands PAGE 176

left
(VTJ/S)

Flights between outlying islands allow visitors to witness wonderful aerial views PAGE 57

below
(OP/S)

With subjects ranging from ever-posing king penguins to wide-open landscapes and colourful buildings, the islands are a photographer's dream PAGE 63

summer months. The small rocky beach on the south side, **Christina Bay**, is a good site to look for kelp geese and magellanic oystercatchers. The banks of kelp that get washed ashore here furnish a comfortable resting place for sea lions.

Towards the end of the Cape, where the tracks almost merge into one, the Falklands Conservation replanting programme, begun some 25 years ago, is showing dividends with some healthy tussac-grass growth now visible. The end of the headland is fenced off to ensure the grasses are not grazed by any straying animals. Southern sea lions come to sleep in the more mature stands or can be seen resting on the rocks near the water's edge. In some of the more sheltered hollows it is possible to find some hardy clumps of thrift and pimpernel. The fast-flowing tides bring a lot of food within the reach of the many seabirds that breed nearby. It is not unusual to see mixed flocks of birds feeding a short distance out to sea. Penguins, gulls, terns and shearwaters are regularly observed from here. This exposed headland has proved to be an ideal spot for keen birdwatchers to observe many of the seabirds that breed in the Antarctic, especially during the equinoctial gales.

Cape Pembroke lighthouse

The lighthouse is a short distance further on towards Cape Pembroke. The waters surrounding the entrance to Port William, stretching along the coast as far as Stanley, are very dangerous, with a strong tidal race, several small islands and rocks, including the infamous **Billy Rock** which has claimed more than its fair share of shipwrecks over the years with many lives lost. The need for some sort of beacon became apparent when Stanley was established during the 1840s. The first markers were not lit and were only of use during daylight hours. The first painted marker was replaced by a larger construction in 1849, followed by the erection of the present lighthouse in 1855. This was a cast-iron structure brought from London. It stands at 60ft (18m) and was first lit on 1 December 1855, its light visible up to 14 miles away. The light was run on rape oil and was turned by a clockwork motor, burning 1,000 gallons of oil annually. At one point, sea-lion oil was unsuccessfully tried as an experiment to cut the costs of keeping the lamp alight. The first lighthouse keeper was William Creed who lived with his family in a cottage built at the base of the tower. All the provisions for the keepers and the light had to be landed by boat at a place known as the gulch, instead of being hauled the 7 miles from Stanley.

Before the advent of telephone and radio, messages in daytime were sent using signalling flags, and at night horses were ridden back to the capital to inform the authorities of any shipping movements and to raise the alarm if any boat was seen in trouble. Horses were kept close to the tower for this purpose. Despite the light, ships in trouble were not a rare occurrence. This system was replaced in 1912 when the wireless station was built in Stanley. The light was modernised during the late 1800s and again in 1906, when it was rebuilt on better foundations. The new paraffin light could reach 16 miles out to sea and continued to function until the Argentine forces landed in Yorke Bay in April 1982. It has remained unlit ever since, having been replaced by an automatic solar-powered light and radar reflector situated a few yards away. The foundations of the keepers' houses can still be seen beside the old lighthouse.

The lighthouse was vandalised after the war, but was refurbished by the Alistair Cameron Memorial Trust. For those wanting to visit, the key from the lighthouse can be obtained from the Historic Dockyard Museum in Stanley (page 77). Once inside, you can climb the spiral staircase to look out over this wild landscape.

Nearby is the propeller from the *Atlantic Conveyor* that was placed here to commemorate those who lost their lives when this merchant vessel, which was part of the task force coming to liberate the Falkland Islands, was sunk in 1982.

SURF BAY For those who have the time, Surf Bay is another stop of interest on the way back to Stanley from Cape Pembroke. It is also a popular spot for a walk for those living in Stanley as it is less than 5-minutes' drive away. Whichever way you approach Surf Bay, it is reached by turning eastwards off the main road at the inland end of the Canache. The long beach is a spectacular sight when the waves are crashing on to the sand, the wind picking off their crests as they reach breaking point. Falkland steamer ducks and scatterings of terns and gulls can be seen feeding on the kelp beds behind these breaking rollers. Most years a small group of elephant seals have come ashore to moult in the small bays to the south of the beach on Hooker's Point. White-rumped sandpipers and two-banded plovers frequent the banks of kelp along the tide line.

KIDNEY ISLAND

Kidney Island is a small tussac-covered island lying at the southern entrance of Berkeley Sound. Opposite this island, on East Falkland, is Kidney Cove (page 94). Kidney Island is a government-owned National Nature Reserve. It is not used as pasturage and, consequently, retains its original flora. The island can be accessed via a boat trip from Stanley which takes roughly half an hour, cruising out through Port William (see opposite).

A visit to Kidney Island gives travellers a good idea of what much of the coastline of Falkland must have been like before sheep and other grazing animals were imported, as there is an abundant lush growth of tussac grass. The number of visitors to the island is limited to 14 at any one time and an approved guide must accompany all parties (see opposite for details). Lying about 9 miles by boat from Stanley, it is a narrow island of around 79 acres – three-quarters of a mile long and half a mile across. Most of the north-facing side of the island is low-lying, but steep cliffs, with one extensive bay, face east between two rocky headlands. The southwestern side of the island is much lower where the tussac grass comes down to the sea, leaving a narrow beach of rock and sand. All landings are made on this sheltered sand. This island has a very dense covering of tussac grass, making it essential for all members of any visiting group to remain within reach of each other

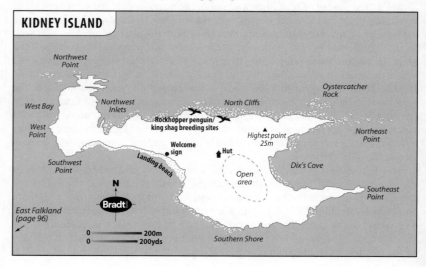

KIDNEY ISLAND

Northwest Point

West Bay

Northwest Inlets

North Cliffs

Oystercatcher Rock

West Point

Rockhopper penguin/ king shag breeding sites

Welcome sign

Landing beach

Highest point 25m

Hut

Northeast Point

Southwest Point

Open area

Dix's Cove

Southeast Point

N

Bradt

East Falkland (page 96)

0   200m
0   200yds

Southern Shore

and their leader – it's easy to get lost! This dense growth makes walking problematic, especially as burrow-nesting seabirds use the whole island. There are also some very boggy areas, so good footwear and waterproof clothing are essential. No food and drink is for sale on the island, so come well prepared.

A visit to Kidney Island is a unique opportunity to see Falkland habitats as they once were, before the arrival of humans. It can be quite a tiring day, but it is certainly a memorable one.

GETTING THERE AND AWAY Boat trips out to the island from Stanley Harbour are quite rare as permission has to be obtained from the Falkland Islands Government Environmental Planning Department (✆ 28480) and the only way to visit is with an approved guide. Boats can be arranged from Sulivan Shipping (✆ 22626; w sulivanshipping.com). Local travel companies such as Falkland Islands Holidays or International Tours and Travel (both page 73) can help you with finding a guide, arranging a boat trip, and getting the government permission; it's quite a jigsaw to fit all the pieces together if you want to organise it yourself. Needless to say, it is worth trying to find a group of like-minded people as the costs to do it by oneself will most likely be prohibitive.

The trip from Stanley usually takes less than an hour and gives visitors a very good opportunity to get some photos of the capital and the surrounding area from the sea. As the boat passes through the Narrows at the entrance to Stanley Harbour, there is a chance of seeing Peale's dolphins as they regularly play in the bow wave of incoming and outgoing boats. Once in Port William there are more seabirds present, mostly rock shags and king shags with accompanying gulls and terns. In late summer, the boat trip can also afford visitors the chance to see a jigger at close range, when their skippers bring them into the sound to renew their licences or to see their agents. These rather strange boats with their long lines of lights running the length of their upper decks show up at great distance at night, as they fish for the squid that come into Falkland waters towards the end of the summer.

Along the northern coastline towards Kidney Island, black-browed albatrosses, gentoo penguins and magellanic penguins start to appear, along with the familiar southern giant petrels. Once round **Mengeary Point**, sooty shearwaters suddenly become the most common bird, shearing low over the sea on calm days or flashing past the boat in a great display of controlled flight. For keen birdwatchers there is a possibility of finding great shearwaters amid the masses of sooty shearwaters. The sheltered water channel between Kidney Island and Kidney Cove is a good place to watch gentoo penguins elegantly negotiating their way to the shore. Two beaches, **Don Carlos Bay** and the small strand to the south of Kidney Cove, are worth inspection from the sea because resting southern sea lions often head there. Gentoo penguins can also be seen landing on Kidney Cove, walking up to reach their colonies at the back of the beach. This area had been heavily mined but is now clear. In the absence of people during that time the penguins took over, so there is a good colony here.

Landing on Kidney Island involves anchoring in the kelp beds on the southwestern side of the island before coming ashore in a rubber dinghy. A sign at the top of the landing beach indicates some of the dos and don'ts of the island. The danger of fire is paramount on account of the abundance of flammable tussac grass, so smoking is consequently banned here. It is also important that bottles, lenses, and lens filters are not lost on the island as their light-magnifying effects could also start a fire.

Trips to Kidney Island are very much governed by the weather and it is not unusual to have to postpone a trip to the island for a day or so. It is therefore a good idea to allow for an alternative date in the itinerary in case the weather causes a change of plans. As the weather may also curtail the time spent on the island, the crew of the boat will usually provide a ship-to-shore radio so that they can reach visitors, should the weather take a turn for the worse. Generally, visitors will be ashore for between 2 and 4 hours.

WHAT TO SEE AND DO As the tussac grass is so tall here it's very easy to get lost; before you land your guide will give you a briefing about staying in one group and following their lead while moving around the island.

Commerson's and, occasionally, Peale's dolphins sometimes follow the rubber dinghy on its way to the shore, often coming very close to the boat. Sometimes a lone sea lion will trail behind the boat, curious to see what is going on. Along the narrow beach, groups of magellanic penguins and Falkland steamer ducks survey each new arrival with interest. As this island has no rodents, there is nothing to prevent large numbers of small birds from breeding. The most obvious are the tussacbirds, which come out to the anchored ships and then follow visitors around the island, picking off whatever insect life is disturbed by passing feet.

There is no defined path through the tussac grass which covers the island. Even with a guide it is advisable, when still aboard the ship, to get a bearing on the roof of the small hut visible on the brow of the hill. This is the island's only building and has been used for many years by those studying the breeding birds and other wildlife. Its most famous use was by Olin Sewall and Eleanor Pettingill, who first stayed here in the late 1950s, when they made a film for Disney about Falklands wildlife. While it has been repaired several times over the years, it could never be classed as luxury accommodation! It is now used by the researchers that come to study the island's wildlife. Once heading towards the hut, the first section is up an incline to the plateau on the top of the island. The highest point of Kidney Island is slightly less than 25m.

Almost all the island is thick with tussac grass, although there are some slightly more open areas to the east of the hut. It is here that wild celery and the indigenous strawberry can be found. The latter grows best on the top of dead tussac grass – the white flowers at their most attractive before Christmas, the bright red fruit ripening later in the summer. These are popular with the Falkland thrushes that feed in this area. These thrushes often indicate the presence of a short-eared owl. This predator is rarely active during the day unless flushed or discovered by the thrushes, which then proceed to mob the owl until it leaves their territory. It is difficult to make quiet progress through the tussac grass, and the resident magellanic penguins are never very impressed by visitors walking past their burrows. The braying call of the 'jackass', as it is locally called, soon becomes a very familiar sound.

Visitors should pause at regular intervals to admire the birdlife overhead, which constitutes a perfect foil to the creatures scuttling around at ground level. **Turkey vultures** are the most prevalent; these huge creatures seem to be able to fly in almost all weather conditions. Southern **caracara** breed on the island, but are very shy and are therefore not so easy to find. Other birds passing overhead include **terns** and **brown-hooded gulls**, both of which breed in small numbers on the ends of the rocky promontories on the southeast side of the island. **Southern giant petrels** do not breed here but seem to enjoy flying low over the island, passing barely above head height on occasions.

By crossing directly to the other side of the island from the landing site, it is possible to reach the **rockhopper penguin colony** on the typical rocky outcrops. These cliffs are 16ft (5m) high and made up of quartzitic sandstone. Some of the flatter ledges to the northern end of the cliff are home to **rock shags** and are also used by roosting **black-crowned night herons**. The main cliffs still have rockhopper penguins breeding on the upper slopes, although their numbers are reducing, with just under 300 pairs counted in recent years. The 200 pairs counted in the 2017 to 2019 seasons is a big reduction from the 3,500 pairs that were estimated to be breeding here in 1936. The unavailability of food is thought to be a major factor in their decline. The occasional **macaroni penguin** joins this colony, especially in springtime. A very rare **northern rockhopper penguin** has been occasionally noted during the summer, joining in with its southern relatives. King shags also breed at the top of this outcrop.

The most prolific seabird on Kidney Island is the **sooty shearwater**, which returns to the island from its winter out at sea in the northern hemisphere during the spring. By midsummer, large numbers gather to the east of the island waiting for darkness to fall. When it is fully dark, these birds fly in over the island before finding their own burrows. Scientists think that their well-developed sense of smell plays a large part in their nocturnal ability to locate their burrows. During the summer the birds take it in turns to supervise the nest, allowing the mate to head out to sea. The reason for this nocturnal behaviour is that they are easy prey on the ground during daytime, so only come ashore after dark to avoid predators such as skuas and the larger gulls. In calm weather, multitudes of shearwaters gather on the sea. They are constantly in motion in windy weather, wheeling spectacularly aloft in large groups before landing again, but rarely settling for long. The only other species of shearwater that breeds on Kidney Island is the **great shearwater**, which can occasionally be seen among the larger flocks of sooty shearwaters. If the flock has been settled for a while, it is quite usual to see rockhopper and magellanic penguins passing through on their way to the shore.

The other notable seabird breeding on Kidney Island is the **white-chinned petrel**, known locally as the 'cobbler', because its song supposedly resembles the sound of a shoemaker cobbling on his last. The petrels breed in burrows on the higher slopes of the island, but they are normally pelagic and so are not easily observed. Every now and then one does come near the island, flying low over the tussac grass before dropping down close to the burrows. These birds can be seen on most visits to the island, if you are observant, but they are never easy to find.

Dix's Cove on the eastern side of the island is a good place to look for some of the smaller birds of Kidney Island. **Dark-faced ground-tyrants** and **Cobb's wrens** are common along the boulder beach with tussacbirds usually never very far away. **Southern sea lions** are not uncommon in this bay and can sometimes come up into the tussac grass to sleep. These resting places have a distinctive, rather rank, smell and the blades of tussac grass are completely flattened by the weight of these huge beasts. Before descending through the tussac grass to the beach, it is a good idea to find a vantage point to check if any are visible, and to listen out for any snorting noises. Meeting a sea lion face to face, although a memorable experience, is neither recommended nor safe – a quiet, steady retreat is the best course of action. The occasional **elephant seal** has been known to come ashore at this site, but fortunately they rarely move far from the top of the beach. Brown-headed gulls and South American terns are very active in defending their territories on the headlands on either side of the beach – skuas and vultures are chased away as soon as they fly over the headland. A few black-crowned night herons can be found roosting along the northern arm of the bay. To get back to the hut there is a short-but-steep climb up out of Dix's Cove before heading west towards the hut and then southeast on to the landing beach. Amid the occasional patches of short tussac grass, the blue form of berry-lobelia, some scattered specimens of Antarctic eyebright and sizeable clumps of cinnamon grass grow wherever the ground is exposed to sunlight.

In late summer, **southern right** and **sei whales** have been recorded in the deeper waters to the east of Kidney Island and in the entrance of Berkeley Sound to the north. These whales are most often encountered by the boats working in the area, but are occasionally seen by visitors to the island and have been subject to studies by Falklands Conservation. In calm weather it may be possible to circumnavigate Kidney Island before returning to Stanley. This gives visitors a superb vantage point over the gigantic flocks of sooty shearwaters and, when these birds gather in large numbers, they are a true wildlife highlight of the Falklands. They are usually seen sitting, waiting for the light to fall before they come ashore. If they are disturbed by a passing boat or skua, they will rise up in a swirling mass before settling again, often only a few yards from where they started. As with any boat trip around the islands, there is always the chance of finding some of the more unusual seabirds or cetaceans that pass through the waters around the Falkland Islands.

There are three other tussac-grass-covered islands between Cape Pembroke and Berkeley Sound that are off limits, but can be viewed from the sea on the way to and from Kidney Island. **Cochon** Island is the largest, lying a mile and a half to the northeast of Kidney Island; the other two, Bottom Island and Top Island, are just to the north of Cape Pembroke.

KIDNEY COVE

Regarded as an important area for breeding seabirds, Kidney Cove is one of the few places on Falkland where four species of breeding penguin can be found. There is no longer any accommodation nearby, but Kidney Cove is easily accessible on a day trip from Stanley.

GETTING THERE AND AWAY Kidney Cove, which was opened for tourists in 1999, is only accessible by land. Permission to visit the area must be given by the owners of Murrell Farm, Adrian and Lisa Lowe (✆31001; m 54665; e allowe@horizon.co.fk; w kidneycovetours.com) and is for experienced drivers only. Therefore, the site is usually accessed by visitors based in Stanley through one of the day trips organised by the Lowes's company, Kidney Cove Tours (page 73). These tours include a 3-hour round trip to Kidney Cove (£50 pp) and an extended 6-hour trip to visit the rockhopper colony on the north shore of their land (£70 pp). Prices include pick up and drop off in Stanley. The drive from the capital to Murrell Farm takes about an hour, after which it takes another 30 minutes to reach Kidney Cove.

 WHERE TO STAY There is the option to stay overnight in Kidney Cove Cabin or Rockhopper Cabin (same contact info as above; **££**), each of which sleeps four in two twin rooms. These are basic cabins – eg: with portable toilets – but are ideally situated for visiting the wildlife in the area, with one near the rockhoppers and the other in the cove. Note that children are not allowed in the Rockhopper Cabin as it is situated near cliffs.

WHAT TO SEE AND DO Near Kidney Cove are the remains of a house used during World War II by the 16 men stationed on Look Out Hill. The base of a naval gun with which they guarded the entrance to Port William can still be seen. There is little left of the house apart from a very solid-looking fireplace, which has stood the test of time much better than the rest of the house. These men also created a garden in the shelter of the hill, traces of which are still visible today.

The beaches and headlands from Kidney Cove back westwards to Sparrow Cove were mined extensively during the 1982 war but have now been cleared. Those minefields presented no obstacles to the gentoo penguins who come ashore at Kidney Cove – they would walk up through the fenced areas until they reached one of the three **gentoo penguin colonies** situated on the grassy bank just outside the minefield. One of these colonies has a small group of king penguins in its midst. The only other noteworthy colonies of this majestic species in Falkland are on Saunders Island (page 156) and at Volunteer Point, on the northeastern part of East Falkland (see below). Elsewhere, such as on Sea Lion Island, there are a few others in smaller – generally non-breeding – groups, but this is the nearest **king penguin colony** to Stanley.

The grass around the freshwater pool behind Mine Cove, only a few yards from the penguin colonies, contains some of the many species of geese that breed on Falkland, while a varied selection of ducks, ranging from upland geese to crested ducks, visit the pool during the day. **Magellanic penguins** breed nearby on the drier slopes behind the coves, and also to the north in the turf-covered summits of the steep cliffs, which are quite a walk from the nearest beach. Visitors who are on the Lowes's full, 6-hour tour will be taken further along the coast, to the north shore of the farm, where there is a large colony of **rockhopper penguins**. These penguins are good climbers and can be seen easily making their way up the steep cliffs that typify this area. The views from here out over Berkeley Sound towards Volunteer Point are superb. To the west of Mount Low is the peak known as Twelve O'Clock Mountain. Apparently, the name relates to the fact that, viewed from Stanley, the sun appears to be directly above this hill at noon, thus signalling time for lunch.

VOLUNTEER POINT

Volunteer Point is named after the *Volunteer*, a ship that visited the Falkland Islands in 1815. This privately owned nature reserve is on a narrow strip of short grass that connects East Falkland to the headland of Volunteer Point itself and is bordered by the 2-mile-long Volunteer Beach to the north and by Volunteer Lagoon to the south. The wardens' house is at the western end of the grassy area, while the king penguin colony is at the eastern end. This colony is one of the highlights of any visit to the Falkland Islands – it is the largest colony of this species on the islands and is still increasing. There are two additional species of penguin, and many other birds breed in this fabulous scenery. As you near the site on the tracks from Johnson's Harbour, the whole area opens up spectacularly before you, revealing the lagoon, penguins and beach. It is possible to stay at the wardens' house, but the majority of visitors will come here on a day trip from Stanley. The 3-hour drive out gives you a good sense what travel was like on the Falklands in years gone by as the last section is over *camp*.

GETTING THERE AND AWAY The majority of visitors who reach Volunteer Point do so via the **road** and track from Stanley – the drive to and from the site is an experience in itself. It is only possible to get to Volunteer Point in a 4x4 and previous experience of driving over the soft, boggy ground that typifies *camp* is essential, as many inexperienced drivers have realised to their cost. The penguin colony is only about 45 miles from Stanley using the road to Johnson's Harbour, after which point tracks over *camp* can be followed. However, this drive normally takes 2½–3½ hours, depending on the state of the track and the route taken. Those with back or neck problems should not undertake this trip as it is a rather rough ride.

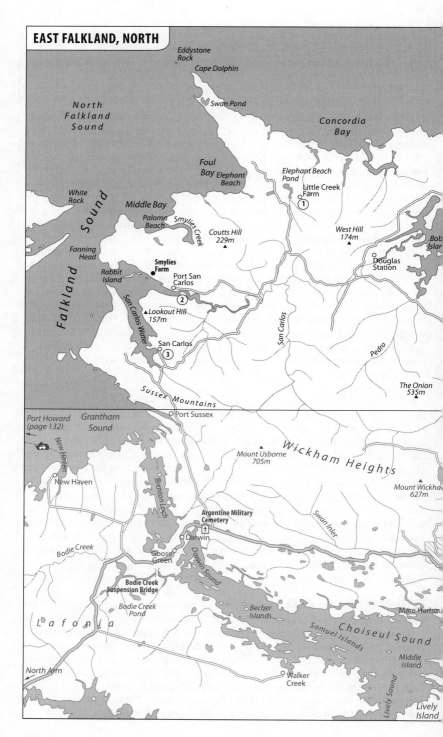

EAST FALKLAND, NORTH

Eddystone Rock

Cape Dolphin

Swan Pond

North Falkland Sound

Concordia Bay

Foul Bay

Elephant Beach

Elephant Beach Pond

Little Creek Farm

①

White Rock

Middle Bay

Paloma Beach

Smylies Creek

Coutts Hill 229m ▲

West Hill 174m ▲

Bob Islar

Douglas Station

Falkland Sound

Fanning Head

Rabbit Island

Smylies Farm ●

Port San Carlos

②

San Carlos Water

▲ Lookout Hill 157m

San Carlos ③

San Carlos

Pedro

Sussex Mountains

The Onion 535m ▲

Port Sussex

Grantham Sound

Port Howard (page 132)

Mount Usborne 705m ▲

Wickham Heights

Mount Wickha 627m ▲

New Haven

New Haven

Brenton Loch

Swan Inlet

Bodie Creek

Argentine Military Cemetery ⓘ

Darwin

Goose Green

Darwin Sound

Bodie Creek Suspension Bridge

Bodie Creek Pond

Lafonia

Becher Islands

Mare Harbou

Choiseul Sound

Samuel Islands

North Arm

Walker Creek

Middle Island

Lively Sound

Lively Island

96

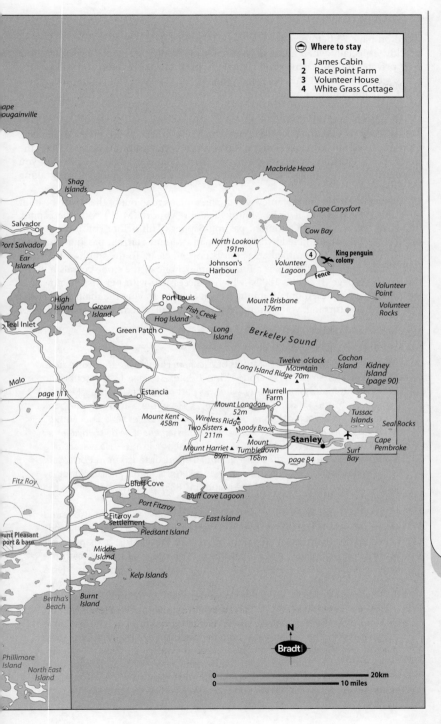

It is advisable to book a seat on an **organised day trip** from one of the operators listed on page 73 before you reach the Falkland Islands as they do get booked up quickly, especially when a cruise ship docks in Stanley. As you will be travelling over private land your driver will have the appropriate permission and will pay the entry fee (£15) to visit this site. These tours typically leave Stanley between 08.00 and 09.00 and return between 16.00 and 18.00, depending on how long you stay at the colony. These trips cost in the region of £200 upwards per person.

For **experienced self-drivers**, vehicles can follow the road from Stanley to Port Louis. To do so, take the Darwin Road, which passes turnings to other settlements en route. It is only tarmacked on the way to MPA – the rest of the drive is along the gravel roads typically found in the rest of the Falkland Islands. Despite this, you can drive all the way to Port Louis in a normal vehicle with a typical journey taking 35–40 minutes.

The Darwin Road from Stanley was the first major road out of the city to be built after the 1982 war and it links Mount Pleasant Airport (MPA) with the capital. The road leaves Stanley Common, passing Sapper's Hill before continuing south of Mount William, Tumbledown Mountain and Mount Harriet, passing what was one of the most heavily mined areas but is now all clear. To the south of the road, only a mile or so out of town, is a fine example of one of the stone corrals built by the gauchos (page 8) in the 1800s, which is accessible with permission now that the mines have gone. About 15 minutes from Stanley, leaving the main road at the first right-hand turning, you then drive through a valley across the eastern end of

RIVERS OF STONE

The dominant geographical features of Wickham Heights are the **stone runs**. These 'rivers of stone' have aroused much interest since first described in 1764 by Antoine Joseph Pernetty, who was part of de Bougainville's 1763–64 expedition to the Falkland Islands (page 7). He wrote a two-volume book about his travels, *Journal historique d'un voyage fait aux Îles Malouines en 1763 et 1764 pour les reconnoître et y former un établissement et de deux voyages au Détroit de Magellan avec une relation sur les Patagons*, in 1769. He was visiting the largest of the stone runs on Falkland, a short distance from Port Louis. This 4-mile, grey 'valley of fragments' was given the name 'Princes Street' by Charles Darwin when he visited the islands in 1833, as it reminded him of the cobblestones in Princes Street, Edinburgh.

These features, most commonly seen in Wickham Heights, are also found on the Devonian Quartzite on East and West Falkland. Seen from the air, they appear as grey patches on the slopes of the hills. They consist of many rough boulders sorted in such a way that the smaller stones are underneath the larger boulders. These stones are not stable, making it impossible to drive a vehicle or ride a horse across them. Where the road cuts across a stone run, the lower stones that have not been exposed to the elements are quite red in colour compared with the pale grey hue of the stones above. Very little plant life can survive in the relatively sterile habitat of the stone run. A few native strawberries and hairy daisy are the only rare plants with any colour, apart from the white flowers of the unique snakeplant which is endemic to Falkland. These flowers are columnar stems with many leaves close together and a white, rounded head. They stand upright in small clumps and remind some of snakes' heads, hence their name.

Wickham Heights, overlooked by Mount Kent on the left and the Two Sisters on the right.

Nowadays, the only material evidence of the 1982 war is the wreckage of Argentinian helicopters that were destroyed by the British forces and the military establishment on the top of Mount Kent. There is a superb view northwards as the road drops down from Wickham Heights towards the next junction, about half a mile ahead; to the left is Port San Carlos, to the right Port Louis. The settlement of Estancia nestles at the head of the very long inlet that enters the South Atlantic far north of here. **Port Louis** (page 100) is only a 5-minute drive from this junction, past the turning to Green Patch settlement, around the head of Port Louis Harbour, from where in clear weather visitors have a wonderful view over Berkeley Sound.

From Port Louis, the made-up dirt road continues to Johnson's Harbour, 20 minutes or so along the track. The remainder of the drive is over white grass and diddle-dee, following the many tracks. One of the side tracks before Johnson's Harbour approaches **Fish Creek**. The shallow waters around the creek are full of small mullet that can be seen zooming away through the water as any vehicle approaches. The deeper water in the creek is sometimes home to silver grebes and the omnipresent speckled teal.

The old route between Fish Creek and Johnson's Harbour settlement varied according to tide. At low water it was possible to drive along the exposed narrow beach, much to the amazement of the upland geese and Falkland steamer ducks. At high tide there was no beach to cross and it became necessary to use the track leading over the headland on the higher ground. This was a slower route than crossing the beach. Knowledge of the local tide times was essential to ensure that it was possible to drive all the way along the beach without getting caught by the tide. The new road, built nearly 30 years ago, means this section is much safer and easier to drive, but it does seem tamer than in the past. At **Johnson's Harbour**, your driver will usually stop for a few minutes for a comfort break. After leaving the picturesque settlement, the tracks lead up the valley between Mount Brisbane and North Lookout. The view from the head of the valley, looking back over Johnson's Harbour Farm across Berkeley Sound to Wickham Heights, is magnificent. In wet years the 5 miles between these hills and the coast can be a very difficult drive: many of the vehicles that have got bogged down have done so in this stretch. As a rule, the shallow peaty pools hereabouts are not very rich in wildlife.

Travelling along this route, the pale blue waters of the shallow lagoon behind the penguin rookeries come into view before long. The approach to the shanty at the northern end of **Volunteer Beach** can be tricky to negotiate due to the small streams that flow from the hills into the lagoon. Temporary bridges are used by locals to span these streams and are moved from one crossing point to another as required.

Once past the shanty the abundant wildlife soon becomes evident. Upland geese and ruddy-headed geese are very common in the grassy valley that leads from the shanty to the lagoon. By late summer if the small lakes on the bank are still present they can contain family parties of speckled teal and crested duck. The track heads up on to the bank that divides the lagoon from the beach and continues past all the penguin colonies towards Volunteer Point. The king penguin rookery is towards the far end of the bank. Vehicles are best parked in the car park on the grassy area to the north. Nowadays, there are some small portacabins where visitors can shelter, but it can still be a very exposed site, so warm clothing is essential. Toilets are also situated near the car park.

In the past, Volunteer Point was on the **cruise-ship** route but, as landing cannot be guaranteed owing to the large swells that crash on the shore, this is now a rare event.

Port Louis was the site of the first French settlement on Falkland and was the original capital of the islands in the 19th century, before the establishment of Stanley. French admiral Louis-Antoine de Bougainville left St Malo in 1763 to establish a colony at Port Louis, formally taking possession on 5 April 1764. Captain John McBride, from the British settlement at Port Egmont on Saunders Island, informed the French of the British colony in 1766. These two colonies continued to coexist until France relinquished its claim to the Falkland Islands at the insistence of the Spanish. Bougainville was paid £25,000 to reimburse the expense he had incurred in setting up Port Louis. The formal transfer to Spain occurred on 1 April 1767 when Bougainville passed control over to the Spanish governor Don Felipe Ruiz Puente.

The Spanish, under the command of Don Juan Ignacio de Madariaga, expelled the British from Port Egmont in 1770. The British settlement was re-established at Port Egmont in 1771, where it remained until the British departure from the islands in 1774. The Spanish remained at Port Louis, known then as Port Soledad, until 1806 when the governor Juan Crisostomo Martinez quit the islands, leaving behind a plaque claiming sovereignty for Spain. The Spanish commander withdrew the remaining Spanish settlers from the islands in 1811.

In 1820 the Argentine Government in Buenos Aires, having gained independence from Spain in 1816, claimed sovereignty over Falkland and possibly sent David Jewett, commander of the *Heroina,* to hoist a flag on the islands, although there is little written evidence of this claim. Don Pacheco, an associate of Louis Vernet, was granted land in the Falklands by the United Provinces Government in 1823. He then requested that one of his employees, Don Pablo Areguati, was appointed unpaid *comandante* of Port Louis. The first attempt at settling only lasted a year, but Vernet's second expedition in 1826 was more successful. In 1828 he was given permission from the United Provinces Government, countersigned by the British consul, to form a colony on East Falkland and was accorded fishing and sealing rights. Vernet became Comandante Polotico y Militar in 1829, using Port Soledad (Port Louis) as his base. He arrested three American schooners for illegal sealing in 1829, the news of which only reached the United States when one of the boats, the *Breakwater*, escaped. Another of the ships, the *Superior*, was released while the third, the *Harriet*, and her captain were taken for trial in Buenos Aires. The American response to this was to dispatch USS *Lexington* under Commander Silas Duncan to the islands. The ship arrived on 28 December 1831, destroyed the settlement at Port Soledad and declared the islands free of any government. Matthew Brisbane, who had been placed in charge by Louis Vernet, was taken to Montevideo in irons.

A new governor was sent to the islands by Argentina in 1832 but was murdered by mutineers shortly after taking up his appointment. The commander of the Argentinian warship *Sarandi*, Don Jose Maria Pinedo, took charge until the arrival of Captain Onslow, with his ships HMS *Clio* and HMS *Tyne*, who had landed at Port Egmont on 20 December 1832, before reaching Port Louis (Soledad) on 2 January 1833. He gave Pinedo written notice that he was exercising British sovereign rights and would be raising the British flag next day. He then requested Pinedo lower the Argentinian flag and leave the islands. Pinedo protested and refused to comply with such demands. The British landed the next day, took down the Argentinian flag, returned it to Pinedo, and raised the British flag. Pinedo left Falkland, taking with him all the Argentinian forces that had been stationed on the islands. Subsequently, the settlement was left in the hands of William Dickson, who had been Louis Vernet's bookkeeper. Matthew Brisbane took over from him when he returned to the islands in April 1833. In August of that year, during the mutiny of a group of seven gauchos led by Antonio Rivero, Brisbane, Dickson and two others were murdered. The surviving settlers escaped firstly to Hog Island and later to Turf Island in Berkeley Sound. They were found on the sealer *Hopeful* two months later. Following the arrival of HMS *Challenger* in January 1834, the gauchos were arrested and sent via Rio de Janeiro for trial in England. This trial never took place and the men were later returned to Montevideo. The first officer of *Challenger*, Lieutenant Henry Smith, and a boat crew were left in charge of the settlement.

In the autumn of 1833, in the midst of all of this upheaval, Charles Darwin arrived in Berkeley Sound on the *Beagle,* under the command of Captain Fitzroy. He visited Port Louis and the surrounding region, collecting botanical and geological samples during his expeditions. He appears not to have liked the islands or their climate, as, for instance, he wrote on the third day of his visit that, 'the whole landscape has an air of desolation'. His descriptions of the countryside and its wildlife were some of the first ever made about the Falkland Islands.

The Colonial Land and Emigration Commissioners proposed the islands' suitability for colonisation in 1840. Two years later, Governor Moody was instructed by Lord Stanley to investigate the potential of Port William as the site of a new town. Captain Ross of the Ross Antarctic Expedition collaborated in this investigation and advised that Port William was suitable. Governor Moody received instructions in March 1843 to establish a new settlement there and work began during the following July, when the move from Port Louis was initiated.

Nowadays, Port Louis is a quiet sheep farm that just happens to have played an important role in the islands' history. Income is derived from sheep farming, with most of the wool being exported to the UK. Like all other farms in the Falklands, it is privately owned – just one family lives in this secluded spot. In many ways it is architecturally typical of a modern Falklands settlement, with brightly painted roofs, white-walled houses and barns being the norm, but some 19th-century houses bear witness to its stint as the islands' capital. The pine trees growing by the main house, in the lee of the prevailing winds, provide relatively secure nesting sites for Falkland thrushes. At low tide, magellanic oystercatchers and blackish oystercatchers favour the bay, whereas speckled teal and crested ducks prefer the brackish water where the stream flows into the sea. A short distance from the site of the original French settlement is the indicator of magnetic north, left behind by the crews of *Erebus* and *Terror*, the ships participating in the Ross Expedition.

Port Louis is now only open for local traffic as there is a bypass for those heading to the north of East Falkland to sites such as Volunteer Point (page 95). In 2019, Port Louis Tours (m 51082; w portlouistours.com) was established to take small numbers of tourists, both land-based and cruise ship-based, on exclusive tours to Seal Bay and the surrounding area on the north coast.

WHERE TO STAY *Map, page 96*

There is accommodation available in Johnson's Harbour and out at Volunteer House. Both options will give you more time at the colonies and are consequently popular choices for photographers. The accommodation at Johnson's Harbour is only a 5-mile drive from the penguins, while the wardens' house is smaller and more basic, but has the advantage of being closer to the colonies thus giving visitors the option to explore the north coast of Berkeley Sound.

Volunteer House (2 rooms) Volunteer Point; 32000; e drp@horizon.co.fk; w volunteerpoint. co.fk. This fully catered small cottage is situated by the gate at the western end of the site & is home to the wardens of the reserve. The 2 twin rooms are up a narrow stairway & have views out to the north over Volunteer Beach from their large windows. Tours can be arranged to nearby sites, as well as transfers to & from Stanley/Mount Pleasant Airport. Fully catered; camping (£) is also possible here for those self-catering. £££

Johnson's Harbour Cottage (2 rooms) Johnson's Harbour; 31398; e mjf_farming@ hotmail.com; w johnsonsharbour.com; contact Martha Molkenbuhr. This centrally heated self-catering cottage situated in the middle of this scenic settlement sleeps up to 8 people in 1 king & 1 twin/dbl room, each with bunk beds. There is also a dbl sofa-bed/futon in the lounge. Meals such as b/fast packs, packed lunches, etc need to be prebooked. There is a minimum 2-night stay. Tours to Volunteer Point & the North Coast can be organised for those staying here. ££

WHAT TO SEE AND DO The main **penguin colony** does move slightly from year to year, but is always located between the valley and the southern boundary fence. These birds are used to the presence of visitors throughout the year but a distance of 7.5m must be respected. It is possible to get close views of the birds by sitting beside their main routes to the sea and waiting for them to come and inspect you. The majority of the inactive birds in the main group are probably incubating their huge, single egg. This egg is sometimes visible on top of the penguin's feet as it awaits incubation, but is hidden when the bird sits down. The penguin's stiff tail feathers help prop the bird upright when it is incubating or roosting. Penguins can also rest by lying prone on the ground but seem to prefer to remain upright, presumably as this gives a better chance of spotting any approaching predators.

The air around the rookery is full of soft piping noises through the summer. This sound is the young calling to their parents. When just hatched these youngsters are small enough to stay hidden under the folds of their parents' skin, especially on cold windy days, but as they get larger, or on warm days, their heads peep out just above the parents' feet. Chicks, which have grown too big to fit under the parent birds, still try to hide by pushing their heads into their former haven. They look a rather comical sight, only their head hidden, the rest of the body exposed to the elements. As they grow, the chicks develop a very fluffy, brown, downy coat to protect them from the cold. Years ago, they were known as 'oakum boys', as the colour of these feathers was reminiscent of the oakum used in caulking ships. These birds look a sorry sight when, at nearly a year old, they lose these feathers and gain their adult plumage, before heading out to sea for the first time.

Adult king penguins have very rich auburn-coloured neck patches and throats. This colour is not so intense in immature birds that are too young to breed (they do not start breeding until between four and six years old). These birds have a singular reproductive cycle which involves breeding early in year one, late in year two and resting for the third year; consequently the rookery contains birds of various ages. Those males that have come ashore looking to mate are the most vocal. They make themselves as tall as possible before pointing their bill up to the sky and trumpeting, finishing with a flourish before slowly subsiding to their usual height. This is always an impressive performance, although the penguin tends to sound like a trainee wind musician.

The main breeding activity takes place around the principal flock, but there are usually several smaller groups nearby. There may be some young birds in these satellite groups, but they are typically non-breeding adults. Males seeking a mate wander around the main group, adopting a very exaggerated strutting walk and batting each other with their flippers. Owing to their staggered breeding cycle there will always be some pairs starting earlier than others, but generally birds will be incubating between November and January with small young being visible from early in the new year until late February, after which they will be much easier to see as they are too big to hide under their parents.

The majority of the birds return to the sea at Volunteer Beach. Some walk in the other direction, to the lagoon, where they can be seen washing and splashing about in the shallows. The low banks above the small beach on the edge of the lagoon make a good vantage point for observing these birds. Sometimes they can be seen swimming in the shallow water and the graceful speed of their movements is in stark contrast to their upright waddling gait on land.

King penguins constitute the main attraction of Volunteers, as the sanctuary is known on the island, but they are not the only penguins breeding prolifically on this grassy bank. Two colonies of **gentoo penguins** occupy the lagoon side of the bank a short walk from the king penguins. The number of colonies has varied over the years. Sometimes two groups of gentoo penguins will merge, while in other years they will remain apart, but the overall number of birds does not vary significantly, with around 1,000 pairs using this site in recent years. By late summer all the young will have been gathered into crèches in the middle of the colony for protection from predatory birds. It is quite a sight when the young race after their returning parents to beg for food. The adult's purpose is twofold: it wants to teach its offspring to feed and also wants to ensure that it is nurturing its own young and not its neighbours'. **Magellanic penguins** prefer the beach side of the bank where the

VOLUNTEER POINT'S KING PENGUINS

King penguins were first recorded at this site in the late 1860s, although they were almost extinct in the islands by 1870, their feathers and their oil making them a valuable resource (page 10). A small colony was reported at nearby Cow Bay in the 1920s, with a well-established rookery at Volunteer Lagoon being noted by the early 1970s. This colony continues to grow and over 1,500 adults have been counted at this site in recent years. Most will be breeding adults with 600–700 young being produced each year. A few of the adult birds have been found to be carrying tags put on them in South Georgia, so new birds coming into the colony from this distant island is a factor in this colony's success story. The penguins make their nests on a grassy strip of land that separates the lagoon from the open sea, linking the headland to East Falkland. The main colony now has a circle of white stones around it to indicate permitted areas. It should be noted that some penguins, particularly the young birds will often come and investigate those sitting outside the circle! If you sit still and quiet they will often come very close before deciding you are not worth investigating and carrying on with their business.

drier, sandy ground is much more suitable for digging burrows than the wet, peaty ground. The bank above the beach is, therefore, riddled with both used and unused penguin burrows.

After the penguin colonies have been visited there is plenty more to see. The **flora** is dominated by grasses thanks to the grazing birds and sheep. Some of the wetter valleys are full of *gunnera*, with its inedible red berries hidden under the leaves in late summer. The most colourful flower is the sea cabbage with its silvery white leaves, fluffy to the touch and topped by bright yellow flowers at the height of the summer. The seeds formed during January are a preferred food of the islands' smallest finches, the **black-chinned siskins**. The sea cabbage grows above the shoreline, anchoring the shifting sands. Their deep roots enable these plants to survive in what must be a very inhospitable habitat when the wind whips up the sand. In the lee of the sea cabbage, small groups of waders gather in late summer, the majority of which are **white-rumped sandpipers** that have come from North America to winter on the islands. The other birds are the resident **two-banded plovers**, which breed above the high-tide mark, so it is sometimes possible to find some of the young racing from one clump of sea cabbage to the next.

Dotted along the long sandy **beach** are clusters of penguins, geese and steamer ducks. Magellanic, gentoo and king penguins have differing requirements as far as choosing a breeding site is concerned, but mixed flocks on the beach are nonetheless quite usual. On windy days they lie down with their backs to the wind and seem to be fast asleep, ignoring the sand drift gathering up behind them. The low elevation of the bank means that it is difficult to watch the penguins swimming to the shore, but it does mean that it is easy to walk out on to this 2-mile-long beach. The penguins appear as if by magic out of the surf as the waves crash upon the beach. Sea lions have been glimpsed trying to catch these birds.

The second most frequent species, after penguins, are **geese**. Upland geese and ruddy-headed geese frequent all grassy areas. By late summer they have gathered into large family groups. Habitually the males gather together flocks of juveniles, irrespective of their parentage or age. According to one theory, this behaviour suggests that the males use unrelated offspring as an avian shield for their own goslings, the probability being that any predator will not detect their young. The predators here are mostly avian; turkey vultures and variable hawks are the most numerous and can be seen around most penguin colonies, while peregrine falcons circle high over Volunteer Point. Scavenging **Antarctic skuas** nest close to their food sources and will take small unguarded penguin or goose chicks as well as any other species nearby. The skuas that breed here are generally very tolerant of people but unfortunately have learnt to scavenge from visitors to this site. This behaviour is not to be encouraged as it teaches them bad habits and disrupts the food chain.

A walk beyond the eastern fence for half a mile or so leads visitors out on to a series of headlands, some with spectacular caves. Rock shags breed on some of the headlands and night herons can often be found feeding in the pools. This walk gives another dimension to this already fascinating area as it is slightly higher and you can look back along the whole of Volunteer Beach, over to the lagoon in the south.

The **small islets** beyond Volunteer Point, although out of sight at the far end of the reserve, are the haunts of **fur seals**; visitors are not allowed to access these areas, but the seals can sometimes be seen zooming through the surf on to the beach. **Elephant seals** have been recorded on some of the sand beaches but, like fur seals, they often pick sites that are not readily accessible to tourists.

CAPE BOUGAINVILLE

Cape Bougainville is situated roughly in the middle of the northern shore of East Falkland. The nearest settlement, Port Salvador, situated to the southeast, has been in the hands of one family for five generations. This beautiful coastline, with its abundant wildlife, has much to offer visitors, and is best reached on a day trip from Stanley, as there is no accommodation nearby.

HISTORY Andrez Pitaluga established the farm in 1838 when he settled in the Falkland Islands. He spent many years obtaining the leases of land in East Falkland, before he set about removing the wild cattle that had been introduced by the sailors and early settlers. The farm was started in the early 1880s and named Gibraltar Station in memory of his birthplace. The fifth generation of his family farms the 50,000 acres in the traditional manner, producing fine wool from sheep of Tasmanian origin.

GETTING THERE AND AWAY The Cape is roughly 2–2½ hours by road from Stanley. Follow the road out of town for 20 miles before turning left at Estancia and continuing for another 30 miles or so. The first part of the journey from Estancia crosses several streams that feed into Port Salvador to the north. They come down from the Onion Range and are good fishing sites, judging by the number of islanders who fish there. Turn north at the far end of Port Salvador and then, after a couple of miles, branch left over *camp* towards Cape Bougainville itself. The countryside becomes much flatter on the last sections of the gravel road, with turnings to Port San Carlos and Cape Dolphin marking the end of the made-up road.

As this trip is not really viable for anyone who does not know the route, it is advisable to book one of the local guides (page 73). They will organise the permission needed to travel over this land from the owners. Visiting here is a full-day trip and is not suitable for those with back or neck problems owing to the fact that you will be driving over rough ground in *camp* for about 30 minutes.

WHAT TO SEE AND DO The main attractions of this area are the penguin colonies along the northern coast, with the large rookeries of rockhopper penguins mingled with king shags found near Cape Bougainville the most accessible. A few macaroni penguins have been noted in these colonies in recent years. It's a very rugged area with high cliffs and narrow, white-sand beaches on some of the coves in between. At Mare Rincon, a few hundred yards to the east of Cape Bougainville, a little further along the coast away from the cliffs, gentoo penguins and magellanic penguins breed in profusion. A careful look through the gentoo penguin colonies may well reveal a few king penguins, especially in late summer when they come ashore to moult. Many species of wildfowl breed in suitable habitat along this northern coast, so the pools are worth investigating. Closer to the farm there is a further small colony of gentoo penguins within easy walking distance across the creek.

The lovely coastline, with its white-sand beaches stretching between jagged rocky outcrops, makes this a superb area to visit. This relatively unknown part of East Falkland is worthy of inclusion in the itinerary of a visit to the islands.

CAPE DOLPHIN

Cape Dolphin is the most northerly point of East Falkland, marking the division between East and West Falkland. It is an infrequently visited site with enormous potential for wildlife. The flat grassy meadows on the way out to the Cape are home to many geese, with Swan Pond being a particularly good area for these birds. The actual Cape itself is a good spot to see sea lions hauled out on the rocks at the tip; various cetaceans, ranging from dolphins to whales, have also been seen by visitors. The majority of visitors reach this active farm on a long day trip from Stanley, which is around 60 miles away. For those who wish to stay longer, there is accommodation nearby. The area is named after the HMS *Dolphin*, the ship belonging to the British explorer John Byron in which he circumnavigated the globe between 1764 and 1766, visiting the Falklands along the way. The farm is owned by a family from Greece, but is managed by the neighbouring Little Creek Farm.

GETTING THERE AND AWAY Reaching this distant headland entails a long drive from Stanley of at least 2½ hours. The section of the route driven off-road, over *camp* is much shorter (8 miles) and not as rough as the drive to Cape Bougainville or Volunteer Point, but it does have its moments and can only be undertaken in a 4x4 with a local driver (page 73) who will have obtained the permission needed to access the farm land.

After following the main road from the capital, you will turn north towards Port Louis and then follow the left fork at Estancia towards Port San Carlos. After driving for around 60–90 minutes, depending on the number of times you stop for photos, you will reach the Cape Dolphin track. This track heads north, passing between West Hill and Coutts Hill before dropping slowly down towards the coast through white-grass-covered slopes, topped with diddle-dee.

 WHERE TO STAY *Map, page 96*

The majority of visitors come here on a day trip from Stanley, but as with many of the headlands on the north of East Falkland a longer stay would be more comfortable as there is plenty to see. For those staying at the accommodation at nearby Little Creek Farm, day trips out to Cape Dolphin can be arranged with the owners.

Visitors can **wild camp** anywhere on Cape Dolphin farmland, but you have to be self-sufficient and pets are strictly not welcome. To arrange a stay, contact Ben and Maggie Berntsen (☏41020; e benebf@horizon.co.fk).

James Cabin (3 rooms) Little Creek Farm; ☏31216; e littlecreekFl@hotmail.com; contact Emily & Mark Gilbert. The cabin, a short walk from the main house at Little Creek Farm (formerly Elephant Beach Farm) & a 10min drive from the Cape Dolphin settlement, sleeps up to 10 guests in 3 rooms: 1 dbl, 1 dbl & bunk bed, & 2 bunk beds. Recently refurbished, it is centrally heated, fully furnished, & provides a well-equipped kitchen for those wanting a self-catering option. Pets welcome as long as kept on a lead & under control. **££**

Kings Ridge Cottage (3 rooms) Douglas Station; ☏31120; e jclarke@horizon.co.fk. A self-catering place comprising 3 bedrooms, 2 containing a dbl & sgl and 1 with 2 sgls plus a 'junior bed' & a sofa bed. **££**

Sand Point (2 rooms) Douglas Station; ☏31120; e jclarke@horizon.co.fk. A smaller property with 2 en-suite rooms with a dbl bed & a dbl sofa bed in the kitchen. **££**

WHAT TO SEE AND DO The Cape Dolphin area is a designated wildlife sanctuary best known for its breeding **southern sea lions**, which breed close to the very tip, but are in much reduced numbers. Also breeding along the headland are gentoo penguins and king shags, with rock shags breeding on the cliff faces.

The largest pond in the area is Elephant Beach Pond, which is close to the dunes that lie behind Foul Bay. The other pool is Swan Pond, situated almost at the tip of Cape Dolphin. Both pools are good places to look for black-necked swans, as although this shy species does not often allow a close approach, it can quite easily be viewed at these locations. Amid the more common waterfowl, pairs of yellow-billed pintails can also be found on both ponds. The only grebes that breed on these waters are the white-tufted on Swan Pond. The short grass around the ponds is a favoured site for large numbers of upland and ruddy-headed geese. On the small headland to the northwest of Swan Pond is a breeding site for southern giant petrels. These birds are sensitive to disturbance, so keep at least 500m from them.

Cape Dolphin Farm and Little Creek Farm have been working with Falklands Conservation on a tussac-grass restoration scheme. This has involved planting tussac during the winter months when the ground is at its wettest and then fencing off the areas to stop them from being grazed. Work started on the 'rustling grass' plantation on North Camp Farm in 2005 and the 'laskaridis plantation' in 2011. The idea is to restore these areas to their former glory before overgrazing saw the removal of the tussac and the subsequent loss of habitat for a wide range of wildlife.

SAN CARLOS AND PORT SAN CARLOS

The Spanish sloop *San Carlos* visited East Falkland in 1768, giving its name to the inlet and the settlements which lie on the western side of the island, 50 miles from Stanley. Both San Carlos and Port San Carlos sit on this western side of East Falkland; the former overlooks San Carlos Water, which was known as Bomb Alley during the Falklands War in 1982. Many of the nearby place names became famous at that time, such as Ajax Bay where the field hospital was situated, and the war memorial at San Carlos is a popular stop for those interested in the events of 1982. These locations are a good 3-hour drive from Stanley meaning a very long day trip with very little time to explore. Accommodation is available in this area and at Port San Carlos; alternatively, use Darwin as a base and travel from there. Although not as well known for its wildlife, the area has a scattering of penguin colonies and the lakes and streams contain a variety of wildfowl. The settlements are small active sheep farms, usually run by the family with shearing gangs coming in to shear the sheep in November and again in January and February.

Port San Carlos is situated on the arm of the inlet that later becomes the San Carlos River, which is one of the best-known fishing sites on East Falkland.

SAN CARLOS Ajax Bay, opposite Port San Carlos settlement, was chosen as the site of a factory to freeze sheep carcasses for export to the UK after World War II. It was a complete financial disaster, and after wasting a great deal of time and money, it was eventually closed down in the mid 1950s. The buildings were still standing in 1982 and were used by the British Task Force as a field hospital after the landings in June that year. The footage of the Argentinian planes attacking the British Task Force in San Carlos Water is some of the most dramatic of that war. The task force started landing troops at 02.00 on Friday 21 May 1982. By the end of the day several thousand men had been landed and had established the bridgehead. During this action HMS *Ardent* was abandoned after a series of air attacks, and two helicopters were shot down. A further 17 Argentinian aircraft and four helicopters were brought down that day. The shore facilities were not attacked until 27 May, by which time some of the British forces were already making their advance on Goose Green. San Carlos Water continued to be a busy port until the Argentinian surrender on 14 June 1982.

Port San Carlos also made the headlines in 1982 when the 3rd Battalion Parachute Regiment landed at nearby 'Green Beach', so called because during the British–Argentinian conflict beaches were colour-coded according to their military significance – green beaches were the preferred beaches.

These days, it is a quiet settlement overlooking a peaceful bay, although reminders of the war are never far away.

Getting there and away San Carlos is a 3-hour (71-mile) **drive** from Stanley along the all-weather road, past the military base at Mount Pleasant before turning north just before Darwin – roughly 1½ hours (58 miles) from Stanley. All gates in the section of road from Darwin to San Carlos should be left in the position that they are found. The gravelled road continues all the way to San Carlos; although it is possible to drive in a non-4x4 here, many of the vehicles seen on the road are 4x4s, as their owner's work requires this type of vehicle. The drive is over the lower slopes of the Wickham Heights, passing Mount Usborne (705m) on the right. The hills then merge into the Sussex Mountains where the road climbs up and over, giving you your first view of San Carlos Water. This is a rather commanding view, looking all the way to Fanning Head in the distant north. On a clear day the hills of West Falkland can be seen out over the Falkland Sound, with Goose Green and Darwin to the south. San Carlos is only a short drive downhill from here, as the track runs parallel to the inner part of San Carlos Water. There is an **airstrip** close to the settlement, which is roughly 25 minutes from Stanley by air by FIGAS (**w** falklands.gov.fk/aviationservice; £85.92; for booking information, see page 58).

 Where to stay *Map, page 96*

White Grass Cottage (2 rooms) ✆32044; **e** McMullen@horizon.co.fk; contact Mathew McMullen. A self-catering cottage at Kingsford Valley Farm (part of San Carlos settlement) sleeps 6 in 1 twin/dbl room & 1 twin room with bunk beds. This basic house has all the expected facilities (oven, microwave, fridge, shower, etc) & is centrally heated. **££**

What to see and do The majority of visitors to San Carlos are interested in the military history of the area. Little remains from the 1982 war apart from the remnants of the field hospital and the memorial. The **British War Cemetery** is a short distance to the north of the settlement overlooking **San Carlos Water**. This well-maintained memorial is a poignant reminder of the lives lost here in 1982. Another relic from the landings is the renovated missile-firing site on Lookout Rocks, to the north of the settlement. A small but well-thought-out **museum** to commemorate the events in San Carlos Water is always open and is free to visitors. Owned by Stanley's Historic Dockyard Museum (page 77), the museum's exhibits include photographs and objects from those hectic days of winter 1982 as well as a display prepared by Falklands Conservation about its work and the islands' wildlife. There is also a section about rural life on the islands prior to the events of 1982.

There are no huge colonies of seabirds in the vicinity, but several species of **waterfowl** can be found along the shore and **Commerson's dolphins** are frequently seen in San Carlos Water. The scenery in this part of East Falkland is superb, from the views across Falkland Sound to the west and to the heights of Mount Usborne, the highest mountain on Falkland at 2,312ft (705m) to the east.

PORT SAN CARLOS Port San Carlos is a picturesque settlement some miles inland from **Fanning Head**, which overlooks the entrance of Falkland Sound. William

Cameron founded a farming community in 1870, which was then called San Carlos North. It stayed intact until 1989 when it was divided into the five individual farms that still exist today.

Getting there and away For those coming from the south, the 23-mile **road** that links Port San Carlos and San Carlos is rather twisting and turning, but is a lot quicker than the old tracks over *camp*, taking just under an hour to drive, allowing you to visit both settlements in a 2WD. Port San Carlos can also be reached direct from Stanley by following the route to Cape Dolphin (page 106) until you reach the western end of Port Salvador, where instead of heading towards the Cape you can turn left. This journey from Stanley can be achieved in just over 2 hours. Alternatively, you can take a 20-minute **flight** from Stanley with FIGAS (w falklands. gov.fk/aviationservice; £84.63; for booking information, see page 58).

Where to stay *Map, page 96*

Race Point Farm (2 rooms) Port San Carlos; ☏41012; e jhjones@horizon.co.fk; contact John & Michelle Jones. This farm has a freshly renovated self-catering cottage that sleeps 8. Each room has a dbl bed & bunk beds. There is a shared bathroom as well as a spacious kitchen/dining room/sitting room with views out towards Fanning Head. Although advertised as self-catering, meals can sometimes be provided depending on the owner's other commitments. Tours to nearby wildlife sites or a coastal tour can be arranged but need to be booked in advance. **££**

Scurvey Grass Snug (2 rooms) Port Sussex; ☏32203; e portsussex@horizon.co.fk; ⓕ Scurvy Grass Snug Self Catering. Sleeps up to 6 in 1 dbl, 1 twin & a dbl sofa bed in the lounge. This new-build

(2022) property is situated in a valley to the west of Port Sussex, with a nice sized deck looking out into the bay and similar views from the spacious, glass-fronted lounge. It also has a hot tub for those willing to brave the elements. **££**

Trout Court (2 rooms) Port Sussex; ☏32203; e portsussex@horizon.co.fk. Trout Court has 2 rooms – 1 dbl & a dbl with a sgl bed – 3 camping beds are also available for larger groups. Situated between the main road & Port Sussex, it's accessible via a low-tide or high-tide route. Ideal for a 'get away from it all' break, & with walking, wildlife watching & good fishing sites nearby. It's just under 2 hours from Stanley & is much closer to MPA, Goose Green & San Carlos. **££**

What to see and do Port San Carlos is one of the premier **fishing** sites on the Falkland Islands. Many visitors come here to fish in the San Carlos River that enters the sea a few miles east from the settlement. The prime time for fishing is from the end of February to the end of April. Falkland mullet and trout can be caught in the river, and the former can also be hooked downstream in the tidal reaches of the river. The current record sea trout for the islands, which weighed 22lb 12½ oz (10kg), was caught in 1992 on the San Carlos River. There are no licensing requirements, and your accommodation provider can arrange permission to fish in the river, if desired. The San Carlos River is wide by Falkland standards, and winds its way down to the sea, eventually becoming Port San Carlos. Further inland it becomes even more convoluted, almost turning back on itself at times.

There is also plenty for the non-fishing visitor to explore. **Fanning Head** lies about 7 miles to the northwest of Port San Carlos. Getting there requires local knowledge as to which track over *camp* to take, so speak to your accommodation provider before travelling. North of the head is a **rockhopper penguin colony** that looks across to West Falkland. **Cetaceans** have been observed from this vantage point as they enter or leave Falkland Sound. The tide race carries food to the surface, therefore when the flow of water is at its greatest, the feeding frenzies of gulls, terns and other seabirds can be seen from the shore. Many of the species of wading birds found on the islands have been seen in this area. These birds regularly commute between the shore and nearby Rabbit Island.

Paloma Beach is approximately a 40-minute drive north from the settlement, up over a mixture of white-grass and diddle-dee heath. The spectacular beach stretches for 2 miles along Middle Bay. This scenic site, with its long stretch of white sand, is situated between two curving headlands, and is home to a **gentoo penguin colony** that occasionally attracts some king penguins. Permission must be sought from Smylies Farm before entering this area, which can be organised by your accommodation provider. Close by, to the west of the beach is **Smylies Creek**, which is a good location to look for some of the island's wildfowl, as are Paloma Pond and Shallow Pond which lie behind Paloma Beach. Black-crowned night herons can be seen creeping along the shallow waters of Smylies Creek. Upland geese and ruddy-headed geese are common on the grasslands inland from the beach. One of the rarest geese on the islands, the ashy-headed goose, has been recorded several times here.

DARWIN AND GOOSE GREEN

The name Goose Green has become one of the most famous in the islands after the events of May and June 1982 (page 13). Darwin and Goose Green are situated less than a mile apart on the narrow neck of land that joins the two sections of East Falkland: the low-lying land of Lafonia to the south and Wickham Heights and the Onion Range to the north. Choiseul Sound opens out to the sea to the east and Brenton Loch flows into Falkland Sound to the west. Darwin is named after the famous naturalist, Charles Darwin, who visited the islands in the 1830s. Goose Green is the centre of a population of over 70 people, while Darwin is a small settlement, even by Falkland standards. Despite this, Darwin is now being promoted as an alternative base to Stanley from which to begin and end a trip to the islands. From here you can hike to the highest point on the islands, Mount Usborne, or simply spend time enjoying the quiet. Visitors can explore the most typical aspects of Falkland life in this region by visiting a working sheep farm and watching wildlife, as well as visiting the site made famous in 1982.

HISTORY There is an idea that the name Darwin comes about from the fact that Charles Darwin made several journeys into *camp* during HMS *Beagle*'s voyages in the Falkland Islands in 1833 and 1844. It is thought that at one point he may have stayed in the area that is now Darwin settlement.

Samuel Fisher Lafone, a merchant from Montevideo, bought the region to the south of Darwin in 1846. The name for this area, Lafonia, is a derivation of his surname. He had also bought the contract to take charge of all the wild cattle in East Falkland, having made his base at Hope Place on the southern side of Brenton Loch. By the time the Falkland Islands Company bought him out five years later very few cattle remained. Hope Place was found to be unsuitable for livestock farming, and in 1859 the settlement was transferred to Darwin, with Goose Green becoming the centre of operations in 1922.

Many of the buildings in Darwin were moved by sledding them to Goose Green, which must have been an impressive sight as these building were jacked up and then put on skids and dragged across the *camp*. The company became the most important sheep owner on the islands and, by 1880, they had 100,000 sheep on East Falkland. This number has reduced and now some 80,000 sheep graze this

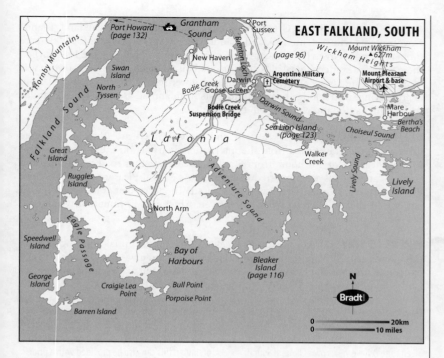

Port Howard
(page 132)

Grantham
Sound

Port
Sussex

Hornby Mountains

Swan
Island

New Haven

Benton Loch

(page 96)

Wickham Heights

Mount Wickham
▲627m

Mount Pleasant
Airport & base

North
Tyssen

Bodie Creek
Goose Green

Darwin

Argentine Military
Cemetery

Falkland Sound

Bodie Creek
Suspension Bridge

Darwin Sound

Mare
Harbour

Bertha's
Beach

Great
Island

L a f o n i a

Sea Lion Island
(page 123)

Choiseul Sound

Ruggles
Island

Adventure Sound

Walker
Creek

Lively Sound

Lively
Island

Eagle Passage

North Arm

Speedwell
Island

Bay of
Harbours

Bleaker
Island
(page 116)

N

George
Island

Craigie Lea
Point

Bull Point

Porpoise Point

Bradt

Barren Island

| 0 | | | 20km |
| 0 | | 10 miles | |

100,000ha farm. In 1922 Goose Green was chosen as the site of an improved sheep-handling operation. Wool sheds, hydraulic presses, dips and pens were moved to the settlement. Sheep were originally farmed for their meat until this proved uneconomical; thereafter wool became the islands' major export. The shearing sheds in Goose Green are some of the largest on Falkland.

During the Falklands War Goose Green played a pivotal role. It was here that large numbers of Argentine troops were stationed. The Argentine troops imprisoned all 114 residents of Goose Green and any visiting civilians in the Community Hall at the centre of the settlement almost a month after the initial Argentine invasion. They were only allowed out for very short periods each day and had to endure these cramped conditions until liberated by the second parachute regiment on 29 May 1982, some eight weeks later. To reach Stanley from the landings in San Carlos water, the British military marched over the Sussex Mountains and engaged in their first short, but very fierce, land battle of the war. The defeat of the Argentine troops opened up the way to Stanley from the south. Goose Green and Darwin were garrisoned with up to 1,400 Argentinian troops. These soldiers were well entrenched and had placed hundreds of mines around the settlement.

After a heavy naval bombardment, the men of the second parachute regiment attacked in what became the first major land battle of the war. Many men were killed, including Colonel 'H' Jones of the 'Paras' and Flight Lieutenant Nick Taylor who was shot down in his Sea Harrier over the settlement. The British men of the parachute regiment, who died freeing Darwin and Goose Green, are remembered by a memorial on the hill overlooking the settlements and by the memorial at San Carlos (page 108). The restoration of the settlement after the war took some time. Some buildings in Goose Green still show bullet holes, a constant reminder of those dangerous days.

Since the war, Goose Green Farm has been sold to the Falkland Islands Government, who set up Falkland Landholdings Ltd to run the 300,000-acre property. Goose Green is not the thriving community it was during the 1980s, when there were fewer mechanical aids such as quad bikes, meaning that farm work was more labour intensive, and nowadays has far fewer residents. In contrast, Darwin is prospering, with a lodge busy with tourists from abroad as well as locals on day trips from Stanley and elsewhere in the islands.

GETTING THERE AND AWAY Darwin and Goose Green are only a 35-minute **drive** along the gravel road from the international airport on the military base at Mount Pleasant, or 1½ hours from Stanley. The all-weather road is drivable in a normal car but 4x4s are more frequently used. As Mount Pleasant Airport is close by, the airport at Goose Green is seldom used. The ferry that runs between East and West Falkland operates from New Haven, which is a 30-minute drive away to the southwest.

WHERE TO STAY Darwin makes an excellent base for an initial first few days on the islands as it is closer to the airport than Stanley and gives you the opportunity to explore not only the Darwin and Goose Green area but also to head west to San Carlos and Port San Carlos and south to North Arm and Bull Point.

Darwin House (6 rooms) Darwin; 📞 31313; e info@darwin-house.com; w darwin-house. com. The 2 dbl, 2 twin & 2 dbl/twin rooms are all en suite & have views over Choiseul Sound, the settlement & the Wickham Heights. This well-appointed property, the former manager's house, has a conservatory where you can sit & look out towards Mount Usborne & then walk through into the lounge which leads further on into the dining room with an honesty bar tucked in one corner. Locally grown, organic produce features on the menu with lamb, mutton & beef sourced from Goose Green, just the other side of the hill. The lodge is only yards from the water, with a close-cropped (by sheep & geese) green on the inland side & a row of red-roofed cottages a few hundred yards away at the base of the low hill between Darwin & Goose Green. Tours, either full day or half day, can be arranged. For those passing through, Darwin House offers *smoko* during the afternoon with a good range of cakes for a light snack. For those wanting lunch or dinner, this can also be provided with a prior booking. **£££**

Bookkeepers (5 rooms) Goose Green; 📞 22699; m 52350; e flh.tourism@gmail.com. A self-catering place in the settlement that sleeps 12: 1 dbl & 1 sgl; 3 sgl beds; 1 sgl; 1 dbl & 2 sgls; & 1 large sofa bed. **££**

Osborne Cottage (3 rooms) Goose Green; 📞 32228; m 55530; e jtlee@horizon.co.fk. This self-catering property situated in the settlement sleeps 6 in 3 rooms – all sgl beds. **££**

The Galley Café Goose Green; ⏰ 08.00–17.00 daily. There is a café in Goose Green that is situated in the former mess hall in the middle of the settlement. It is a typical British café, well known for its tea & Full English breakfast fry-ups. **£**

WHAT TO SEE AND DO There are opportunities to watch the wildlife of this area using Darwin as a base. **Fishing** and **horseriding** are popular pastimes when staying here and can be arranged through Darwin Lodge. It is also possible simply to relax in the peaceful atmosphere as, although the busy farm of Goose Green is not far away, Darwin seems to have its own peaceful ambience. You can wander around the shores of Darwin Harbour, or, for the energetic, arrange a lift to the base of Mount Usborne and climb the highest peak on the islands.

A short walk back along the entrance road from Darwin House (see above) you will find the renovated **corral**, built in 1874. This suffered some damage in 1982 and was repaired in 1998. The gauchos used this circular building in the 1800s for gathering cattle. Adjacent to the corral is a stone building, the **Galpon**, built in 1849, which was home for the gauchos and their horses. The shore around this area and the small pond at the western edge of the green only 150yds from the lodge are favoured haunts of ruddy-headed geese and upland geese. Magellanic oystercatchers and blackish oystercatchers can be seen performing their display flights during the summer over the lagoon in front of the lodge.

The road from Darwin towards Goose Green cuts through the **Boca Wall**, only a 5-minute walk from the lodge. This gorse-covered bank of peat marks the division between the two settlements and was built in 1849. A little further along the road is Darwin Hill where there is a **memorial** to the 17 men of the second parachute regiment who died in action. The open grassy slopes to its right saw some of the fiercest battles including that in which Lieutenant Colonel 'H' Jones was killed (page 14). By turning left at the first junction and continuing to walk for 5 minutes (100yds) along the track, you can see a low **cairn**, which is his memorial, on the bank of a low hill. On the slope above this marker the remains of the foxholes that he was attacking when he died can be seen. A few hundred yards to the south and close to the airstrip used for inter-island flights, is the grave of Flight Lieutenant Nick Taylor.

Goose Green is just over half a mile to the south of Darwin, continuing along the road. It is a much larger settlement than Darwin and has a proportionately larger quay where all the wool from Goose Green Farm was loaded in the past. The end of the quay is built over the remains of a boat named the *Vicar of Bray*. This is the last extant ship to have participated in the Californian Gold Rush. Legend has it that the *Vicar of Bray* was in San Francisco Harbour during the great earthquake of 1906, and it is now owned by the San Francisco Museum. Black-crowned night herons can be found roosting on the timbers inside this hulk. Rock shags are often quite approachable as they roost on the bollards at the end of the quay. The wreck of the *Garland* is visible from the quay, 3 miles across Choiseul Sound. This 18th-century iron ship, built in Liverpool, was wrecked here in 1911.

The **Community Hall**, where the residents were locked up during the war in 1982 (page 111) can be visited. There are very few artefacts from this period here, as it is an active community hall. There is, however, a small memorial room which contains a photo of Margaret Thatcher and a signed letter sent to the farm after her visit in 1983. Inside is also a list of all those imprisoned here at that time, as

DARWIN'S CEMETERIES

For those with a particular interest in the local history, there are two cemeteries you can visit in this area. The first, on the outskirts of Goose Green, is the disused **Darwin Cemetery**. The other is across the neck of land to the north of Darwin beside the main access road from Stanley. This is the **Argentine Military Cemetery**, which lies on the opposite side of Choiseul Sound and contains the graves of Argentinians who fell during the 1982 war. There are a couple of hundred white crosses here as well as a row of marble slabs on which are engraved the names of all of those from Argentina who lost their lives. Many of the crosses were marked 'soldado Argentino – solo conocido por dios' ('known only unto God'), but recent work taking DNA samples from these graves has meant that many of them have now been identified and visiting relatives now have a known resting place for their loved ones. It is a rather poignant place, reminding us how many lost their lives here.

well as a framed Union Jack flag with '2 Para Goose Green' written in large letters, with many of the soldiers' names and comments written on it. Otherwise, there are photos and plaques around the walls from the various military stationed here at that time.

One of the iconic images of the war in 1982 was the large black shearing sheds with 'POW' written on them. These have now been repainted so the lettering is no longer visible. During shearing season, these sheds are full of sheep so the noise of them bleating and the whirring of the shearing gang's wool clippers make this a very noisy place. There is still wildlife here, however, as a pair of barn owls can often be seen roosting on the roof beams at the back of the shed. I wonder what they make of it all when it's busy?

One of the highlights of a visit to the area is the **Bodie Creek Suspension Bridge**, one of the most southerly suspension bridges in the world. It involves a 15-minute drive to the south of Goose Green to the Bodie Creek. The track bends sharply before the inlet to reveal this rather magnificent bridge, built in 1924–25 to span the 400ft (122m) gap. It was constructed to reduce the time taken to drive sheep from the southern parts of Lafonia to the shearing sheds in Goose Green, thus avoiding an arduous detour around the inlet. The bridge is now closed but is still a superb sight, although a little incongruous in this setting with no other structure made by humans in sight.

LAFONIA

The flat, low-lying land of Lafonia is unlike anywhere else on the Falkland Islands. Goose Green and Darwin are a metropolis compared with Lafonia's wide-open spaces, where the white-grass slopes seem to run for miles and miles. **Walker Creek** is a small settlement on the southern side of Choiseul Sound, to the west of Darwin and New Haven. North Arm, another hour's drive south from Walker Creek, is located at the head of the Bay of Harbours. Another 2-hour drive over *camp* leads you to Bull Point, one of the Falklands' premier wildlife sites. Owing to the distances involved, few first-time visitors come this far south, but for those on subsequent visits it is a popular choice. The sights here are not practical on a day trip from Stanley or Darwin and, as such, most visitors stay at North Arm.

The large working farm of over 530,000 acres at **North Arm** has its settlement on the inland (northern) end of the Bay of Harbours and is situated within a largely flat landscape. The small lakes that typify this area are a good place to look for various species of waterfowl. Staying here is a chance to experience **farm life**, especially at shearing times in November and late January and February when everything seems to be happening at once with big flocks of sheep being moved in and out of the shearing-shed pens. One of the main aims of any time spent here is to visit the wildlife-rich site of **Bull Point**, now designated an Important Bird Area by BirdLife International and situated 2 hours south from North Arm driving over *camp*.

GETTING THERE AND AWAY There is only one road south from Goose Green for the 1-hour drive (so 2½ hours from Stanley) to the North Arm settlement. The **drive** is over the typical Falkland gravel roads, across low-lying land, where occasional small ponds can be seen. As it is so flat it is relatively featureless by Falkland standards, so most visitors just concentrate on reaching their destination rather than sightseeing. Most of the road traffic you will see is heading to West Falkland via the ferry from New Haven, to the tiny settlement of Walker Creek on the south side of Choiseul Sound, or to North Arm to the south. These are the only roads; local farmers will otherwise drive over *camp* to reach their sheep pastures. Driving from **North Arm to Bull Point** takes you over some very soft ground that tests the skill of any driver and should only be undertaken by 4x4 and by those who have the local knowledge, so is best done as part of a tour from Stanley (page 73).

WHERE TO STAY For further details of George House and Creek House, contact Emma Reid (📞 32030; m 52027; e north.arm@horizon.co.fk). The settlement store can be opened at weekends but please ask. The local club is usually opened at weekends for those wishing to taste the social life of the area.

Creek House (4 rooms) North Arm. A self-catering place, that sleeps 10, with 2 dbl & 6 sgl beds. It was refurbished & opened in 2021. **££**
George House (4 rooms) North Arm. This is the largest house in the settlement; it's of a basic accommodation style but is clean & well maintained throughout. Guests sleep in 1 dbl &

3 twin rooms. As with many of the houses in the islands, you get the impression that this house was designed as it was built, but it doesn't take long to find where everything is. **££**
Sleepy Hollow (2 rooms) North Arm; 📞 22699; e flhtourism@gmail.com. This newish house sleeps 5 in 1 twin & a family room. **££**

WHAT TO SEE AND DO There is a small **museum** in the settlement at North Arm that is dedicated to the history and agriculture of the area and displays various photographs of the settlement from days gone by, as well as some of the old tools used on the farm and in the houses. The museum is always open for visitors to look round and the building that now houses it was originally the settlement store before becoming the farm foreman's office.

This area is one of the best places to look for some of the **rarer waterfowl** on the Falklands, with coscoroba swans being seen reasonably regularly over the years on some of the pools. One well-vegetated pool is only a 5-minute drive south of the settlement and is worth a look as you never know what could be there. There is a good range of waterfowl species including silver teal and yellow-billed pintail and also the chance of seeing a black-necked swan every now and then. There's also a possibility of spotting species such as cinnamon teal and red shoveler, both from South America, or just to enjoy seeing so many birds feeding undisturbed.

A trip down to **Bull Point**, a designated Important Bird Area (IBA), is a true highlight for those that journey this far south. A wide range of birds inhabit the area, from penguins to land birds to other waterfowl in some superb lowland coastal scenery. Gentoo penguins occupy sandy beaches while magellanic penguins can be found on the drier heaths. Long-tailed meadowlarks and dark-faced ground tyrants are also common here. You can easily spend the whole day wandering or driving around exploring the area. The long, winding drive takes you through terrain covered in white grass and diddle-dee before reaching a narrow neck of land with a sand beach to the north and a stony shore to the south. The headland to the south of here is called **Craigie Lea Point** and the remains of the wreck of the ship of the same name that sank here in 1879 are still visible on the shore.

The headland at the other end of this area, to the west, is a good site to look for plant fossils, including tree stumps, where even the growth rings can still be seen. The final part of the drive to Bull Point passes small sandy beaches, low cliffs and banks of tussac grass. There has been some active tussac regeneration work by the farm in conjunction with Falklands Conservation to return this area to what it once was. The tussac areas have been fenced off to allow them to grow to their former glory. Gentoo and magellanic penguins breed here and the occasional king penguin comes ashore to moult from time to time. The small pools in this area are home to silver teal, Chiloé wigeon, silvery and white-tufted grebes and a few black-necked swans. The drier heaths are good places to look for rufous-chested dotterels, white-bridled finches and dark-faced ground-tyrants; scout the beaches for two-banded plovers and both magellanic and blackish oystercatchers. The short cropped grassy coastal greens are busy with upland geese and ruddy-headed geese, often in large groups late in the summer after the breeding season. There is also the chance of finding some **southern elephant seals** or **southern seals** hauled out on the beaches on the southern and eastern sides of the headland. The latter are often seen near the small unmanned lighthouse at the most easterly point – **Porpoise Point**, just south of Bull Point itself. Offshore, both Peale's dolphin and Commerson's dolphin are seen regularly and some lucky observers occasionally spot orca, fin or sei whales. On a calm day it's well worth keeping a watchful eye out to sea, looking for a spout or a fin breaking the surface.

BLEAKER ISLAND

Lying to the southeast of Lafonia, Bleaker Island was on the tourist map for many years only as a stopping point for some of the cruise ships visiting the islands. However, the opening of high-class self-catering accommodation nearly 30 years ago opened up the island to all visitors, from both land and sea. This long, thin island is over 12 miles (19km) long, but is only 1 mile (1.6km) wide at the widest point. It is still stocked with sheep but has a very good range of wildlife, including three species of breeding penguin, and as such has been designated an Important Bird Area (IBA) by BirdLife International. The northern part of the island is a

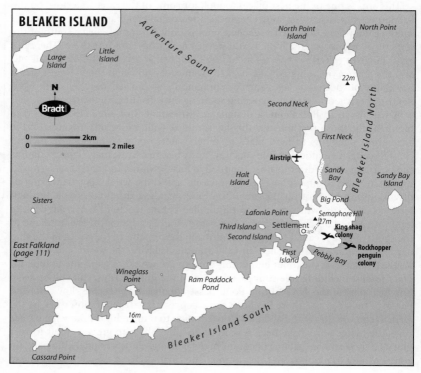

National Nature Reserve. Although it is not as famous as some of the other wildlife sites around the archipelago, Bleaker Island has plenty to offer and is well worth including in any itinerary. The modern accommodation is centrally placed and is ideal for exploring as it is only a short walk away from a huge king shag colony, with the rockhopper penguins also nearby. Here, visitors get a real sense of being away from it all.

The island's headlands and bays have a variety of names; some are descriptive such as Pebbly Bay or Sandy Bay, while others have a historical connection – for example Cassard Point is named after a French sailing vessel that was wrecked there in 1906. This is the nearest point to East Falkland as Driftwood Point is only half a mile away.

GETTING THERE AND AWAY In the past, the majority of visitors who reached this island did so via the smaller **cruise ships** that are able to get in close enough to land people. Now there is accommodation on the island, independent travellers are able to access what the island has to offer, too. It takes 30 minutes to **fly** to Bleaker Island via FIGAS from Stanley (w falklands.gov.fk/aviationservice; £88.50; for booking information, see page 58). The airstrip is a 10-minute drive from the accommodation; transfers are available as the owners drive out to meet every plane.

WHERE TO STAY Bleaker Island's two properties (✆ 32490; e bleakerislandfarm@ horizon.co.fk; w bleakerisland.com; contact Nick Rendell; ⊕ 1 Oct–30 Apr) are close together so can be booked together by visiting groups or individually. Both are on the settlement and can be either self-catering or full board.

Cassard House (4 rooms) Sleeps up to 8 in 4 en-suite bedrooms – 3 twins & 1 dbl. This property, built in 2011 & upgraded in 2021, has incorporated many environmentally friendly, energy-conservation ideas, including triple glazing & underfloor heating, which creates a very cosy place to stay. The large lounge opens out into a large conservatory with a deck out front for those rare calm days, allowing visitors to sit outside & enjoy the sunshine. This house has Wi-Fi connectivity throughout. **£££**

Cobb's Cottage (2 rooms) This cottage can accommodate 4 guests. It was originally built in 2001 & was upgraded in 2013 to incorporate 2 twin, en-suite bedrooms, a sun lounge & a lounge/dining room. There is no Wi-Fi connection, but guests can connect to Cassard House's. For those wanting FB, meals are usually served at Cassard House. **£££**

WHAT TO SEE AND DO A lift can sometimes be arranged to various points on the island – a chat to your accommodation provider is the easy way to organise this. Vehicle hire can also be arranged, as can a tour to see the lay of the land at £40 per person.

The highlight of this island is the **rockhopper penguin colony** of some 720 pairs that is situated only a short walk from the settlement, although for many the colony is rather overshadowed by the 9,000 pairs of **king shags** situated on the flat ground in the centre of the island, not far from the settlement. The sheer number of birds flying in and out of the colony along with the attendant gulls and skuas rather dominates the skies. You have to pass these king shags in order to reach the rockhoppers, and it is worth spending a bit of time watching this bustling community. The rockhopper colony is situated on the low cliffs on the eastern side of the island just over half a mile from the settlement at Long Gulch. Further south, a colony of **gentoo penguins** can be found, along with a scattering of **magellanic penguins**. **Rock shags** also breed on the outer cliffs.

The pools on the island contain both **white-tufted** and **silver grebe**, as well as many **wildfowl**, including the occasional black-necked swan. Big Pond, a 20-minute stroll north of the settlement, is an excellent spot for wildfowl including silver teal and white-tufted grebes and can hold the odd ornithological surprise such as white-tufted coot from South America. In rough weather many of the gulls that would normally be feeding out over the kelp beds will come and roost beside the pool. Sadly, summertime droughts have lowered the water levels considerably so that some of these pools now occasionally dry out.

There are patches of tussac grass in various locations about the island, which are home to a population of **grass wren**. There are also some small tussac islands offshore; First Island, Second Island and Third Island are in the bay by the settlement, and Sandy Bay Island and North Point Island are home to some of the birds that can occasionally be seen on Bleaker Island, including Cobb's wren and tussacbird.

Birds of prey are well represented on Bleaker Island, with breeding southern caracara and the occasional striated caracara, which have probably come from Sea Lion Island to the southwest. **Southern sea lions** can often be seen hauled out on the rocks but do not breed on the island. Up to 40 have been seen at any one time, although this number does vary.

The islands' meandering coastline means that there are miles of open country for **walking** and long sandy beaches for those who like to potter along the strand line. You can walk straight down the middle of the island from one end to the other, but then you would miss out on the various pools, sheltered bays and the wildlife that uses these locations. It's a rather low-lying island, with a high point of only 27m at Semaphore Hill, but to get to each bay you will walk over slightly elevated ground so the views are varied. As it is also a narrow island you can zig-zag up and down, looking for flora such as lady's slipper as well as yellow orchid and dog orchid. These are at their best in late November and early December.

On some of the headlands facing west into Adventure Sound, southern giant petrels can be found nesting. These birds are very shy and are easily disturbed; in order to avoid causing them to fly, keeping a safe distance of 200m is suggested. They will often look like large rocks sat on the flat ground in the distance so can be easily missed.

BERTHA'S BEACH

Situated a few miles from the military base at Mount Pleasant Airport (MPA) at the northern entrance of Choiseul Sound, this white-sand beach with abundant wildlife, including penguins, has long been a favourite site for those working at MPA. It has now been recognised as an Important Bird Area as well as a RAMSAR site due to the range of wildlife found here and as such has become a more popular stop for those visiting the islands. There is no accommodation here as it is only a short drive from MPA, 40 minutes from Darwin and about 1¼ hours from Stanley. As this is a working farm (Fitzroy Farm), visitors are asked to take special care during the lambing season (mid-Oct–end Dec) as the ewes on the greens (the flat grassy areas behind the beach) are susceptible to disturbance and could potentially abandon their lambs. Visitors are also asked to avoid walking on the moorland further inland.

HISTORY As with many locations on the Falkland Islands, this bay was named after a shipwreck. In this case it was an iron barque called *Bertha* that ran aground here in 1892. It was carrying a cargo of cedar logs which were washed ashore, some of which can still be seen along the beach or up on the short grass area favoured by grazing geese behind the shore. There is a local story that the barque ran aground because it was off course due to a magnetic anomaly that occurs around Direction Island, a tiny island situated about a mile offshore in the centre of the bay.

GETTING THERE AND AWAY The journey to the beach is about 6 miles from MPA and about 40 miles from Stanley. Driving **from Stanley**, you will reach a crossroads only a mile from the base at MPA. The right turn is labelled to MPA, the other to Mare Harbour, the British military harbour. Arriving **from Darwin**, the road bypasses MPA to reach the main road junction above; follow the sign to Mare Harbour. Drive towards Mare Harbour until you reach a fenced-off area on the left, after which turn left on to a rough track and drive over the *camp* to the beach just under 2 miles away. There is a locked gate close to the road. Those staying at MPA can get a key from 12 Faculty Reception while all other visitors should ring the landowner, Falkland Landholdings Ltd (📞 32384). If visiting on an organised tour your drivers will arrange this for you.

WHERE TO STAY Fitzroy settlement makes a good base from which to explore Bertha's Beach.

Cook House (4 rooms) Fitzroy; m 51655; e fitzroy.farm@horizon.co.fk. Situated in Fitzroy settlement, this large house sleeps 13 in 1 dbl & a trpl room downstairs, & 1 trpl & a room with 2 bunk beds upstairs. Bedding not provided. **££**

Peat Stack Flat (2 rooms) Fitzroy; 📞 31313; e fitzroy.farm@horizon.co.fk. Also in Fitzroy, this smaller property of 2 bedrooms sleeps 4 in a dbl & in bunk beds. **££**

WHAT TO SEE AND DO Having parked in the car park, you can walk either north or south along the beach. Visitors are asked to stay on the beach and to avoid the dunes at the back of the shore. From the beach, wildlife can be easily observed. At any point along this coast there is a chance of spotting **Commerson's dolphins** playing in the surf. They seem to delight in surfing in on the rollers as they crash on the shore after a southerly or southeasterly gale. Peale's dolphins can also be seen here, but can be harder to find, although their taller fin should make them stand out more than the shorter, more rounded fin of the black-and-white-bodied Commerson's dolphin.

At the far end of the northern part of the beach there is a colony of gentoo penguins, while magellanic penguins can be seen breeding on the drier sections behind the beach. There is a large pond just before the gentoo colony, which is a good spot to look for black-necked swans and Chiloé wigeons among the more expected species including speckled teal and crested ducks. Silvery grebe are also sometimes seen here. As elsewhere, the run of drier summers has much reduced the water levels on many ponds here.

Falkland steamer ducks are widespread across the beach, with groups forming late in the summer season after breeding. This area has also been a good site to look for some of the more unusual species found on the islands; coscoroba swans have been seen here on more than one occasion.

The southern end of the beach connects some small islets which are also breeding areas for magellanic penguins. Here, the beach is a good site to look for wintering white-rumped sandpipers from North America and has been a reliable location to see sanderling, another wader that occasionally winters in the Falkland Islands. On occasion, South American terns nest here; they are very vocal, so you know when you are getting near a colony. Visitors are asked to give them plenty of room, as they are a species that can easily be disturbed from their nesting site.

Also at the southern end of the beach, there is a track that leads west over the drier ground to another gentoo penguin colony. There are some small pools here that can be good for water birds; as with the pond at the northern end of the beach, silvery grebe are sometimes seen here.

The beach is also a good site to explore the botany of the Falkland Islands; over 80 different flowering plants have been recorded here. Spring and early summer, when the plants are in bloom, are the best times to go looking for species such as the yellow violet, Falkland lavender and the emblem of the islands, the pale maiden. One of the rarest plants on the Falklands is also found here – Dusen's moonwort fern. It's not an easy plant to identify but a challenge for those of a botanical mind. Somewhat easier to find is coastal nassauvia, a low-growing flower that blooms between mid-December and February; it will often grow in low clumps and has the most wonderful sweet smell.

BLUFF COVE LAGOON

This inlet on the west side of East Falkland become famous during the 1982 war as it was the site of the secondary landing of the British forces and where two of the British Navy ships were hit, leading to some of the most dramatic images from this period. Nowadays, though, Bluff Cove is better known as a visitor site for the many cruise ships to the Falkands. Although only accessible by cruise-ship visitors, Bluff Cove has become increasingly popular in recent years due to its abundant wildlife not far from Stanley, as well as the facilities at the site such as the café and the small museum and shop.

HISTORY This area of East Falkland was little known to the outside world until it was chosen as the second landing point by the British Forces in 1982. Even then, it would not have become so well known as it is today if the landing had happened without being attacked. The images of the helicopters hanging over the burning hulks of the *Sir Tristram* and the *Sir Galahad* will remain with all those watching the news at that time. These two troop carriers had been attacked by Argentine aircraft on 8 June 1982 and set on fire. Many lives were lost that day, with many others suffering severe injuries, especially burns. Thankfully the area has since returned to its peace and quiet with only a memorial on the cliff to the south of Bluff Cove Lagoon at Bluff Cove to remind one of the terrible events of that day.

GETTING THERE AND AWAY This site is only open to passengers on cruise ships who have booked through those companies. Minibuses collect passengers from the car park next to the Public Jetty in Stanley to take them on the 30-minute drive to Bluff Cove Lagoon. The driver/guides will give a commentary (vehicles have a good PA system on board) about the areas they are passing through on the main road south before turning off on the newly built access road to the site. The guests are then given a short briefing by an on-site guide before having 2 hours to explore. This is ample time to have a good look around, as well as enjoy the complimentary hot drink and cake in the café and have a look at the shop and museum.

WHAT TO SEE AND DO Having been briefed, it is the nearby penguin colonies that catch the eye, as there are c1,000 pairs of **gentoo penguins** only yards away. A little further on one can see the small colony of **king penguins** that are now calling this area home. Some 20 pairs of these magnificent birds are now breeding but others come and go, so there is hope that this colony will continue to grow. **Magellanic penguins** also breed nearby so are often in the vicinity. Other species of penguin can occur from time to time but are rare. A walk across the site leads one to a long sandy beach which is also usually a good place to watch the penguins coming and going to the sea. **Southern sea lions** can sometimes be seen here, and **Commerson's or Peale's dolphins** can be sighted in the surf if conditions are right.

Southern Giant Petrels are also seen out to sea, along with a variety of gulls. On land, the shore of the lagoon can attract **wading birds** such as magellanic oystercatcher, two-banded plover and white-rumped sandpipers among others. A good mix of **geese** like the short grass at the site, with large numbers of upland geese and ruddy-headed geese grazing near the penguin colonies, and the occasional pairs of kelp geese along the rocky shores at the end of the beach. A mixture of small birds also visit the site, including Falkland thrush, long-tailed meadowlark and dark-faced ground tyrant.

A wide variety of **flowers** also occur here, especially in springtime when the national flower of the islands, the pale maiden, can be found. More obvious throughout the year is the sea cabbage after which the café is named. This is found along the shore above the high-tide mark.

It's a good idea to leave enough time to explore the museum, which is between the shop and the café. It houses a fascinating collection of exhibits, covering everything from the events of 1982 to the early days of farming, including equipment used in those bygone times. The complimentary hot drink and cake are very welcome on a cool windy day – Hattie's cakes are justifiably famous and leave one wanting more. The shop has a real mix of products for sale, many of which are handmade (often by members of staff) and all exclusively commissioned for this shop.

For those on a short stop from a cruise ship this site is ideal as it covers many aspects of the Falklands and still leaves time to get back to Stanley to explore the capital of the islands before returning to the ship.

6

Sea Lion Island

Sea Lion Island, one of the smallest islands in Falkland, is one of the most popular destinations for visitors. Lying 10 miles (17km) from East Falkland, this island forms a plateau rising to approximately 100ft. It is 5 miles long and just over 1 mile at its widest point. From Bull Hill, at the western end, the island slopes gently down eastwards to the open sandy beaches. There are a number of pools on the island. The tussac grass extends around some of the coast away from the cliffs, while inland the habitat is grassy turf. This island has the most accessible breeding colonies of southern sea lions and southern elephant seals. It also has one of the highest densities of breeding birds on the islands. It is one of the best places to see one of the most endangered birds of prey in the world, the striated caracara, locally known as the Johnny Rook. There are also many small birds on the island in the absence of any ground predators. In early and late summer there is the chance of seeing killer whales close inshore. The island was recognised as a National Nature Reserve in 2011 and is also a RAMSAR site – a wildlife-rich area designated in the Convention on Wetlands treaty (named after the first of these sites, Ramsar in Iran) – due to the high numbers of waterfowl found here. The sheer abundance of wildlife in such a small area makes Sea Lion Island a must on even the shortest of trips to the Falklands, but especially for those interested in photography: many of the published photographs of Falklands' wildlife have been taken here. In 2017, Micky Reeves and Sarah Crofts, operating as Wild Falklands Ltd, bought a 99-year lease for the island with the aim to establish high-end ecotourism and nature conservation.

The small, nearby offshore tussac islands of Brandy, Whisky and Sea Lion Easterly are uninhabited and were bought by the Antarctic Research Trust (w antarctic-research.de) in 2004 to protect their future.

HISTORY

This is the most southerly inhabited island in the Falkland Islands. The original settlers, who came to farm the island as well as to take penguins and seals for their oil, built their house on the slight rise between Cow Bay and Elephant Corner so that it would be possible to signal to passing ships or to the settlements on the mainland. The farmhouse, which can be found at this site, was built from timbers salvaged from the shipwreck of a British ship, the *Viscount*, in 1892.

A system of bonfires, used to signal to the mainland, was used in Falkland until the arrival of radio in the 1950s. Three fires in a row meant that help was needed, but the low-lying island is difficult to see from the mainland, so the effectiveness of this system was questionable, as was shown in 1929, when a Frenchman employed on the island, one Alexander Douglas, committed suicide. After trying to alert the authorities using the bonfire system and receiving no response, his workmates thought about trying to reach the mainland. However, they didn't have a boat so

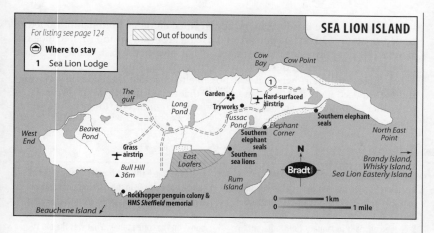

For listing see page 124

Where to stay

1 Sea Lion Lodge

Out of bounds

SEA LION ISLAND

Cow Bay

Cow Point

The gulf

Garden

Hard-surfaced airstrip

Long Pond

Tryworks

Tussac Pond

Southern elephant seals

West End

Beaver Pond

Southern elephant seals

Elephant Corner

North East Point

Grass airstrip

East Loafers

Southern sea lions

Bradt

Brandy Island, Whisky Island, Sea Lion Easterly Island

Bull Hill ▲36m

Rum Island

N

Rockhopper penguin colony & HMS *Sheffield* memorial

Beauchene Island

0 — 1km

0 — 1 mile

one of the men, Benny Davis, built a raft from wooden barrels and set off through the surf. He launched this boat just after dark and reached Speedwell Island, nearly 30 miles away, roughly 12 hours later. It is said that he simply headed west until he could smell the seabirds on Annie Island, which lies to the west of Speedwell Island, to the south of Lafonia.

Sea Lion Island, now owned by Wild Falkland Ltd, was owned by the Falkland Islands Development Corporation from 1990 and the Clifton family prior to that and was actively farmed until 1997, when wool farming on this small scale became uneconomic. The island used to be home to the Falkland Islands' stud sheep flock, but following the cessation of commercial farming, the last sheep were removed in the early 2000s. The hardship caused by the island's geographical isolation cannot be underestimated. Until the introduction of the inter-island float planes in the 1950s, the only connection with the rest of the islands was one or two visits a year by ships calling in to pick up wool and to leave mail and provisions.

Since 1982 things have changed dramatically; cargo boats now call in three or four times a year and Islander aircraft fly in and out almost daily during the summer. The hard-surfaced airstrip close to the lodge has largely superseded the grassy runway at the western end of the island, though the grass strip is still used in certain winds. The island was not greatly involved in the Argentine occupation of 1982. There is a memorial to those killed on HMS *Sheffield* on Bull Hill. The ship was hit on 4 May 1982 but did not sink until 10 May, when it was under tow to a safe anchorage in South Georgia. The recently refurbished grave near the garden on the hard-surfaced airstrip's northwestern slopes is of Mrs Susan Whitley, one of the three Falkland Island civilians in Stanley killed on 11 June 1982.

Nowadays, the island's lodge is open during the summer months, and two nearby houses are used by the staff and the elephant seal researchers – the only people who live here – making it a busy place. In the winter months, meanwhile, the lodge is closed and the island is very quiet.

GETTING THERE AND AWAY

The majority of visitors arrive by **plane** on the 35-minute FIGAS flight from Stanley (w falklands.gov.fk/aviationservice; £109.14; for booking information, see page 58) or from other places on Falkland. These local flights operate daily on demand. Those arriving by air are met and taken to the lodge where they are given

6

a short time to settle in and then, if they wish, taken on an optional introductory guided 4x4 tour (£50) which points out the main areas to visit and what to look out for on a 1–2-hour drive around the island's major sites. In the past, cruise ships have called here, but at present the island is closed to visiting ships.

For those with their own **boat** it is possible to visit, but there are no moorings and the exposed nature of the island means that anchoring is at your own risk. As with other islands on the Falklands, it is advisable to contact the lodge before sailing (see below).

WHERE TO STAY *Map, page 123*

Sea Lion Lodge (12 rooms) ☎32004; e sealion_lodge@horizon.co.fk; w sealionisland. com; ⊕ 1 Oct–31 Mar. The only place to stay on the island, the lodge was purpose-built in 1986 & opened officially in January 1998, adjacent to the existing farm buildings, & sleeps guests in spacious, mostly en-suite rooms. Accommodation comprises: family room (containing 1 dbl, 2 sgls); 5 dbl/twin rooms (1 dbl bed &1 sgl bed); 2 dbl rooms (dbl beds); 2 sgl rooms with en-suite bathroom & 2 sgls with shared bathroom. The lodge is centrally heated throughout & operates on a FB basis, with the option of taking a packed meal or coming back to the lodge at lunchtime. The 3-course evening meal is of a high standard & caters for all tastes & diets. This single-storey building has bedrooms off the main corridor in the eastern arm with the lounge/bar situated at the other end of the lodge. The superb views from the lounge/bar allow guests to watch the distant elephant seals at all times of the day &, in the evenings, magellanic & gentoo penguins can be seen arriving in great numbers. There's also a good selection of reference books on the coffee table. What was the old TV lounge is now the dining room, thus giving more room in the main lounge for all guests to enjoy the views from here. The lodge has a Wi-Fi hotspot with internet & phonecards available. There are also 2 public toilets near the entrance to the building. As with all accommodation outside of Stanley, you must remove outer footwear before entering the building. There are shoe racks in the conservatory which you pass through on the way into the main building. Since 2018 there has been a steady programme of upgrades to the lodge, including a new roof in 2019 & new wall cladding & windows in 2023, plus the usual continuous decorating. **££££**

WHAT TO SEE AND DO

Walking around Sea Lion Island on the open, grassy turf is fairly undemanding but, as everywhere, there are some essential ground rules. At the lodge, and on the introductory tour, advice is given regarding the ground rules for the welfare of the wildlife. This enables visitors to approach both animals and birds safely, without causing the wildlife any distress. For more information on ground rules for wildlife encounters, see page 47. There are now some marked paths near the lodge due to the successful tussac grass regeneration making it harder to find a route; be aware that some of the grassy slopes above the cliffs at the western end can get very slippery in wet weather. In the Bull Hill area in particular, the cliffs themselves are steep, so care is needed in windy weather. Tussac grass can be very thick and is often above head height, making progress and orientation difficult on occasion.

In sheltered spots there is also the chance of meeting sleeping **sea lions or elephant seals**. Upon arrival, visitors are given a rough map of the island from the lodge, on which one area, **East Loafers** on the southern coast, is marked as being out of bounds as this is the main breeding area for southern sea lions. These are dangerous animals and are best viewed from the top of the cliff. **Southern elephant seals**, easily seen around the sandy shores of the eastern end of the island, are a different matter as they are less aggressive. However, you must keep a respectful distance from them – the standard advice is to remain at least one of their body lengths away, and to make sure that they always have access to the sea, never getting between them and the water. Despite their size they can move very quickly and with very little warning. The elephant seals have been studied here since 1995 by a team of Italian researchers focusing on the ecology, behaviour and genetics of this population. For more information, see w eleseal.org.

Of the 50-plus species of birds in the Falklands archipelago, two found here deserve a special mention. The **Falkland skua** can be very energetic in defence of its territory, by dive-bombing any intruder. Most of the skuas nest in the open grass at the western end of the island, with a few nesting just off the main track from the lodge towards the island's eastern end. These large birds can be seen on the nest and are best admired from a certain distance. This distance will vary from bird to bird, but when they start to sit up and take notice of you, it is the time to find an alternative route. The other species is the **striated caracara** – these beautiful, inquisitive birds of prey have a strong liking for shiny or brightly coloured objects so when they're in the area, it is a good idea to keep a close eye on your possessions.

Although Sea Lion Island has the best reputation for seeing **killer whales** on Falkland, it is by no means guaranteed. They are most often seen at the eastern end of the island, usually cruising past where the gentoo penguins come ashore to reach their colonies, or where the elephant seals have their pups – on the sandy areas east of the lodge. They can also be seen near the sea lion colony at East Loafers. The best chance of seeing them is when the elephant seals and sea lions have their pupping seasons. Keeping an eye out to sea is essential, especially if there is any disturbance of gulls, terns and shags at the edge of the kelp. These birds often follow the killer whales in the hope of some scraps.

WALKS This small island offers a wide variety of walks, although there are few marked paths or signs to follow. It is possible to walk around the whole coast in one day; however, this would mean missing many of the spectacular sights that make this island so unique. A minimum stay of two nights is recommended, but to enable you to revisit favourite spots, three would be a better idea.

Cow Point, North East Point and Elephant Corner
It is possible to explore the eastern end of the island before lunch. The closest beach, **Cow Bay**, can be reached by cutting across the field to the north of the lodge and continuing down a shallow valley through the tussac grass towards the sand. Many magellanic penguins nest in this area, including one pair often seen using a burrow almost under one of the old stiles. At the western end of the beach a few elephant seals can be seen, hauled out above the tide line, when they come ashore to moult at the end of the breeding season. A walk westwards along the beach should find upland geese and kelp geese, as well as several noisy groups of magellanic oystercatchers. After Christmas many of these have young and are often seen in small family groups along the water's edge. There is no safe access to the western end of the island from this beach.

Turning around and heading east, one can walk along the sand towards **Cow Point**. The sand does disappear in places and it becomes necessary to walk over flat rocks. Two stretches of large boulders, around 100yds along the beach, can be difficult to navigate so take care. For those wishing to avoid this section, you can return to near the lodge and head east for 10 minutes, before rejoining the long sand beach. This area has many small birds, including Cobb's wrens, popping in and out of the stones at your feet, while elegant dark-faced ground-tyrant catch flies at the top of the beach. From Cow Point, small numbers of gentoo penguins can be seen porpoising their way back to land through the banks of offshore kelp. These penguins are making their way to the long sandy beach that stretches eastwards from here. This flat area between the north and south beaches is regularly swept over during the winter gales. Breeding gulls and terns often use the higher ridges; therefore, it is preferable to keep at a reasonable distance from these areas to avoid disturbing them. The large gentoo colony is a dominating presence at the top of the beach and is clearly designated, with a wire fence ensuring that the penguins are not disturbed. It is always worthwhile looking at this colony to see if there are any king penguins. Most years, one to two of these birds are present, although as many as five have been noted in the past.

Behind the sand beach, shallow temporary pools can sometimes be seen, formed when high tides coincide with windy days to push water into this area. When the pools are present, many small wading birds can be found feeding in them. Along with the two-banded plovers, there are often many white-rumped sandpipers that have come here from their North American breeding grounds. Continuing east for less than 10 minutes to the far end of the beach, there is a small colony of southern giant petrels. These are shy birds and are very easily disturbed; keep at least 500m from them at all times. The area between the colony and **North East Point** is dominated by clumps of tussac grass growing in fine loose sand. There is usually one pair of striated caracara in this area and a strong possibility that one of the resident peregrine falcons might pass overhead. Despite the presence of these birds, this end of the island has less abundant wildlife and it is more difficult walking through the tussac than on the sand so, if time is limited, there are more rewarding areas to explore on this island.

A few minutes' walk south from the giant petrel colony takes you to a beach that both magellanic and blackish oystercatchers can be found nesting at the top of. As their nests are well camouflaged, walkers must watch out for displaying adults and thus avoid the nesting sites. The beach is also another favourite haul-out site for elephant seals, with one favoured site at the eastern end of this beach, and even more found at the western end, a 20-minute stroll away.

Just beyond the big haul-out site, you can walk around 100yds on to some grassy slopes (a super place to watch both upland and ruddy-headed geese), behind which there is a small bay, the aptly named **Elephant Corner**. Here, visitors can push through the tussac grass on the path of least resistance in order to reach a low promontory in the middle of the cove. The elephant seals can be viewed in safety from here and it is an excellent spot for photography. The fence line along the edge of the tussac grass behind Elephant Corner is a good site to watch some of the smaller birds, such as black-chinned siskin and white-bridled finch, especially in springtime. It has also been the temporary home to several vagrant birds over the years, including a white-crested elaenia. As with all vagrants, they are not an annual occurrence, but this is a good place to look, just in case.

Tussac Pond, Long Pond, Bull Hill and Beaver Pond
The western tip of Sea Lion Island is much further from the lodge. It may be possible to get a lift from the lodge to the Bull Hill area and walk back, or to set off in the morning, take a packed lunch and explore the whole area on foot, returning mid-to-late afternoon.

Beginning from the lodge, the garden is a short walk west from the airstrip. The hedges shelter a good variety of small birds and protect all the vegetables grown by the lodge. Turkey vultures are often found sitting on the higher hedges at the back of the garden. Between the airstrip and the gardens are the remains of the tryworks – the brickwork is all that remains of the site where penguins were rendered for oil. Each penguin rendered approximately half a pint of oil, which was used for lighting. Hundreds of penguins were taken for this purpose in the late 1800s and early 1900s.

The first pool, **Tussac Pond,** is tucked away in the tussac grass on the southern side of the island, a 5-minute walk south from the tryworks. This pool is home to several species of duck such as Chiloé wigeon and speckled teal. It is also a great place to watch magellanic penguins zooming through the shallow water, as they are not this easy to observe when in the sea. The overhanging tussac often hides a few black-crowned night herons. Snipe can be found feeding in some of the wetter grass. In springtime, grass wrens and white-bridled finches can be heard singing from their elected song posts. Outside of the summer breeding season, grass wrens are hard to find, unlike the Cobb's wrens that advertise their presence with frequent chattering. Among other species seen on this pool are the elegant silver grebes. Although these can be seen on many of the pools on Falkland, you are much closer to them at this site. On the seaward edge it is a good idea to listen out for any snorting or snoring as elephant seals can often be found asleep, hidden in the tussac grass.

By heading west, following the line of the inner edge of the tussac grass, it does not take long to reach a low cliff from where the southern sea lions can be viewed on their breeding beach down below. During January and February, pups can be seen with their mothers at the top of the beach. The 'beach master' males are very aggressive in protecting their harems from the younger males who await their chance in the shallow water just off the edge of the beach. It is at this time of year that killer whales can occasionally be seen patrolling the shores. This grassy slope can be dangerous in high winds or when wet. When walking in this area, visitors are usually accompanied by Falkland thrushes and tussacbirds. The path then turns northwards towards the middle of the island, and joins one of the few tracks, from which you head west for 15 to 20 minutes towards a lower section of the island.

It is here that the next pond, **Long Pond**, is found. This is a much more open pond, the only shelter being a narrow strip of reeds on the western bank. It is on the borders of these reeds that most wildfowl tend to congregate. At first glance, there may appear to be very little birdlife on the pond but, in fact, a good variety of water birds breed here. The grassy banks are one of the favoured areas of upland geese and ruddy-headed geese and have been good sites for some of the rarer species of bird that occasionally visit the island, such as aplomado falcon or Chilean flamingo. The open heath in this area is a good site for rufous-chested dotterels and Falkland pipits. If the wind is from the north, there are some nice sheltered areas to have lunch in the next area of tussac grass overlooking East Loafers. Though it is always advisable to have a look around for dozing sea lions before settling down to eat!

The most visited sites on this end of the island are the **memorial to HMS** *Sheffield* and the nearby **rockhopper penguin colony** in the Bull Hill area. The walk from Long Pond to these sites takes between 20 minutes and half an hour. After following the edge of the tussac from East Loafers past the end of the grass airstrip, visitors need to be on the lookout for nesting skuas. The only building visible as you near Bull Hill is the corrugated iron shack that is used as the fire control point for the airport. The memorial is less than 100m away from the hill, high on the cliff overlooking the area in which HMS *Sheffield* was lost. The cross, with its associated wreaths and ship's badges contained in a glass-fronted case, commemorate this Royal Navy ship that was attacked by Argentine aircraft on 4 May 1982, when it was acting as a guard ship to the southeast of the Falkland Islands. It was hit by a missile which caused a fire, resulting in the ship being abandoned. Six days later, it was under tow to South Georgia for repair when inclement weather caused more water to breach the hull, resulting in it sinking here, southeast of Sea Lion Island. Some 20 men lost their lives in this attack. Although the rockhopper colony behind the cross is not as large as in former times, it is still an impressive sight. Among the penguins are a large number of king shags. The sights, sounds and smells make this a memorable place. There is a constant melee of activity: small groups of rockhoppers bounce their way from the steep cliff access point to the colony and back again. Standing down wind of the colony, you can't help but notice the pungent odour. Shags are also prevalent; their noisy greetings as they encounter their mate or chicks fill the air with a cacophony of raucous sound. Owing to the high number of breeding birds here, many scavenging species are also present, including striated caracara and the ever-present tussacbirds. This is also one of the best places on the Falkland Islands to see snowy sheathbills. A macaroni penguin, never an easy species to see here, has visited the rockhopper colony in recent years, so is worth keeping an eye out for. It often pairs up with a rockhopper penguin and produces a hybrid young but was not successful in 2022–23.

Offshore, many black-browed albatrosses pass the island on windy days. Over 100,000 pairs breed on the island of Beauchene, which lies 30 miles south of Sea Lion Island and can be seen on the horizon on clear days. It is the most southerly and also the most isolated of the Falkland Islands and was discovered in 1701 by Jacques Gouin de Beauchêne and named after him. Large numbers of sooty shearwaters arrive during the breeding season in order to breed on the offshore tussac islands such as Sea Lion Easterly, and are easy to see as they fly offshore of the rockhopper colony.

The far west of the island has a few more king shag colonies but little that cannot be seen elsewhere. Since the late 1990s, a tussac-grass replanting programme has been initiated with particular emphasis on this more eroded end of the island. The new growth seems to be establishing itself quite well and, hopefully, will eventually look as good as the established tussac elsewhere on the island.

By heading north from the Bull Hill area, on a 20-minute walk down a gentle slope towards the island's northern shore, you eventually reach **Beaver Pond**, so called after the Beaver float planes that landed here from the 1950s until they were replaced by the Islander aircraft during the early 1980s. This peaty pool is worth investigating; it has good numbers of geese nearby and often has breeding gulls and terns along the boulder beach on the seaward side. The grassy slopes to the east of here are populated with many breeding pairs of Antarctic skuas. On returning to the lodge along the northern side of the island, it is best to avoid the tussac grass, as this can be impenetrable in places. There is one track, a half-hour walk away from Beaver Pond, that leads through the tussac grass to the gulf where all the island's freight is landed. Many birds can be seen feeding along the edge of the tussac grass, perching on the higher tufts. It is important to follow the tracks on the way back to the lodge, as there is a boggy area between the garden and the hard-surfaced airstrip that is best avoided unless you are looking for the snipe that like to frequent this area.

7

West Falkland

West Falkland is generally more rugged than East Falkland, the highest point being Mount Adam at 2,297ft (700m). The three main hilly areas are the Mount Adam/Mount Robinson range which runs east to west ending at Byron Heights, the Hornby Mountains which run parallel to Falkland Sound to the west of Port Howard, and the high ground in the Port Stephens area. West Falkland is mostly composed of Palaeozoic sedimentary rocks, quartzite, sandstone and shale. Some of the higher peaks show signs of glaciation during the most recent glaciation period, known as Pleistocene (2.58 million–12,000 years ago), with cirques remaining from hanging glaciers and a less jagged outline than seen on other peaks, such as at Wickham Heights on East Falkland. The wide-open spaces between the mountain ranges give a different feel to the countryside compared with East Falkland or the smaller islands. The eastern coast along Falkland Sound is very linear, while the coastline to the west is deeply indented and rugged cliffs reaching 700ft (213m) dominate. There are many shallow lakes and streams in West Falkland. The habitat is mostly grasslands in the wetter areas, described as oceanic heath formations (page 23), but this gradually changes as the ground dries into diddle-dee and *blechnum* fern heaths. In these two habitat types a variety of other plants occur, ranging from yellow orchid through to vanilla daisy, depending on the soil type and the amount of water present.

The main settlements are Port Howard (see below), Fox Bay (page 136) and Fox Bay West, Port Stephens (page 140), Chartres, Hill Cove (page 141) and Roy Cove. Flying over West Falkland, a scattering of shepherds' huts can be seen away from these settlements. Although not as rich in wildlife as some of the smaller islands, there is still plenty to see – the Lyn Blake Reserve at Hawk's Nest Ponds is one of the best sites to look for waterfowl, and the penguin colonies on the north shore and at Fox Bay are well worth a visit.

There are also various artefacts from the Falklands War to be seen, either in the small museum at Port Howard (page 134) or by visiting the various crashed aircraft sites close to the road between Port Howard and Fox Bay and Chartres.

Port Howard makes the ideal base from which to explore the island because it has a wide choice of accommodation and tours regularly run from the settlement. For those wanting to stay a little further afield, the far reaches can be explored from a variety of smaller settlements such as Port Stephens, Fox Bay, Port Edgar, San Carlos, Port San Carlos and Shallow Bay.

PORT HOWARD

The settlement, home to 22 people, is situated at the base of 2,400ft (660m) Mount Maria at the head of its own sheltered harbour. Although this is the largest settlement on West Falkland, you can still walk from one end to the other in

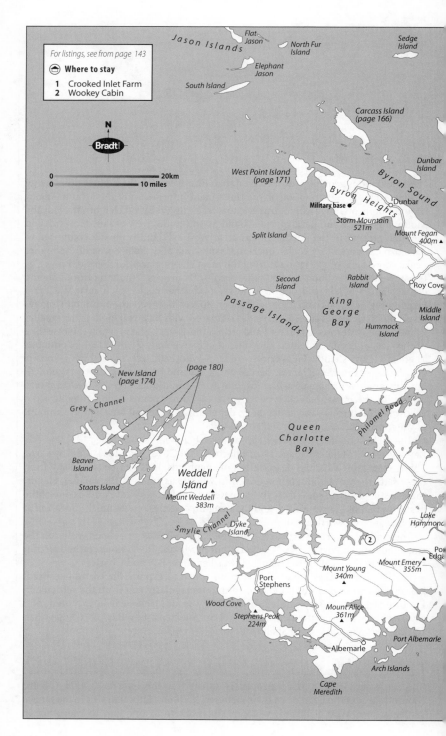

For listings, see from page 143

⊝ **Where to stay**
1 Crooked Inlet Farm
2 Wookey Cabin

N

Bradt

| 0 | | 20km |
| 0 | | 10 miles |

Jason Islands

Flat
Jason

North Fur
Island

Sedge
Island

Elephant
Jason

South Island

Carcass Island
(page 166)

Dunbar
Island

West Point Island
(page 171)

Byron Sound

Byron Heights

Dunbar

Military base ●

Storm Mountain
521m ▲

Mount Fegan
400m ▲

Split Island

Second
Island

Rabbit
Island

Roy Cove

Passage Islands

King
George
Bay

Middle
Island

Hummock
Island

New Island
(page 174)

(page 180)

Grey Channel

Queen
Charlotte
Bay

Philomel Road

Beaver
Island

Staats Island

Weddell
Island

Mount Weddell
383m ▲

Lake
Hammond

Smylie Channel

Dyke
Island

②

Port
Edga

Mount Emery
355m ▲

Mount Young
340m ▲

Port
Stephens

Wood Cove

Stephens Peak
224m ▲

Mount Alice
361m ▲

Port Albemarle

Albemarle

Arch Islands

Cape
Meredith

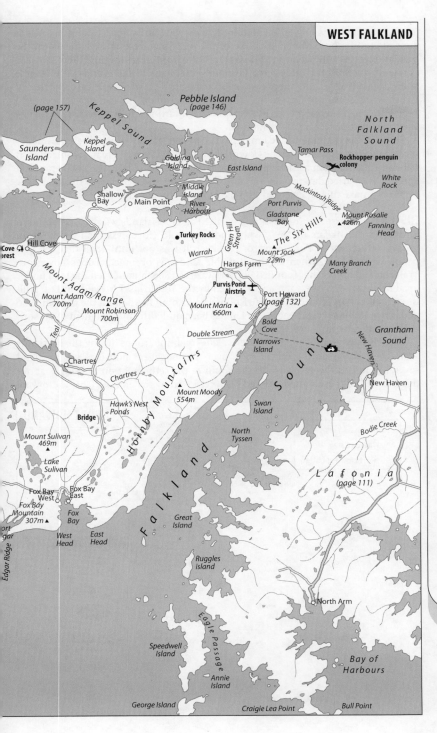

(page 157)

Pebble Island
(page 146)

Keppel Sound

Saunders
Island

Keppel
Island

N o r t h
Falkland
S o u n d

Golding
Island

East Island

Tamar Pass

Rockhopper penguin
colony

White
Rock

Shallow
Bay

Main Point

Middle
Island

River
Harbour

Port Purvis

Gladstone
Bay

Mackintosh Ridge

Mount Rosalie
▲426m

Fanning
Head

Cove ⚓
orest

Hill Cove

Turkey Rocks

Warrah

Green Hill Stream

The Six Hills

Mount Jock
229m

Many Branch
Creek

Harps Farm

Mount Adam Range

Mount Adam
700m

Mount Robinson
700m

Purvis Pond
Airstrip

Mount Maria ▲
660m

Port Howard
(page 132)

Bold
Cove

Grantham
Sound

Teal

Double Stream

Narrows
Island

New Haven

New Haven

Chartres

Chartres

Hawk's Nest
Ponds

Bridge

Hornby Mountains

▲ Mount Moody
554m

F a l k l a n d   S o u n d

Swan
Island

Bodie Creek

Mount Sulivan
469m
▲

Lake
Sulivan

North
Tyssen

L a f o n i a
(page 111)

Fox Bay
West

Fox Bay
East

Fox Bay
Mountain
307m ▲

Fox
Bay

Great
Island

ort
gar

Edgar Ridge

West
Head

East
Head

Ruggles
Island

North Arm

Eagle Passage

Speedwell
Island

Annie
Island

Bay of
Harbours

George Island

Craigie Lea Point

Bull Point

20 minutes and it is only a few hundred yards wide at its widest point because it runs alongside the harbour. It is one of the most picturesque settlements on the Falklands, especially when the gorse is in full bloom in springtime. Port Howard is one of the few remaining large farming settlements in the islands. The farm is some 200,000 acres and supports 40,000 pure-bred Corriedale sheep. Outside of the shearing season of December, January and February, life can be very peaceful here but, when shearing is in full flow, Port Howard is a hub of activity, with the shearing shed the centre of operations.

Some of the outlying islands may have a greater variety of wildlife in a smaller area than Port Howard but the potential of this area is very great – you can visit habitats ranging from freshwater pools to coastal cliffs and thus see a wide range of species. The varied day-trip options and the comfort and welcome at the lodge (see opposite) make this an essential stop on a tour of the islands.

HISTORY The first recorded landing on the Falkland Islands was by Captain John Strong on the *Welfare* in 1690, who landed at Bold Cove, less than a mile from today's settlement at Port Howard. However, it was not until 1868 that the first people settled here, when all the available land was occupied. James Lovegrove Waldron and his brother founded Port Howard in 1866, but they left the land under local management. The company founded by the Waldrons, J L Waldron Ltd, built the school in Port Howard in 1956. Rodney and Robin Lee bought the farm in 1986 and, since Robin's retirement in 2004, it has been under the management of his sons – Miles and Christopher Lee.

Port Howard was occupied by over 1,000 Argentine troops during the Falklands War. Their commanding officer took over the manager's house as his base and several minefields were placed to the south of the settlement on the slopes above the jetty. All of these minefields had been removed by the end of 2020. There were

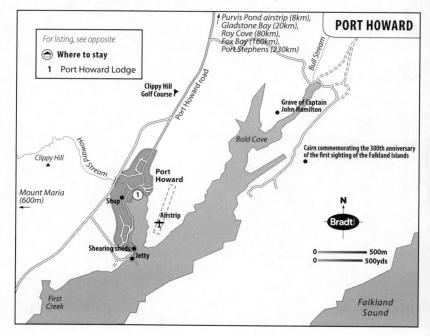

several British airstrikes at Port Howard: one, on 26 May 1982, resulting in at least four Argentine deaths. There was also one British death: Captain John Hamilton was based at a secret SAS observation post on a ridge above Port Howard, which was discovered by Argentine forces on 10 June 1982. The resulting fire fight killed Captain Hamilton, who is buried on the slopes overlooking Port Howard. On 15 June, one day after the Argentine surrender in Stanley, the Argentine forces surrendered to a company of Royal Marines. The small Nissen hut in the garden of Port Howard Lodge holds a collection of artefacts from the war, ranging from a parachute hung from the roof to various firearms and personal kit from the Argentine forces stationed at Port Howard.

GETTING THERE AND AWAY There are two **airstrips** serving Port Howard, the nearer of which is only a few minutes' walk from the lodge, on the other side of the bay. The other, Purvis Pond Airstrip, is a 10-minute drive from the settlement. Both are used by FIGAS (**w** falklands.gov.fk/aviationservice; currently £107.85 from Stanley; for booking information, see page 58) to get visitors to the settlement. The flight from Stanley takes approximately 30 minutes depending on wind strength and direction. If you are staying at the lodge, transfer from the airstrip is included in the cost of your stay.

Visitors may also **drive** from one of the other settlements on West Falkland, the majority of which are serviced by their own airstrip, or arrive by **boat** on the *Concordia Bay* ferry (**m** 55299; **w** workboat.co.fk). This has been running since 2008 and links New Haven on East Falkland to the jetty in Port Howard, transporting vehicles and passengers between the two islands. As it can be busy at peak times it is advisable to book your journey before travelling and to check the website for the latest schedule. If you are staying in Port Howard when it arrives or, indeed, are a passenger on the ferry itself, keep an eye out for Commerson's dolphins, who like to play in the bow wave of the ferry's wake. The dolphins can often be seen hanging around the harbour after the ferry has docked, waiting for it to make its onward journey. The same ferry also ships cargo for the small outlying islands around the archipelago.

TOUR OPERATORS Locally based Kelper Tours (☎ 41194 **w** thecovefalklands.com) run excursions around West Falkland.

WHERE TO STAY *Map, opposite*
Port Howard is the ideal place to stay to explore West Falkland as it offers the opportunity to see a working farm, is home to a small museum, and has good access to the wildlife sites elsewhere on the island.

Port Howard Lodge (7 rooms) ☎ 42187; **e** porthowardlodge@horizon.co.fk. The lodge consists of 2 dbl, 3 family & 2 twin rooms, all en suite & with views either overlooking the bay or up to the mountains behind the settlement. There is also 1 separate shared bathroom & 1 public toilet. Built in 1952, this was originally the farm manager's house & it has retained many of the furnishings of that period, with a very smart wood-panelled hallway that leads from the kitchen to the dining room on one side, & the lounge & bar area on the other. The original telephone with a wind-up handle is still in place on the wall before the lounge, next to a dresser full of all sorts of artefacts, such as fossils, shells & memorabilia from days gone by. You enter the building through the conservatory, where you leave outer footwear before going on to the carpeted flooring inside. There is a very grand staircase at one end of the downstairs hall that leads to the upstairs hall & the upstairs bedrooms, & there is a narrow staircase to the other end of the long hallway. The lodge is well known on the islands for its food & hospitality & is fully catered so b/fast & dinner are taken in the dining room, which is decorated with many photos, cups & awards won by farm animals at past judging events. The food often includes locally caught trout & mullet as well as local lamb & beef, accompanied by vegetables grown in the garden only a few yards from the building. A packed lunch can be made ready for any excursions. For drinks, there is an honesty bar attached to the lounge. The lodge's managers will take you on a walk around the settlement, including a visit to the shearing sheds so you can get a feel of what it must be like to work here. There is a small shop nearby containing many basic provisions, but it does not have a huge range of stock. Tours to a variety of destinations are available from the lodge, whether it be an hour's drive to Gladstone Bay or further afield to the northern shore at White Rock or southwards to Fox Bay. The last includes visits to some of the crashed aircraft sites from the Falklands War. These tours are usually arranged at the time of booking the accommodation & cost £55 for a half day or £110 for a full day & £15 for a farm tour. A very relaxed atmosphere, created by hosts Sue Lowe & Wayne Brewer, makes this an extremely comfortable place to stay. **£££**

WHAT TO SEE AND DO Staying at Port Howard gives you the opportunity to explore the area around the lodge. A gentle stroll along the main tracks takes in the sites and the settlement's birdlife, but with a little more time you can walk further to Bull Cove or southwards along Port Howard Harbour. A 4x4 tour allows you to explore the rest of the island and, while the majority of people will visit the sites on West Falkland on a tour organised through their accommodation, Kelper Tours (❨ 52194; e mpmwl@horizon.co.fk; w thecovefalklands.com/kelper-tours; contact Peter & Shelly Nightingale) will organise self-catering accommodation and drive visitors on a guided tour around the various sites. Prices start from £180 per person per day for a full day tour.

The **sheltered gardens** of the lodge are a veritable suntrap, and a good place to look for some of the smaller birds – black-chinned siskins often sing from the hedge tops and Falkland thrushes feed on the open grass. On the lawn, beside the lodge is the small **museum** (⊕ daily; free entry). Port Howard was occupied by approximately 1,000 troops during the 1982 war with Argentina and much of the equipment left behind after their departure is displayed here. The museum is always open, and the collection gives an idea of what life must have been like during the occupation.

From the museum, the **jetty** is only a 10-minute direct walk through the settlement, along the track that follows the edge of the harbour. However, you can take your time and spend anything up to a couple of hours wandering around, watching wildlife or just admiring the view. The bridge and ford that cross Howard Stream, a few hundred yards along the track, are a good place to look for black-crowned night herons feeding in the stream. Small groups of black-chinned siskins can be seen in the low bushes on the slope above. Where the stream enters the nearby inlet, a flock of speckled teal are usually feeding in the shallows. The track winds past the **shearing sheds** to the quay. The shearing sheds are used several times during the summer, so it is often possible to see how the wool is processed. The track then continues for another 100yds or so before reaching the jetty used by the ferry that links East and West Falkland. From here, it is possible to walk on a short higher track that loops back towards the lodge, passing some of the residential houses, before rejoining the main track before the bridge. There is also a new link road that leads from the ferry terminal directly to a new road behind the settlement, and then joins the main road away from Port Howard.

Another walk takes you northeast from the lodge, along the main road to Fox Bay and the rest of West Falkland. After 100yds, before the newer farm sheds, leave the road and bear right for another 200yds as the track you're now following rises up towards the airstrip overlooking the settlement. Walk up over the airstrip and along the inlet on the far side of it and, after another 600yds or so, you will reach a small headland and the **cemetery** where the grave of Captain Hamilton, who lost his life during the Argentinian occupation in 1982, can be found. **Bull Stream** flows into the far side of this inlet, helping to make the area very rich botanically. Many plants from northern Europe have been accidentally introduced with cattle fodder in the past, such as yarrow and common daisy, and there is also some interesting local flora including vanilla daisy, dog orchid and Christmas bush. Flocks of long-tailed meadow larks are often found feeding in this area – their rather drawn-out squawk flight call is very distinctive. From here, you can retrace your steps or take the track that crosses Bull Stream and return to the main road before heading south back to the lodge, which will take another 15–20 minutes. Alternatively, you can also walk for another 10–15 minutes to overlook Bold Cove and then continue for a similar amount of time up the hill opposite Port Howard – one of the most scenic areas on West Falkland, where there is a cairn to commemorate the 300th anniversary of the first sighting of the Falkland Islands. West from here you can see Port Howard laid out before you and out over the Falkland Sound towards East Falkland on the other side. The highest point on the Falklands, Mount Usborne (705m), is visible on a very clear day.

There is a nine-hole, 18-tee **golf course**, Clippy Hill, a 10-minute walk out of the settlement on the main track from the lodge. The course is free to visitors, clubs are available at the lodge and it is always open to play.

For those with a 4x4, there are several points of interest that can be reached **beyond the settlement**. These sites can also be walked, but bank on a full day of walking from

FISHING

Port Howard is one of the main centres for fishing in Falkland. The two most popular species of fish with anglers in Falkland are the sea (brown) trout, which was introduced between the 1940s and 60s, and the Falkland mullet. The former is found in the freshwater rivers, while the latter is found in tidal waters, often following the tide as it comes in over shallow ground. The most frequently fished rivers are the Warrah and the Chartres, with sea trout being the target fish. The **Warrah River**, which cuts through the white-grass plain between the Hornby Mountains and the Mount Adam range, is a 45-minute trip from Port Howard, travelling west along the only road for most of the trip until turning off over a grass track for the last mile or so. As with all fishing trips from Port Howard, the lodge will assist you with transport, a fishing guide, ghillie and food. No licence is required to fish here, although there is a maximum of six fish per angler per day. The fishing season is 30 September until 30 April, with the best times to fish being in September, October, February and March. It is also possible to fish in the river's main tributary, **Green Hill Stream**, which is a few miles closer to Port Howard, or a little nearer to the lodge in **Many Branch Creek**, a 30-minute drive north from the lodge. The **Chartres River** is about 90 minutes' drive, following the only road south from Port Howard. It can be fished from Little Chartres Farm for around 2 miles onwards until the river starts to open out. **Mullet** can also be caught in many of the creeks around Port Howard. Rod hire from the lodge is £3 per rod; ghillie hire is £110 per day. Transport to the fishing venues varies from £110 to Hill Cove, Roy Cove or Fox Bay to £30 for the Warrah River.

the lodge and be sure to carry all supplies you will need with you. The main channel to the south, Port Howard Harbour, is reached by a short, easy walk along grassy tracks by the water or a drive from the settlement. The furthest reaches of the channel are 5 miles from the lodge. Magellanic oystercatchers and blackish oystercatchers feed along the shore, along with a scattering of two-banded plovers. It is sometimes possible to observe Commerson's dolphins cruising in the shallows, while further out there are southern giant petrels zooming low over the water. **Double Stream**, just over halfway to the far end of Port Howard Harbour, enters the sound in a broad expanse of stone and mud. The views from here are fantastic, looking out from Port Howard Harbour into Falkland Sound. On the return trip, a detour up to **Freezer Rocks** on the side of Mount Maria is well worthwhile. This line of rocks jutting up through the diddle-dee and ferny vegetation is in a commanding position above the settlement. The views from here are superb – on a clear day you can see over the ridge that is the eastern boundary of Port Howard Harbour, out into Falkland Sound and beyond to East Falkland. The grass track up to the rocks is quite rough so is slow going in a 4x4, but is an easy (albeit uphill) walk of 20 minutes or so. From here it is a short journey, again over a rough track, back to the settlement, making this trip an easy half-day 4x4 tour from the lodge, or part of a longer, full day's walk.

FOX BAY AND AROUND

Fox Bay East and Fox Bay West are smaller settlements than Port Howard, with the main jetty lying to the south of Fox Bay East. The small airstrip that services these two communities lies between the two and there is also a small helipad that is sometimes used by the British military.

While a trip to Fox Bay from Port Howard, passing the Hornby Mountains to the east, can take as little as an hour or so, the round trip is over 100 miles and there are many places to visit on the way so the trip can easily fill an entire day. A short 5-minute drive by 4x4 from Port Howard, along the only gravel road, takes visitors past a small **quarry** in which variable hawks have occasionally nested and, if they are present, can be seen from the road. A mile or so further along the road are the old **peat diggings**. The settlement at Port Howard does not use much peat nowadays, but stopping here gives a good sense of the sheer scale of the diggings.

Continuing for 5 miles, on the western side of the road, there are the **remains of two of the aircraft** shot down by British Harrier jets during the 1982 war. The first, an Argentine Skyhawk, is easy to find as part of the wing has been stood up near the road. It is only a few hundred yards off the road to the actual crash site of this plane, where you can walk around the remains of the impact crater where the engine and other aircraft parts are easily identifiable. The other site is several hundred yards further off the track and takes local knowledge to find. This is the remains of an Argentine Dagger that was shot down on 21 May 1982. The pilot ejected and survived, but his plane is a real mess – you can still see the mangled cockpit and the remains of the engine, a little further on. These planes were using this wide-open valley between the Hornby Mountains and Mount Adam range to try and bomb the British forces landing at San Carlos Water on East Falkland. By staying low in the valley they were trying to avoid radar detection. There are nine other wrecked planes on land owned by Port Howard Farm, although these are not generally accessible by tourists. The area around the wreck sites is a good place to look for Falkland pipits, and yellow orchids have been found here in summer. The road then carries on for another mile or so, past Harps Farm. Southern caracara have been seen along the ridges that border some of the streams in this area.

The road continues for some 20 miles from the lodge, through fairly level ground before descending on a steep bend that emerges on to a bridge over a stream. Just beyond the stream is the layby created by the road crew when they extracted the hard core necessary for building the road. This is a wonderful site for geologists or, indeed, anyone with an interest in fossils. The broken rock towards the rear edge of the flattened ground is full of trace fossils. There have been at least three species of *trilobite* and five species of *brachiopod* and *crinoids* found here. The rock is part of the Fox Bay Formation, which is early Devonian in age (Emsian period), some 407–397.5 million years old.

As these stops can occupy most of the morning, it is just as well that there is a good picnic lunch spot at the **Lyn Blake Reserve at Hawk's Nest Ponds** some 20 miles away, after the road crosses the Chartres River either by ford or a narrow bridge, with the turning to the ponds another 5 miles or so on the east of the track. This scenic spot by the bridge often has a good number of waterfowl on the river, including speckled teal and Chiloé wigeon, particularly on the upriver (eastern) side. The Hawk's Nest Ponds are not visible from the road, but there is now a sign beside the track indicating where they are. Following the sign, it's a 5-minute drive to the first of two reed-fringed pools that have a great diversity of waterfowl. This is also one of the best sites on the Falklands to look for scarce species such as yellow-billed pintail or flying steamer duck. Care should be taken when approaching the first (northern) pool, as the track can be rather wet, making it easy to get bogged down. The track leads to the reed bed at the northern edge of the pond. A good variety of wildlife can be found feeding along the edge of this reed bed, especially if the ground behind is flooded.

Although this is primarily a good site for waterfowl, when flooded the area can also be good for wading birds such as magellanic snipe and rufous-chested dotterel. The reed beds have also occasionally been inhabited by a few black-crowned night heron. Close to the edges of the pool it is possible to see speckled teal, silver teal and white-tufted grebe, whereas the flock of Chiloé wigeons are usually found out in the middle. Among the most attractive water birds on Falkland, black-necked swans (page 37) breed on both of the Hawk's Nest Ponds. After Christmas, the young are quite well grown and can be seen following their parents across the pool. These are very shy birds and will not allow observers to approach closely. As with any patch of water on Falkland, there is always the chance of an unusual bird turning up; for example, an ashy-headed goose was once seen in with the flocks of upland geese.

The southern pond, only a few hundred yards to the south, over a slight rise, also has reed beds. Two small areas of reed can be explored – one on each of the western and southern sides of the pool. This pool is much wider and is therefore favoured by the flying steamer duck (page 38) – a species that can be difficult to see on the islands. At least one pair has bred on this pond in most years. Although there are fewer water birds in number on this pool compared with the northern pool, there is a greater variety of species, including the yellow-billed pintail (page 39). The white grass around the pool is a good place to see breeding Falkland pipits (page 44); their tuneful song can be heard on sunny spring days. Although called Hawk's Nest Ponds, birds of prey are not common. It is, however, not unusual to discover at least one variable hawk (page 40) quartering the ground in the far distance.

The drive from the pond to Fox Bay passes through some of the wettest areas on West Falkland, but although the habitat seems ideal for a range of waterfowl, there is usually little worth stopping for apart from some very tame rufous-chested dotterels that often feed right beside the road. The last mile before reaching the settlements at Fox Bay provides some of the more spectacular scenery of the trip as the bay opens out in front of you, looking south between East Head and West Head. Shortly after, the road forks: to the left is **Fox Bay East** (population 11) and to the right is Fox Bay West. During the shearing season, Fox Bay East is a very busy place with farmers from some of the outlying farms coming to help, as well as the shearing gangs who move from farm to farm. There is also the small **Post Office Museum** (free entry) here, which gives an insight into how life was lived on the islands prior to the modernisations that have occurred since 1982, with special emphasis on the history of the post office. In the bay between the two settlements are a small number of tussac-grass islands. Magellanic penguins gather on the rocky ends of these islets, while Peale's dolphins can be seen cruising around the edges of the shallow water or playing in the kelp around the coast of Fox Bay.

To the southeast of Fox Bay East, the track continues past a derelict old wool mill and leads through a series of gates (which should be left in the position you find them) out into a long passage between fields. At the end of this passage, bear right around the bay, until on the south-facing cape called **Kelp Point**. Park here and walk on to the slight rise, where there is a memorial to commemorate the 25-year anniversary of the Falklands War. It is a simple cross on a plinth, made of the local Fox Bay stone, upon which there is the inscription 'From the sea Freedom'. The sound of the braying calls of the displaying male penguins should lead you to **the gentoo penguin colony** which moves its location slightly every year. Early in the season the black-and-white adults with their orange bills and white flash over the eye will be lying or standing over their pebble-built nests, incubating their eggs, but by January the young will be making their presence felt. The larger chicks are very curious and will often come to see visitors if they are sitting down. Although they will rush back to the colony at any sudden movement, they will sometimes come right up to your feet. The old breeding sites can be seen by locating the bright green circles of grass, enriched as their droppings have increased the nitrate levels. As with all colonies, keep at least 6m from the birds, even though the penguins themselves may not heed the rule! Always ensure that you are not blocking them coming to and from the colony by standing away from their track to the sea.

Follow the birds back to the beach to see many more on the rocks where they come ashore – they often stand around here for a while when preening, moulting or resting. The occasional king penguin can also be seen coming ashore to moult. If unable to find their own species for company, king penguins will make do with the next best, which is often a gentoo penguin colony. The low cliffs to the west of the penguin route are often home to a pair of variable hawks that nest in this area. They will usually let you know if you are too close to the nest site by screaming and flying a few yards above you, making their presence felt. If this happens, back away and they will settle down again. If the wind is blowing from the south, look for black-browed albatrosses zooming over the water. In springtime, southern fulmars have been seen feeding in the bay prior to their move down to Antarctica to breed. The main bird activity in the bay involves large numbers of rock and king shags. On the rocks below the low cliff, small groups of snowy sheathbills can be found, in among large numbers of Falkland steamer ducks and kelp geese. In good visibility the scenery here is superb, with Fox Bay in front of you and coastal ridges curling around the back of the bay, ending in the East and West heads.

When standing a few hundred yards west of the gentoos, a further gentoo penguin colony is located across the bay, to the south of Fox Bay West – in one of the most unusual sites on the Falklands – on Fox Bay Mountain (307m). The penguins are only visible with a fairly powerful pair of binoculars or a telescope, as they trudge their way up to the colony, nearly at the top of the hill.

At the end of the visit to the Fox Bay area you can head back north again, where the late afternoon light on the **Hornby Mountains** gives quite a different perspective over the landscape from the morning drive south – the change in the angle of light creates a golden hue over the white-grass slopes.

WHERE TO STAY A stay in the Fox Bay area allows visitors to explore further afield without having to drive back north to Port Howard. For those wishing to do so, Fox Bay East and Fox Bay West make ideal bases to explore Hawk's Nest Ponds or to venture out for just over 2 miles northwest to the largest lake on the Falklands, Lake Sullivan. Fishing is a popular pastime here – the Malo River running south out from Lake Sullivan is one of the prime sea trout and mullet locations.

Black Shanty House (3 rooms) Fox Bay West; m 52008; e helenmarsh@horizon.co.fk; contact Helen & Leon Marsh. This centrally heated property was recently modernised. It is a typical Falklands 2-storey house that sleeps 6. All the rooms are double glazed, there is 24hr power & it is in an area of mobile-phone coverage. The owners provide courtesy transport to & from the airport, a short drive away. **££**

Coast Ridge Cottage (2 rooms) Fox Bay East; ◟ 42602; e nualaemckay@yahoo.co.uk; w coastridgecottage.com; contact Keith & Nuala Knight. This property was opened in Jan 2018 & has a modern-furnished dbl room & a twin room. It has a large open-plan kitchen, dining room & living room & can be booked as FB (£85 pp per night) or as self-catering (£55 pp per night). There is also a spacious conservatory for those who fancy watching the world go by. The low pine trees that form the fence around the property create a welcome sheltered garden. It's only a short walk from here to the store that opens twice a week for 30mins & the Southern Cross Social Club that is open every w/end. The owners of this property also offer a dbl room in their own house, which is available on a FB basis. This newly decorated room, located in the roof of the property, gives views out over the settlement. The owners also offer tours of the farm & some of the nearby wildlife sites & fishing trips. **££**

FURTHER AFIELD FROM FOX BAY To the southwest of Fox Bay is a mountainous area that does not get as many first-time visitors as the rest of the Falklands. However, those on their second or third visit to the islands will often come to explore this part of the archipelago either independently or as part of a tour. Port Edgar is only about 10 miles from Fox Bay as the crow flies, although it is nearly 30 miles away by road. Port Stephens lies further away; to reach here, visitors can either fly via FIGAS (w falklands.gov.fk/aviationservice; £174.93 from Stanley; for booking information, see page 58) or drive for well over an hour from Fox Bay, nearly 40 miles away.

To reach both of these locations, leave Fox Bay East or Fox Bay West on the only road heading southwest. The first part of the road heads west, where you get views looking out over **Queen Charlotte Bay** to the west and the first views of the hills and mountains to the south, including Mount Young (340m), Mount Emery (355m) and Mount Alice (361m).

To the south of the track is Lake Hammond, which, like many other lakes in the Falklands, is often a good site for waterfowl such as speckled teal and crested duck. The lake can also be home to flying steamer ducks or maybe a black-necked swan or two. The turning to **Port Edgar** is just past the lake on the left and the track skirts the higher ground until you start to see the southern end of Falkland Sound ahead of you. The settlement at Port Edgar is situated halfway down the southern arm of Port Edgar itself, sheltered from the open sea by Edgar Ridge.

When staying at Port Edgar there are various walks you can take, both to the north and south along the shore of the port, or you can climb Mount Emery (355m) to the west of the settlement. There is a gentoo penguin colony a couple of miles to the southeast of the settlement, lying on the shores of Falkland Sound and, as with every little-known area, who knows what other wildlife may turn up? Port Edgar is also a popular fishing area, with many of the streams good sites for both mullet and sea trout.

By continuing on the main road, you will eventually reach **Port Stephens** settlement, which lies at the head of Port Stephens, a wide, open bay with a narrow inlet to the South Atlantic Ocean to the southeast. This small settlement does have its own airstrip, and the flight from Stanley would also give good views over the mountains. While staying here you get a view southwest across the corner of Port Stephens towards Stephens Peak. The folded strata close to this peak has been given the name The Indian Village, as the sharp angles at the top of each section look somewhat like the angles at the top of a tepee. If you walk in the direction of the peak from the settlement for about an hour you can reach the south coast overlooking Wood Cove. A rockhopper penguin colony is situated just before here, on the higher cliffs, as is usually the case with this species. In the past this has been another good site to see macaroni penguins that have come to mingle with their smaller cousins. For those wanting to see more penguins, both gentoo and magellanic penguins breed back at the head of the bay, not far from the settlement. Walk for just over a mile to the northwest of the settlement, past the airstrip, and you will reach the first part of the Fegan Inlet. As with many of the inlets on the Falklands it's a very peaceful place, and a good location to watch Falkland steamer ducks cruising along the shore, with kelp gulls and dolphin gulls never very far away.

 Where to stay

Moelwyn Cottage (3 rooms) Port Edgar; 📞42010; e portedgar@horizon.co.fk; w moelwyncottage.com; contact Fayan Alazia. This self-catering accommodation has been refurbished & expanded with the addition of another bedroom. It is situated in the sheltered bay at Port Edgar – an excellent site for walking, wildlife & fishing – & sleeps 7 in 2 dbl rooms & 1 room with a sgl & a bunk bed. Views from the lounge look out over the bay. Discounts are available for longer stays. Fresh produce such as meat & vegetables are available. Pets are not welcome. **££**

Port Stephens Cottage (2 rooms) Port Stephens; 📞42307; e par@horizon.co.fk; contact Peter & Ann Robertson. A self-catering cottage that sleeps 5 with the option of meals being provided on request by prior arrangement with the owners. From here it's only an hour or so's walk to Wood Cove to view rockhopper & gentoo penguins with the rather unusual rock formation known as The Indian Village a short distance around the coastline. **££**

A CIRCULAR TOUR TO THE NORTH OF WEST FALKLAND

For those staying at Port Howard, taking another full-day trip to the north is recommended. Although it is a long journey in a 4x4, the views of the rolling landscape as you travel along the grassy tracks are superb, and the large rockhopper colony sea-cliff scenery will more than reward your efforts.

The route takes you a few miles along the main gravel road out of Port Howard before turning north to the house at Many Branch Farm. From here, continue heading northeast for about 5 miles until you reach the small, disused Mount Rosalie House. This corrugated metal (known locally as wriggly tin) house is now slightly rusty and looks very picturesque situated at the base of the hill that gives it its name, with the remains of various farm implements around the grounds. It was used by the shepherds as an overnight stay when they were gathering sheep in the days of horseback, but with 4x4s, quad bikes and trials motorbikes, the shepherds are much more efficient and can usually get home before dark.

From here, head up the low pass to the west of Mount Rosalie, another 5 miles down the track. From the top, you get views out towards Port Purvis and beyond, to Pebble Island. The track then drops for a couple of miles to a small pool at the eastern edge of Port Purvis. This is home to the usual collection of ducks – including speckled teal and crested – and can occasionally be a temporary home to vagrant birds such as the lesser yellowlegs. From here, the track climbs slowly, twisting and turning around some rocky outcrops for the next mile or so. It is here that your driver's local knowledge of the route and how to drive over such ground as Mackintosh Ridge comes to the fore.

When you reach the top of Mackintosh Ridge you can see the sea to the north, with cliffs extending in either direction. To the west is the point called White Rock and the Tamar Pass between West Falkland and Pebble Island to the west. On a clear day the Eddystone Rock, situated away to the northeast, off the tip of Cape Dolphin on East Falkland, can be seen. The last part of the route to the large rockhopper penguin colony that is situated between the Tamar Pass and White Rock is only another mile away. You know that you are getting near the colony by the hive of gulls, skuas and turkey vultures that are typically found scavenging overhead.

Once parked it is usual to have a picnic lunch before spending the next couple of hours strolling around this site. As is usual with rockhopper penguins, the colony is situated at the top of steep cliffs inaccessible to their predators. Rockhopper penguins are quirky characters, always fussing and fighting or displaying by opening their beak and squawking away while shaking their fiery-coloured eyebrows to the world. It is worth spending some time at the main colony (there are several smaller satellite colonies nearby), looking for the distinctive large yellow and orange crest, found on the foreheads of the slightly larger macaroni penguin. This has been a reliable site for this species, which has its stronghold on South Georgia, several hundred miles to the southeast of the Falklands. King shags also nest here; their colony might not be in the exact same place each year, but it is never far from the rockhoppers.

It's worth keeping an eye out to sea as black-browed albatrosses are ever present and there is always a chance of a royal albatross gliding by. In late summer, sei whales have been seen at a distance off this vantage point and Peale's dolphins can sometimes be seen cruising closer to shore.

Eventually, you have to tear yourself away from this cliff-top abundance of wildlife for the journey back to Port Howard. The trip back takes you over the same route as on the way out, but of course is now from a different perspective so photo stops to look over Purvis Pond from the top of Mackintosh Ridge and again from the slopes of Mount Rosalie looking towards Falkland Sound are a popular and a welcome chance to stretch your legs before arriving back at Port Howard in time for dinner.

A CIRCULAR TOUR FROM PORT HOWARD TO HILL COVE, MAIN POINT AND TURKEY ROCKS

Another full-day, 4x4 tour from Port Howard takes you towards the northern shores of West Falkland. While there is less wildlife and fewer historical sites of interest, this scenic tour gives visitors a very good view of the geography of the island. As the final stretch is over *camp*, local knowledge is essential; your driver will organise permission to travel over the land on the way back from Main Point to Port Howard.

The road initially follows the route towards Fox Bay, as described on page 136, until, about 40 minutes from Port Howard – having passed the airstrip at Purvis Pond, the crashed aircraft site and the fossil site – the right turn towards Hill Cove is reached. This track follows the lower slopes of Mount Adam over Teal River before rising up over the valley between Mount Adam and Mount Fegan. To the southwest, the settlement of Roy Cove, which was founded in 1872, and King George Bay can be seen from the road.

In spring, the bright yellow gorse hedges that surround Roy Cove's houses make the settlement easy to see from this distance. The turning to Roy Cove heads left to the south of Mount Fegan while the road to Hill Cove continues uphill for another 4 miles or so. Cresting the rise above Hill Cove, the view looking north is spectacular. On a clear day Saunders Island and Carcass Island can be seen across Byron Sound, while over the top of Shallow Bay House, Keppel, Golding and Pebble islands are

NARROWS ISLAND

It used to be possible to take a boat trip to Narrows Island from Port Howard; however, at the time of writing this was no longer an option. This thin island on the western edge of Falkland Sound is just over 1 mile (1.9km) long and up to 240yds (220m) wide. The boat ride was a wonderful experience, especially during the summer months, as it is at that time of year that many Commerson's dolphins come into the shallow waters at Port Howard, where they are very keen to play alongside any boating activity.

The **flora** on this island is much more diverse than many of the other islands in Falkland Sound, as it has not been seriously overgrazed. There are a great variety of habitats, from diddle-dee heath to stands of tussac grass. So far 63 species of plant have been recorded, of which six are endemic – these are Falkland cudweed, coastal nassauvia, snakeplant, smooth ragwort, woolly ragwort and Falkland rock cress. This is the only site where snakeplant is found on West Falkland. The tussac grass at the northern end of the island is a favoured resting site for southern sea lions, although they can occasionally be found on some of the beaches. Some of the largest balsam bogs on Falkland occur on the slope just above the landing point. The Falklands' more flamboyant flowers can be found here during the spring and summer months, including lady's slipper orchid, almond flower and thrift.

There are 18 species of **breeding bird** on Narrows Island. The eastern coastal cliffs have a small colony of rock shags tucked out of the wind. On the top of the island, in one of the two colonies of kelp gulls, a small group of dolphin gulls also have their nests. Antarctic skuas breed on the higher slopes, keeping a watchful eye on the gull colonies for any unattended young. Magellanic oystercatchers and blackish oystercatchers nest at the top of the beach on the open shingle areas, while the two-banded plovers nest in the more open, sandy areas. There are no penguins nesting on Narrows Island, although they often fish offshore, as can a few black-browed albatrosses. On calm days, Commerson's dolphins can easily be seen from the island. Other cetaceans, including killer whales, have also been seen in these waters, but are a rare event.

visible to the southwest. It is only a short distance down the hill to the **Hill Cove forest**. This impressive stand of trees was originally planted in the 1880s to the west of Hill Cove settlement, but was substantially enlarged in 1925. These trees are amazingly tall and healthy compared with those seen elsewhere on Falkland – so often on the islands the trees all lean away from the prevailing wind direction, but the trees in the forest seem to protect each other, with some reaching 20m tall. The whole area is full of birds – mostly black-chinned siskins and Falkland thrushes – flying around and calling. The far side of the forest contains some smaller trees, including some apple trees, and there is also a small **cemetery**. The road continues past Hill Cove settlement, only a few hundred yards to the east of the trees, the turning lying just beyond the forest. Before the road follows the edge of Byron Sound, it passes a marker which commemorates the completion of 80km of road from Port Howard.

Beyond this, about 30 minutes away from Hill Cove, is **Shallow Bay House** and then **Main Point House** at Main Point Farm (w mainpointfarm.com), where the road finishes. This farm is home to the only British miniature horses on Falkland. Permission is needed to continue past this point over their land to make the round trip back to Port Howard.

To reach Port Howard, there is no easily defined route between Main Point House and Turkey Rocks along the edge of River Harbour and so a driver with local knowledge is essential in these parts. The drive over *camp* gives wonderful views out towards Pebble Island and the many smaller islands beyond the river. **Turkey Rocks** is a valley that divides two escarpments of sheer rock and has a stone run through the middle. The area is named on account of the turkey vultures that breed on the crags on either side. Variable hawks and peregrine falcons are also seen in this area on a regular basis. This is an excellent site for a picnic as it is a peaceful valley with only the birdlife and a few sheep for company. In late summer small numbers of native strawberries can be found on the western flanks of the valley. If you plan to return to Port Howard from here, the route descends some rather steep slopes and crosses through the Warrah River before rejoining the main road. This will take the best part of an hour, depending on how wet the ground is.

WHERE TO STAY   *Map, page 130*

Visitors looking to spend more time in this little-visited and secluded area can base themselves in one of several self-catering options.

The 3 C's (7 rooms) Hill Cove; m 52918; e karen@bluegrass.co.fk. This huge property sleeps up to 18 in 7 rooms, which are a mixture of dbls, twins & bunks. This was formerly the RAF bunkhouse but was refurbished & opened in 2018 with great views out into Byron Sound from its new decking built on to the upstairs living quarters. **£££**

Boxwood Pod (1 room) Boxwood Paddock, Hill Cove; 41194; m 52194; e shelly@horizon.co.fk, mpmwl@horizon.co.fk; w thecovefalklands.com. Opened in Feb 2022, this is a true pod situated on the water's edge of Byron Sound, which is viewable through the glass front or in sunny weather from the decking outside. There are 3 sgl beds, 2 at low

level & the other above one of the low beds. No pets. No Wi-Fi in pod but a Wi-Fi hotspot is nearby. A variety of tours can be booked visiting many of the sites in this part of West Falkland. **£££**

Crooked Inlet Farm (4 rooms) Roy Cove; 41111; m 51901; e crooked.inlet@horizon. co.fk; contact Joy & Danney Donnelly. Self-catering accommodation with 1 dbl, 1 dbl with a sgl bed, 1 bunk bed, & 1 sgl room. From here one can get wonderful views out towards Rabbit, Hummock & Middle islands in King George Bay. **££**

Shallow Bay Cottage (2 rooms) Shallow Bay; m 55035; e daepeck@horizon.co.fk. This self-catering accommodation consists of 1 dbl/twin & 1 twin room & is in one of the older stone-built buildings in the settlement. It is situated on a slight rise, meaning it offers views out over the area from either side, as well as up to Mount Adam to the south. This settlement is only accessible by road as there is no airstrip. **££**

Wookey Cabin (2 rooms) Carew Harbour, Stoney Ridge Farm; ☏ 42014. A self-catering cabin sleeping 4 in a dbl & a twin, plus a sofa bed if more space is needed. This is an away-from-it-all place nearly 100 miles from Port Howard. **££**

Green Hill (4 rooms) Chartres; ☏ 42212; e josie. kenneth@horizon.co.uk. A newly opened self-catering place at Chartres, which is situated to the west, halfway along the road from Port Howard to Fox Bay. 1dbl, 2 sgls & a family room that sleeps 3 & has views over Christmas Harbour. **£**

GLADSTONE BAY

Gladstone Bay is reached on a half-day tour from Port Howard. Getting there involves driving for an hour or so north, past Many Branch Farm, about halfway (10 mins) along the track, before climbing the slopes of Mount Jock. The views from here are superb, looking back to Port Howard and Falkland Sound to the south and over Purvis Harbour out to Pebble Island to the northwest. There are some small examples of stone runs on the higher slopes. The track over the grass and diddle-dee runs down to the shore of Purvis Harbour, where Gladstone Bay is situated. Fossils can occasionally be found on this pebble beach, but it is otherwise a mix of glacially deposited material of many different origins. Consequently, some very pretty rocks can be seen here. The main purpose of this trip is to visit the colony of gentoo penguins that breed on the diddle-dee, a few hundred yards inland, and to see the large numbers of waterfowl that frequent Gladstone Bay – mostly Falkland steamer ducks and crested ducks – with colonies of king shag and rock shag along the low cliffs to the west. Black-crowned night herons breed in the small clumps of tussac grass that cling to the sides of the cliff. Southern sea lions can sometimes be found on the flat rocks on the point to the west of the beach.

8

Pebble Island

Comprising 22,000 acres, Pebble Island is the third-largest offshore island in the Falklands and is situated to the north of West Falkland. The farm here is some 24 miles long and about 6 miles at its widest point. The landscape varies greatly, from large ponds and moorland to long sandy beaches and high cliffs. The majority of the wetlands are on the eastern part of the island and the three major hills, First Mountain, Middle Peak and Marble Mountain, at the western end. The island gets its name from the semi-precious stones which are found along the coast. These pebbles are mostly translucent or semi-translucent and are made of quartz, an agate. When held up to the light, these pebbles let varying amounts of light through. Opaque stones of varying colours can also be found on the island. For the naturalist, Pebble Island is a superb place to watch the greatest concentrations of wildfowl and wading birds on the Falklands. It also has four species of breeding penguin most summers: rockhopper, gentoo, magellanic and macaroni. In addition, king penguins have been occasionally observed here, and the very rare erect-crested penguin was seen here in the late 1990s.

HISTORY

John Henry Dean from England bought Pebble Island, along with the nearby Golding, Middle and East islands, in 1846 for the grand sum of £400. The sheep farm, which he established across the whole island, is still run as an active farm today, with some 5,750 sheep, nearly all purebred Corriedale stock famous for their high-quality wool. Migrant gangs of shearers, from a variety of nationalities, visit each island in turn during the summer months to carry out shearing. Many of these shearers come from New Zealand and travel to the sheep-farming areas of the world during the various shearing seasons. The quality of the grass means the island has one of the highest stock ratings on the islands, grazing one sheep to every 1.5 acres.

During the Argentinian occupation of 1982 a number of Pucara and Mentor ground-attack aircraft were based on the airstrip, this being one of the better strips on Falkland. The Argentinians changed the name of the island to Isla Bourbon and garrisoned several hundred troops here to protect the airstrip. Eleven of these aircraft and their fuel dumps were destroyed during a daring night raid on 15 May 1982 by the SAS, under cover of naval gunfire. All the people of Pebble Island, 19 in total, were then imprisoned in the farm manager's house shortly after this attack and remained there for the duration of the war. The other major action during the conflict near Pebble Island was the sinking of HMS *Coventry* by Argentinian aircraft on 25 May 1982. It and HMS *Broadsword* had been stationed to the northwest of Falkland Sound to draw off the Argentine aircraft that were attacking the main British landing at San Carlos. This was initially successful, but these two ships were then targeted themselves which resulted in HMS *Coventry* being sunk 14 miles

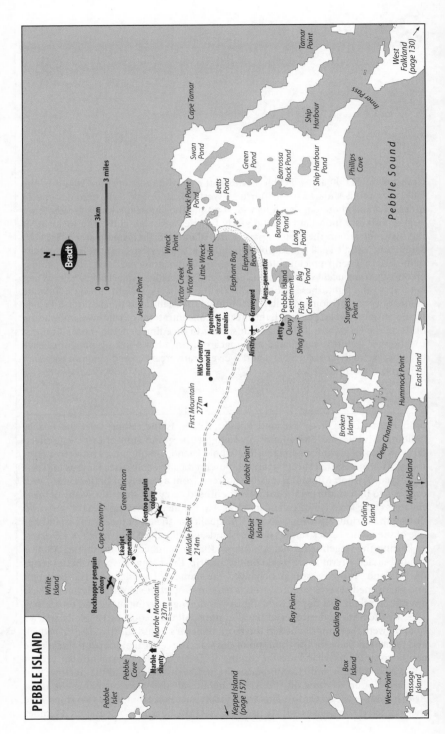

PEBBLE ISLAND

White Island

Pebble Islet

Pebble Cove

Cape Coventry

Rockhopper penguin colony

Learjet memorial

Marble shanty

Marble Mountain 237m

Middle Peak 214m

Green Rincon

Gentoo penguin colony

Keppel Island (page 157)

Jenesto Point

First Mountain 277m

HMS Coventry memorial

Rabbit Point

Rabbit Island

Bay Point

Box Island

West Point

Passage Island

Golding Island

Golding Bay

Middle Island

Broken Island

Deep Channel

Hummock Point

East Island

Sturgess Point

Shag Point

Fish Creek

Argentine aircraft remains

Airstrip

Graveyard

Jetty

Quay

Pebble Island settlement

Aero-generator

Big Pond

Long Pond

Barrossa Pond

Elephant Beach

Elephant Bay

Little Wreck Point

Victor Point

Victor Creek

Wreck Point

Betts Pond

Wreck Point Pond

Swan Pond

Cape Tamar

Green Pond

Barrossa Rock Pond

Ship Harbour Pond

Ship Harbour

Phillips Cove

Pebble Sound

Inner Pass

Tamar Point

West Falkland (page 130)

N

Bradt

0   3km
0   3 miles

north of Pebble Island, with the loss of 20 of its crew (19 at the time and one later in hospital). There were also 30 injured who, along with the rest of the crew, were rescued by HMS *Broadsword*.

The farm manager's house, the largest house in the settlement, was originally built in 1928 and was converted into the lodge in 1987, with a new property built for the manager nearby. During the summer months up to five people live on the island, looking after the active sheep farm and Pebble Island Lodge (see below).

GETTING THERE AND AWAY

The airstrip, situated at the narrowest part of the island, only a 5-minute walk from the lodge, is one of the best grass-landing strips on the islands. In wintertime, the long sandy beach close to the settlement, Elephant Beach, can double up as a landing strip at low tide if the main airstrip is too wet to be used. The **flight** direct from Stanley (w falklands.gov.fk/aviationservice; £118.17; for booking information, see page 58) takes 40–45 minutes. All flights to Pebble Island give wonderful views over East and West Falkland, particularly as you near the island and the surrounding smaller islands.

If you are visiting in your own **boat** you can land at the jetty, but permission must first be sought from the farm managers (✆ 41094; e Alexgould1973@gmail.com; f The Nest, Pebble Island).

WHERE TO STAY

Pebble Island is a popular destination with both tour groups and those travelling independently, so the accommodation does tend to get booked up quite quickly. The accommodation on the island is open during the austral summer – from early October until the end of March.

Markham House (4 rooms) Pebble Island settlement; ✆ 41094; e alexgould1973@gmail.com; contact Dot & Alex Gould. This newly opened self-catering property in the settlement sleeps 8 in 2 dbl & 2 twin rooms with a spacious lounge/dining area. **£££**

Pebble Island Lodge (6 rooms) Pebble Island settlement; ✆ 41093; e manager.pebblelodge@horizon.co.fk; w pebblelodge.com; contact Riki & Berna Evans. This lodge used to be the farm manager's house & is the largest building in the settlement. The majority of the island's visitors stay here as it can accommodate up to 15 people. It has 1 sgl, 1 dbl, 3 twin & 1 family room. All rooms are en suite & have tea- & coffee-making facilities. There is 1 public toilet which is available for all visitors to the island. The large lounge has an open peat fire & an honesty bar in one corner – to be used by guests here – with views across the island to Elephant Bay & Wreck Point. There is also a deck looking out in the same direction; the garden below is a magnet for small birds such as black-

chinned siskin & long-tailed meadowlark. Home-cooked meals are eaten in the separate dining room. These meals often include locally reared lamb, mutton, beef & fish, as well as goose, pâté, Falkland squid & a range of local jams, including diddle-dee. Typically, guests have b/fast & dinner at the lodge & spend the rest of the day on a tour (page 148), on which there'll be the opportunity to have a picnic lunch with *smoko* (usually a hot drink & a variety of cakes & biscuits). The large rooms & super views out over the settlement & further across the island give guests a feel of what it must have been like to live here as manager, knowing you were in charge of everything you could see. The lodge is centrally heated throughout & Wi-Fi is available by using a pre-paid card (available at most lodges across the islands & in shops in Stanley). The warm welcome visitors get on arrival at the lodge plus the knowledgeable guides leading tours of the abundant wildlife & interesting historical sites make for a memorable visit. **£££**

The Nest (1 room; plus dbl sofa bed) Pebble Island settlement ✆41094; e alexgould1973. gmail.com; contact Dot & Alex Gould. This self-catering cottage, situated in the settlement, sleeps 2–4 people in 1 bedroom where the bed can be made as a twin or king-size dbl & 1 dbl sofa-bed in the sitting room. It was originally renovated to be used by the visiting owners, but is now available for visitors. The main room is a kitchen-diner at one end & a lounge at the other. The managers can provide some basic food provisions, including local meat such as lamb or beef, milk, cream & local vegetables (when available). They can also assist with ordering any provisions from Stanley. The nearby lodge can provide meals & tours (page 147) to self-catering guests, but these need to be pre-booked. There is no TV or Wi-Fi. **££**

WHAT TO SEE AND DO

Pebble Island has so many different sites of interest that a stay of several days is needed to explore them all. The lodge provides a map, which indicates the main areas and the layout of the fences on the island. The deeper ponds on the flatter eastern half of the island are home to large numbers of waterfowl, while the wading birds prefer the shallow pools and the sandy expanses of the 6-mile-long (6.5km) Elephant Beach. Some of the more mountainous scenery can be found on the western half of the island. Driving on Pebble Island requires a high degree of concentration to avoid the softer patches in which it is easy to get bogged down, so the skill and local knowledge of your driver is essential.

Big Pond, Long Pond, Elephant Beach and the memorial to HMS *Coventry* on First Mountain are all only short walks from the settlement, and are easily reached by following the vehicle tracks over the *camp*. Otherwise, although fairly easy walking, most of the other sites of interest on Pebble Island are quite a distance from the lodge so going on a **guided 4x4 tour**, booked in advance with the lodge, is the only practical way of reaching them in a day. These tours cost £85 per person per full day. Drop off at various locations is also available from the lodge for up to £30 per person, depending upon your destination. This can happen in conjunction with a tour, if numbers permit. The tours follow grassy tracks over the island; your driver and guide know all the best places to visit and will give lots of information about the wildlife and historical sites.

It is also possible to utilise this pickup and drop-off service by going on several **day hikes** around the island – taking a packed lunch and returning to the lodge each night.

To get the best from Pebble Island it is advisable to spend at least one day exploring the island west of the settlement and one day east as they are so different with plenty to see.

AROUND THE SETTLEMENT The largest building in the settlement is the lodge. Nearby is the farm manager's modern house. The other houses are used by visiting sheep shearers and in the past for school staff. The latter, known as camp teachers, travel around the more isolated settlements, teaching school-age children before they move to the school in Stanley at the age of ten or 11. Between visits, the children are taught over the telephone from school in Stanley, although in the near future this will be replaced with online teaching. The shearing sheds and associated gathering pens are near the quay, as are the main farm buildings. The island's power is provided by the oil-fired generator situated towards the quay as well as wind power from a wind turbine. The lodge also has its own generator to supply electricity during the main part of the day. Water is obtained from the streams that run down from First Mountain. During the shearing periods in November, January and February, large numbers of sheep are driven to and from the gathering pens, so this area is best avoided at this time. Horses and cattle are found on the large grass fields near the settlement and do not usually take any notice of visitors. The island's graveyard is between the western end of Elephant Bay and the end of the airstrip.

Fish Creek, Shag Point and Sturgess Point One recommended walk from the settlement goes out to Sturgess Point via Fish Creek and Shag Point. Leaving the lodge, it's a short walk to the jetty, initially along higher ground, before dropping down. From here, take the track that heads towards the large shearing sheds, around 200yds away, and out along the shore on the southern side of the settlement. A further two jetties just before the sheds are ideal places to look for black-crowned night herons. They can be easily overlooked, as they remain motionless for so long while waiting for fish to swim by. The path continues south, following the coast past **Fish Creek**, only a few minutes' walk away, before climbing the slope that leads to **Shag Point**, a few hundred yards further on. Some 10 minutes further up this gentle slope, you will reach **Sturgess Point**. The views back over the settlement to the north and out over West Falkland in all directions are superb on a clear day, when the distant peaks of the hills in West Falkland can be seen standing up over the low-lying Golding and Middle islands. This is a good site to sit for a while, in calm weather, and look for any passing cetaceans. Commerson's dolphins are the most likely, but Peale's dolphins are also possible.

Elephant Beach and Big Pond In order to reach Elephant Beach, visitors must follow the track leading from the gate beside the sheepdog pens some 100yds from the lodge; cross the field past the aero-generator and the gorse-hedged fields, before heading towards the gap in the dunes behind the small pond. Walking or driving east towards Big Pond behind the sand dunes, this first pool is usually home to a pair of flying steamer ducks along with the more expected speckled teal and crested ducks. The short turf around this small pool, and around most of the ponds on the island, is cropped short by the upland geese and ruddy-headed geese that prefer these areas to the white-grass- or diddle-dee-covered areas.

There is a gap in the dunes between the small pond and the beach that brings you out on to **Elephant Beach**, a 4-mile-long stretch of hard sand which is used as the 'motorway' for those taking a 4x4 tour to reach the eastern parts of the island. Visitors can take a short walk west along the beach or stride out and take a longer walk to the northeast along the sand. In either direction there are usually flocks of Falkland steamer ducks waddling along the beach or surfing in the waves. Kelp gulls are ever present, sometimes on their own, but often in small groups, with brown-hooded gulls and dolphin gulls occasionally joining the flock. A scattering of crested ducks and magellanic oystercatchers can also be seen, and if you are lucky there may be some Commerson's dolphin out in **Elephant Bay**. Depending upon how much time you have, it is nice to amble west for a couple of hours and then cut back across to the lodge at the far end of the beach. There are no routes as such; it's just a matter of aiming for the very visible lodge situated on the bank at the top of the settlement. Those venturing away from the settlement, along the beach to the northeast, can walk for nearly 3 miles to Little Wreck Point, where you can watch Falkland steamer ducks waddling along the sand or small flocks of oystercatchers flitting to and fro. There may even be the chance to spot a dolphin or two playing in the surf. Alternatively, find a gap in the dunes at the top of the beach and cut back across to the track, from where you can head back to the settlement, eventually rejoining the track used at the start of the walk.

To reach **Big Pond**, stay on the grassy track that leads away from the small pond – a good place to look for long-tailed meadowlarks feeding in the rough grass – for a few minutes. The red-breasted males are surprisingly difficult to see at first but are worth the search as their bright red fronts make them a very attractive bird. Variable hawks can often be found perched, tucked out of the wind, high up on the bigger dunes. Big Pond, as the name suggests, is one of the largest on the island. It is also quite deep, which favours the diving birds that can be found here such as the many white-tufted grebes and the occasional rare species including great grebe. The shallow waters on the edge of the pond – close to the dunes on the seaward side of the pool – are the best location if looking for Chiloé wigeons among the numbers of grazing geese. These very wary birds do not usually allow close approach, especially if a variable hawk is nearby. By following the grass track, visitors will come to the small promontory on the western side of the pond, which has a profusion of almond-flower blooms in midsummer; both white and blue colour forms can be found here. The remains of the small jetty on this promontory are from the days before the airstrip was constructed; Beaver float planes landed directly on Big Pond until the late 1970s. From here, the track then continues between the dunes and the pond, giving visitors a good angle to look over the shallow part of the pool in case there is anything they've missed.

To visit all the other ponds on foot is rather impractical owing to the distances involved, as they are spread over a wide area. It is possible to get dropped off by Land Rover to explore these areas before being collected later in the day (page 148).

Victor Creek The second area within walking distance from the lodge is Victor Creek, a shallow creek created by Victor Point that juts out into the western side of Elephant Bay. Although a little further from the settlement, it is still only a 30-minute walk out over the white grass, along a little-used grassy track. To reach this site, follow the tracks up and over the airstrip, bearing right through a gate on the north side. This passes some of the fir trees that were planted in the 1980s. To reach the headland that forms the eastern arm of the creek (Victor Point) there is no track, but the walking is easy going. The area is full of magellanic penguin burrows so care has to be taken to make sure you do not tread in or step on top of one. At low tide, the creek is a good place to look for magellanic oystercatchers and numerous two-banded plovers. The latter can also be found roosting at the tip of Victor Point.

Heading back on the Elephant Bay side of the headland, the strand line is full of all sorts of odds and ends – from scrap-metal relics dating back to the 1982 war, to huge bones belonging to some very large whales that were stranded here many years ago. Some of the rib bones are so old that they look like lengths of curved timber thrown up by a recent gale. As with elsewhere in the Falkland Islands, any metal objects found here are best left alone. If you think they might be unexploded ordnance, make a note of the position and tell the staff at your accommodation. The old adage of taking only photos so that future visitors can see what you saw applies here, no matter how tempting to take that shell, bone or pebble might be.

THE EAST OF THE ISLAND A visit to the majority of the ponds on the eastern side of the island, the rockhopper penguin colonies and the sea lion site is a full 4x4 day trip from the lodge (page 148). The tour typically starts by visiting the Elephant Beach and Big Pond area (page 149) before heading further east. As there are a variety of routes there is no definite order to the sites visited, but the local knowledge of your driver will ensure you do not miss anything.

Betts Pond, Green Pond and Swan Pond A day can easily be spent visiting all the pools between Ship Harbour and Wreck Point. For **birdwatchers**, **Betts Pond** and **Green Pond** have the greatest variety of species, including both white-tufted grebes and silver grebes along with most of the ducks that breed in the Falklands. One of the specialities of Pebble Island is the large quantity of black-necked swans that breed here. They breed on many of the more suitable ponds, so that by late December many small cygnets can be seen following their parents in the middle of the ponds. Once these have reached maturity, they gather in large flocks, which can total over 100 individuals by the end of the breeding season. By midsummer, large numbers of wading birds have reached Pebble Island. At this time of year some of the pools are rather shallow, especially in drought years, which suits the shorter-legged species, such as white-rumped sandpiper and the occasional rarer species, such as Baird's sandpiper. Pebble Island also has a well-deserved reputation for attracting some of the rarer species of bird from South and North America. These have included white-winged coots, rosy-billed pochard, pectoral sandpipers on the pools and a variety of South American land birds around the settlement or on the few sheltered cliffs and tussac-grass banks. Such land birds have included tropical parula and the eastern kingbird. **Swan Pond** is the largest pond on the island but, despite its name, it is not always one of the best places to see swans. Good numbers of wildfowl can be seen along the sheltered edges, but it does not generally have as much to see as some of the smaller ponds, where speckled teal are common and smaller numbers of yellow-billed teal, silver teal and the ever-present crested duck can be found.

Tamar Point, Cape Tamar and Wreck Point The habitat beyond Swan Pond changes to a drier diddle-dee heath as it climbs to form the sea cliffs in the **Cape Tamar** area, a 10–15-minute drive away. There are several sites worth visiting along this rocky coastline. By following the track from the southern end of Swan Pond, having gone through the gate at the head of the pond, towards Tamar Point, along the eastern edge of Ship Harbour, large numbers of Falkland steamer ducks and a scattering of magellanic oystercatchers can be seen. Once past the next fence, there is a small rockhopper penguin colony at the edge of the cliff. A little further along the track there are more impressive rockhopper colonies to be seen, which soon become visible on the next headland. Almost every year there are two colonies of rockhopper penguins at this site, and large numbers of king shags also nest here. The king shags tend to move from colony to colony, so that they are in slightly different sites each summer. The presence of these breeding birds attracts scavengers such as dolphin gulls, kelp gulls, Falkland skuas and turkey vultures, making this a place of constant activity. In the late afternoon, many of the king shags come back to the colony, so there is a continuous stream of birds coming in to land.

By sitting on the small outcrop close to the aforementioned main rockhopper penguin colony, visitors can watch them come ashore and then hop their way up the cliff. Small groups of rockhoppers can be seen swimming around beyond the outer edge of the kelp beds that fringe the coast, before diving and reappearing at the base of the cliff. The small crags on the seaward side of the colony are a favourite haunt of peregrine falcons and southern caracara, although both species are rather shy and are not easy to see when perched. If the wind is onshore, good views can be obtained of black-browed albatrosses and sooty shearwaters as they pass by. In spring and autumn, a wider range of seabirds can be seen from here as onshore winds bring such species as southern fulmar and cape petrel within viewing range. In late summer there is the chance of seeing some of the few royal albatross that visit the region at this time of year. Becalmed, these mighty birds dwarf their nearest albatross neighbours.

Another couple of miles to the east is **Tamar Point**, a low headland looking across to West Falkland. This area is much to the liking of the many magellanic penguins whose burrows are everywhere, making the track difficult to follow as it twists and turns around them. The resident penguins are often stood watching the arrival of visitors, only to duck into their burrows as they pass by. The tidal stream can reach 10 knots between Tamar Point and West Falkland and this attracts large numbers of birds and the occasional southern sea lion. King shags and rock shags feed in large flocks when the tidal stream flows fastest, with black-browed albatrosses and sooty shearwaters skimming low over the water. With luck, prions or diving petrels can sometimes be observed in the rougher water. A telescope is very useful here to give you the best views of any distant wildlife.

Returning through the gate and following the rather vague track brings you out on to the **Cape Tamar** headland. Falkland thrift flowers in profusion most years along the cliff top. This is also an excellent site to watch southern sea lions. They are viewed from the ledges in the tussac grass above the rocky outcrop where they come ashore. It is not an easy scramble to the ledge above them, and should not be attempted by those who do not like heights. The sea lions haul themselves out on some sloping flat rocks close to the base of the cliff. Between these rocks and the cliff is a shallow pool in which they are often seen playing. Lumbering beasts on land, they are transformed into lithe, agile predators in the water. The steep rocks to the left of the viewing ledge harbour a small colony of rock shags. By late summer the wheezing calls of the young can be heard as their parents bring food to their growing brood. More black-browed albatrosses can be seen passing close by, especially in an onshore wind.

It is possible for your driver to take a different route back to the settlement by following the track out past **Wreck Point**. Between Wreck Point and the top of Elephant Beach are a large number of cetacean skeletons. These are the remains of pilot whales that were washed ashore, or 'wrecked', in the early 1980s, with at least one orca skeleton a little further along the beach. The teeth of this amazing predator are still as sharp as razors on its bleached skull. The journey back to the lodge along the hard sand of Elephant Beach is the easiest driving on the island. However, your driver will not always follow a straight line as there are some small, sharp rocky outcrops, and many birds use this beach, so it's not always a straightforward blast for home. The gap in the dunes back to the lodge can be difficult to see at times, as sand occasionally obscures the entrance, but from here it is only a 5-minute drive back to the lodge.

Phillips Cove and Ship Harbour Pond

For those with more time on the island and wanting a much longer walk (or drive), the track from Sturgess Point continues along past three more fences in a easterly direction inland of the low cliffs that look out towards the south. The track becomes rather difficult to follow at times, as it is little used so not so obvious to spot, but eventually leads to the scenic beach at **Phillips Cove** after around 30 minutes' driving. This narrow cove descends towards the sea – its mouth in a gentle curve with a small stream running down its length. It's a very lush area with many upland and red-headed geese feeding here. The steep sides of this site mean that it is often more sheltered than some of the island's other beaches, including Elephant Beach. It was at this beach that the SAS landed when they came to attack the Argentine aircraft on the airstrip in May 1982. The stream and small pool behind the shingle beach contain a variety of waterfowl including speckled teal and crested duck. In the past, king shags have nested on the low cliff to the south side of the beach and may reappear in the future so it's worth a look to see if they are around. Driving eastwards, the journey from Phillips Cove to **Ship Harbour Pond**, where black-necked swans and a few ducks can usually be found,

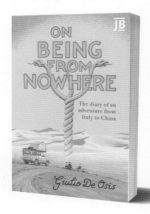

Extraordinary Experiences Designed by Experts

DMC/Local Operator for the Falkland Islands
Tailor-made Itineraries, Wildlife, Landscapes, Trekking & Hiking, Culture & Heritage, Adventure

An abundance of wildlife in its natural habitat (no man-made walkways or viewing platforms) that you are guaranteed to see, combined with very few humans (there is only about 3,500 of us!), and wide open spaces with big blue skies make the Falklands a mecca for keen naturalists and photographers, or for those just looking to get off the beaten track and enjoy a wild and unspoilt environment.

Discover the Falkland Islands and let us plan your trip to all the different destinations. We can guarantee a trip of a lifetime to some of the most natural habitats with abundant wildlife, amazing landscapes and some incredible adventures.

WELCOME TO
THE FALKLAND ISLAN

THE FALKLANDER travel

📞 00 52510

36 Ross Road, Stanley,   🌐 thefalklander.com   ✉ enquiries@thefalklander.com

takes around 10 minutes. The pond is shallow with a rocky edge and is situated in open terrain, with no nearby banks or hills. It is only a few minutes' drive from here to the main track near **Ship Harbour**.

THE WEST OF THE ISLAND The landscape on the western half of Pebble Island is much more arid than that on the east; there are no large pools, only small streams running towards the coast that can be difficult to ford without getting bogged down. Visiting this end of the island is usually done as a full-day driving tour, beginning at the lodge. This tour usually starts by visiting various sites on the northern coast, and eventually reaches the rockhopper penguin colonies at the Marble Mountain end of the island. The drive back in the afternoon usually takes visitors straight back to the lodge and takes around an hour.

Northern coast The northern coast to the west of the settlement is typified by rocky headlands and white sandy beaches as befits such an exposed landscape. The first stop when heading west is on the shoulder of **First Mountain** (277m) – only a 10-minute drive but a good 30-minute stiff walk for those wanting a post-dinner hike – where the **memorial to HMS** Coventry is situated, on a narrow outcrop overlooking the northeast of the island. At the site there is a cross and various memorial wreaths, held in a case. In clear weather, this vantage point gives an excellent view back over the settlement and then on out to West Falkland. In late spring and early summer several of the small, berried plants are in bloom at this site. One of these, the native strawberry, has edible fruit, which can be picked in late summer, assuming the local birds have not already eaten them.

The headlands on the northern coast can be worth a visit if time permits. These can be reached by turning off the main route to the west and following one of several vague grass tracks that are in this area. The local race of peregrine falcon, Cassin's falcon, favours these rocky outcrops. Often the only sign that a bird is present are the plucking posts where they have removed the feathers from their latest catch. Many small birds feed alongside the track, including white-bridled finches and Falkland pipits. If you are lucky, you may even see a grass wren or two. After roughly an hour's drive west, visitors will have reached the large colony of **gentoo penguins** that nest close to the track situated to the north of **Middle Peak** (214m), just inland from the headland known as Green Rincon. The track to this site heads north towards the coast just beyond the long fence running north to south and takes 5 minutes to drive. The birds make their nests on the level ground, a short distance from the beach to the east of the headland. They have moved their nesting site several times over the years, but still follow the same route back to the sea. The colony is surrounded by lush green circles of vegetation, which have prospered as a result of the penguin guano being dropped on the site, thereby enriching the soil below. When seen from the air these could be interpreted as Falkland's first crop circles!

There is much additional activity in the vicinity of **Green Rincon**, making this an ideal place to break the journey west. On the eastern slopes of the first beach you reach when travelling away from the gentoo penguin colony is a small colony of **southern giant petrels**. These birds should not be approached as the adults are very shy and will leave the nest at any sign of human interference; their young are then left at the mercy of the weather and any predators that happen to be in the area. The adults usually move away to sit on the sea and wait there until the cause of their panicked flight has moved on. It is possible to walk out to the headland behind these birds by keeping below the skyline on the east side of the Cape. There is a small colony of **rock shags** tucked away on the lower cliffs and a pair of

variable hawks is often in the area. Usually your driver will drop you here and drive around to pick you up at the far (western) end of the beach, giving you the chance to stretch your legs. The easiest way on to the beach is to follow the small valley at the eastern end. The worn track in the middle of the beach is the runway that the gentoo penguins use on their way to and from their colony. There are usually a good number of birds loafing on the sand at the water's edge, some asleep, others preening ready to go back to sea. There are always a few birds moulting as the immature penguins change their feathers in the summer, earlier than the breeding adults, ready for the rigours of winter. **Falkland steamer ducks** are also found along the shining white sand along with a scattering of **magellanic penguins** and a few **magellanic oystercatchers**. All these birds are potential prey for **sea lions**, which can occasionally be seen cruising through the shallows, hunting for any unwary bird. Their presence is usually signalled by a small mob of gulls and shags that tag along behind hoping for any leftover scraps.

Green Rincon, the headland, an easy stroll up from the beach, is a good spot for a picnic, with several rocky outcrops providing shelter and superb views over the island, looking either southeast towards First Mountain; southwest towards Middle Peak or west towards Marble Mountain. **Southern caracara** can sometimes be seen around this headland along with the occasional juvenile **striated caracara** that have left their breeding grounds on the Jason Islands to the northwest.

Around Marble Mountain

The track west from Green Rincon drops down on to the western beach for several hundred yards before climbing back up on to the plateau. Some of the bright green slopes near Marble Mountain are very wet and, therefore, can be very difficult to cross in a vehicle, but your driver will know where to do so. Trying to pick out the route before they drive over it is a good challenge for those interested. About half a mile from the beach, the track passes a small **memorial** that is situated behind white fencing. This marks the crash site of an Argentinian Learjet that was shot down by HMS *Exeter* during the war in 1982. The fence surrounds the stone memorial topped with a cross. Two outlines of white stones on either side mark the graves of the two airmen buried here.

The largest **rockhopper penguin colony** on the island is on the coast to the north of Marble Mountain. By following the right-hand fork in the track, visitors round a small hill to find a mass of birds on the grassy slopes at the top of a rocky headland. Although the cliff is not as high as the site this species of penguin uses near Cape Tamar (page 151), it is still a difficult climb for these charismatic birds. It is an easy walk on which to sit at various points around the colony to watch all the comings and goings. As with the other colonies, there are many different scavenging birds present. The **turkey vultures**, for instance, take off when approached, while others, such as **kelp gulls** and **dolphin gulls**, just keep a wary distance. Many penguins can be seen at the bottom of the cliff using the rock pools as a communal bath.

At least one pair of **macaroni penguins** has been breeding in this colony over the years, and is occasionally joined by other lone birds. They are slightly larger than their rockhopper cousins but the best features to look for are the thicker, brighter bill and the distinctive orange-yellow crests, which meet above the eye. The crests of the rockhopper penguins are thinner, more yellow and do not meet above the eye. They have tended to use the same area in the colony, furthest away from the main access path to the sea. This species breeds in small numbers in the Falkland Islands and, as such, is never easy to see – this site, along with those on Saunders Island, is the most reliable visitor site for macaroni penguins. This island was also the summer home of an erect-crested penguin from 1997 to 2007. This much rarer species is normally found on the sub-Antarctic islands of New Zealand and was probably only the third record on Falkland.

Some of the best **pebble beaches** are at the far western end of Pebble Island. These can be reached by rejoining the main track near the rockhopper penguin colony and heading west for half a mile or so. As the track bends around Marble Mountain, there is a faint track towards a gate on the slight rise to the right. By following this track along the valley below for a few hundred yards, visitors come to a small pool, which can be a good site for **speckled teal** and the usual scattering of **upland geese** and **ruddy-headed geese**. There is no defined path through to the beach, and beyond this point there are several wet areas to be avoided before reaching the shore, but your driver will circumnavigate any such problems. The shingle beach, Pebble Cove, changes profile after each storm. This constant movement results in very rounded pebbles, some of which are very attractive and well worth searching for, but refrain from taking any as souvenirs. **Southern sea lions** can be seen in the distance on the shores of **Pebble Islet**. The gap between the two islands is a favoured short cut for **rock shags** and **king shags**. **Magellanic penguins** nest in the drier ground between the valley and the beach; the burrows often destabilise what looks like firm ground, making walking a little treacherous at times. As ever, where magellanic penguins are nesting it's worth spending a moment to look for the route through them that causes the least disturbance, either by going around the area altogether or plotting a path through the least-dense part of the colony.

The only building at the far end of the island is the rather run-down **shanty** which you will pass on the way to the beach. The gorse bushes that have been planted here sometimes harbour some of the smaller birds, for example **black-chinned siskins** and **white-bridled finches**. Heading back up on to the main track, the route then follows around the contour on the southwest side of Marble Mountain back towards the settlement.

Southern shore

A non-stop drive back to the lodge takes over an hour from the Marble end of the island. Along this route, you can look out southwest over the ocean; on a clear day Saunders Island can be seen beyond the nearest island, Keppel.

The tracks on the southern side of the island, near Middle Mountain, tend to be more braided than those on the northern side of the three hills. This is often due to sections becoming too wet to get through, so alternative routes have been created. Time and weather permitting, it might be worth visiting the area around **Rabbit Island**, which can be a good site for ducks, geese and the occasional flock of waders such as white-rumped sandpipers and two-banded plovers. This area is reached by following a track leading towards the western end of the island, only 5 minutes off the main track. Although it is not possible to visit the island without a boat it's worth spending a few minutes looking for the species mentioned. The southern side of Pebble Island is much more sheltered than the north shore, and therefore has more sandy and muddy bays with a greater variety of marine life than could survive on the more exposed coasts, with a variety of bivalves and invertebrates dwelling in the mud. It is in these bays that kelp geese and black-crowned night herons can be found, along with several pairs of blackish oystercatchers.

The last part of the journey back to the lodge crosses the airstrip, where the remains of some of the Argentine aircraft blown up on the ground by the SAS during the night raid on 14 May 1982 can be seen beside the runway. There is also a small memorial plaque to this assault at the eastern end of the airstrip, a few yards from the shed housing the fire tender. From here it's a 10-minute walk or 2-minute drive back to the lodge – the end of an excellent day out.

9

Saunders Island and Keppel Island

These two mountainous islands are situated to the northwest of West Falkland. Keppel Island is no longer inhabited and can only be reached by those with a boat as there is no airstrip, although at the time this book went to print this private island allowed no access to visitors. Saunders Island, meanwhile, is an active sheep farm with self-catering accommodation used throughout the year and has one of the best airstrips away from the major settlements. Both islands have black-browed albatross colonies along with colonies of rockhopper, gentoo and magellanic penguins.

SAUNDERS ISLAND

This island, lying 3 miles off the northwest coast of West Falkland, comprises 30,000 acres with just over 66 miles of coastline and is operated as one farm. It is historically important in the islands as it was the site of the first British settlement in 1765 (page 7). The present-day settlement is situated at the base of a range of hills, the highest of which is Rookery Mountain (1,384ft/422m). The high cliffs to the north of this range are home to many breeding seabirds, in particular black-browed albatrosses and rockhopper penguins. These hills are separated from the highest peak on the island, Mount Harston (1,421ft/436m) by a sandy isthmus known as The Neck. The southwestern part of the island reaches 1,220ft (372m) at the summit of Mount Rees. The lower land between the settlement and Mount Rees has some pools and is the site of the island's airstrip. The island has become well known as being home to one of the most accessible black-browed albatross colonies on Falkland situated along the northern coasts. However, Saunders Island has much else to offer, with The Neck area in particular having a diverse selection of breeding seabirds, including a small colony of king penguins.

HISTORY The first British base on Falkland, about 30 minutes' walk along the coast from the present-day settlement, was set up at Port Egmont in 1765 by Commodore John Byron, who was in command of the British expedition to explore Falkland. A British Captain, John McBride, established a proper settlement there on 8 January 1766. This settlement was attacked by a Spanish force commanded by Don Juan Ignacio de Madariaga in 1770, after which the British returned home, having signed an article of capitulation when it became obvious they were outnumbered. (In 1998, the British military forces on Falkland restored the graves of the Royal Marines buried at Port Egmont; page 161.) After lengthy negotiations – under the threat of war – between Britain and Spain, an agreement was signed on 22 January giving Port Egmont back to the British. The Spaniards surrendered possession on 15 September 1771, passing control of the settlement to Captain Scott who was commanding the frigate *Juno*, the sloop *Hound* and the store ship *Florida*. The British withdrew from

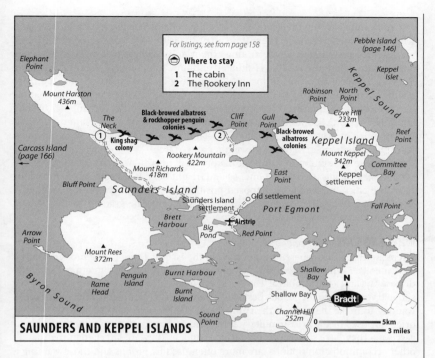

For listings, see from page 158

⊖ **Where to stay**
1 The cabin
2 The Rookery Inn

Elephant
Point

Mount Harston
436m

The
Neck

Black-browed albatross
& rockhopper penguin
colonies

King shag
colony

Cliff
Point

Gull
Point

Black-browed
albatross
colonies

Pebble Island
(page 146)

Keppel
Islet

Keppel Sound

Robinson
Point

North
Point

Cove Hill
233m

Reef
Point

Keppel Island

Mount Keppel
342m

Committee
Bay

Carcass Island
(page 166)

Bluff Point

Saunders Island

Mount Richards
418m

Rookery Mountain
422m

East
Point

Old settlement

Saunders Island
settlement

Port Egmont

Keppel
settlement

Fall Point

Arrow
Point

Mount Rees
372m

Brett
Harbour

Big
Pond

Airstrip

Red Point

Byron Sound

Rame
Head

Penguin
Island

Burnt Harbour

Burnt
Island

Shallow
Bay

N

Shallow Bay

Channel Hill
252m

Bradt

Sound
Point

0   5km
0   3 miles

SAUNDERS AND KEPPEL ISLANDS

Falkland in 1774, leaving behind a flag and a plaque at Port Egmont that claimed ownership of the islands. There was no direct action here during the war in 1982.

Since the 1990s, the island has widened its economic base by opening up to tourism, with the provision of two self-catering cottages (one in the settlement and one at the Rookery) and a portacabin at The Neck. Generally, there are only four to five people living on the island at any one time, who are usually busy transporting visitors between the settlement, The Neck and the Rookery, as well as looking after the accommodation. The island also welcomes cruise-ship visits, where visitors are met on the beach by the owners and welcomed to the island.

The island has been an active sheep farm continuously since the 19th century and nowadays is thriving with some 6,000 sheep. During the shearing periods (December, January and February), when the visiting shearing gang are at work, the settlement is a hub of activity.

GETTING THERE AND AWAY As with the other outlying islands, there are two ways for tourists to reach Saunders Island – via boat or by air. Travellers can get to the island by **air** using FIGAS (w falklands.gov.fk/aviationservice; £137.52 from Stanley; for booking information, see page 58), booking seats on its daily service around the islands. A direct flight from Stanley takes around 40 minutes. Flights can also go via other settlements (at no extra cost) depending on demand. Visitors will be met at the airstrip, one of the best on the outer islands, and taken to the accommodation. For those staying at the settlement there is no transfer fee, but for those staying at the Rookery Inn and in the cabin at The Neck transfer fees apply (£30 return to the Rookery Inn and £70 to The Neck). The self-catering house in the settlement is only a 5-minute drive from the airstrip, whereas the properties at The Neck and the Rookery take longer to reach – the former can take up to an hour.

Cruise ships visiting the island land at either side of The Neck (depending upon which is the sheltered side). There is no quay, so visitors are transferred to the beach via Zodiacs, resulting in a wet landing. The island's owners will meet guests there and explain where the wildlife is situated and how to maximise the time available. They also have a selection of local, homemade gifts and postcards for sale from a suitcase in the back of their vehicle. These Zodiac landings usually only allow visitors to stay on the island for a morning or an afternoon, as the ship has usually combined visiting Saunders with other islands such as New, West Point or Carcass. The number of cruise ships visiting the island varies from year to year, but most visits typically happen between November and March.

For those **sailing** around the islands on their own boat, there is a jetty at the settlement which is used by the inter-island freight boat. It is also possible to anchor near The Neck, but this is an exposed position so a careful eye on the weather is needed. Before landing on the island permission must be granted by the owners (☎41298; e saunders@horizon.co.fk; w saundersfalklands.com).

🏠 WHERE TO STAY *Map, page 157*

There are three sites where one can stay on the island. There is one property in the settlement, a 5-minute drive from the airstrip; one at Rookery Mountain, a 40-minute drive away; and a portacabin at The Neck, a good hour's drive away. The latter two are situated very close to the island's best wildlife and are very popular with photographers wanting to make the most of their time here. The properties in the settlement were originally used by the British military as rest and recuperation centres for the Falkland garrison. They have since been modernised and, as they are larger than the island's other accommodation options, are more often used by groups and those wanting a fully catered option. These are very popular and usually have to be booked well in advance of your arrival in the Falkland Islands. In fact, it is inadvisable to travel to Saunders Island at all without having pre-booked your accommodation.

The accommodation on the island is usually self-catering, but full board can be arranged for the properties in the settlement on request. For those opting for self-catered accommodation, the farm can usually provide milk and eggs (although it is a good idea to check before departure whether this will be the case during your stay). The farm animals are quite inquisitive about any visitors on the island and, for those staying in the settlement, it's not unusual to find a horse looking in the sitting-room windows as they graze the grass between the settlement buildings. There is also a small store that has a limited selection of basic supplies including food and drink.

It is also possible to **camp** on the island (£20 pp/night), as long as permission has been granted by the owners. As it is wild camping there are no facilities. The locations for camping will vary through the summer depending on which areas the sheep are using at any given time. For all accommodation contact David and Suzan Pole-Evans (☎41298; e saunders@horizon.co.fk; w saundersfalklands.com), the island's owners.

The cabin (2 rooms) The Neck. The accommodation at The Neck is of a more basic nature in a 2-room portacabin, which is capable of sleeping 8 in 4 bunk beds. The building is carpeted throughout & is fully equipped, including 24hr power & Wi-Fi. It is quite probable that visitors will see no-one else while staying here. A small radio transceiver is available on request. There is an ordinary radio provided to enable you to listen to the daily flight announcements, news, etc. The wildlife in this area is superb, the majority of which is within easy walking distance of the portacabin, making it a popular place with photographers. For those wanting longer walks from the property, there are elephant seals & spectacular scenery at the far northwest end of the island at Elephant

Point (page 163). There is no minimum stay, but to take full advantage of this fantastic area, 1 night is not enough. **££**

The Rookery Inn (2 rooms) Rookery Mountain. This is the newest property on the island & is on the northern side of Rookery Mountain, on the northeast of the island, close to the albatross, penguin & cormorant colonies. The fully equipped building sleeps 4 guests in 2 twin bedrooms. It was purpose built as tourist accommodation & is therefore more modern than the accommodation in the settlement. Other than the bedrooms, there is a toilet, shower & sink, & a kitchen/dining area. As it is self-catering accommodation, you have to plan ahead to make sure you have everything you need for a stay here – it's a very long walk back to the settlement! The property has a real away-from-it-all feel to it, & guests will appreciate having the surrounding wildlife all to themselves. It is only a few mins' walk to the albatross cliffs & a little further to the rockhopper penguin colonies – an evening stroll to watch the young albatross is a nice way to end the day. In case of an emergency, the owners leave a handheld radio, allowing guests to call the settlement if needed. **££**

The Settlement (5 rooms) Saunders Island settlement. A refurbished bunk house, this self-catering cottage can sleep 10 people in 2 twin, 1 dbl, 1 sgl & 1 trpl room. There is central heating throughout, a shared shower room, bathroom & 2 toilets plus another separate shower room. There is also a well-equipped kitchen & a sitting room with TV, radio & Wi-Fi that works throughout the building. This is a quirky building that feels much bigger on the inside than it looks from the outside. The front door leads into the main room with the main bedrooms to either side, whereas the back door leads directly into the kitchen, from where the sgl room can be accessed. When the weather is inclement there is plenty of room for all guests to sit in the lounge & watch the outside world from the comfort of the easy chairs. Bed linen & towels are provided. **££**

WHAT TO SEE AND DO There is superb walking in the vicinity of the house in the settlement. It is possible to book 4x4 excursions from the settlement; both The Neck and the Rookery – the two main sites on the island – are easily reached on day trips from here. Tours out to The Neck are only run for those spending a minimum of two nights in the settlement. At busy times of year on the farm, during shearing periods, for instance, these trips may be curtailed by an hour or so, depending upon other demands on the island owners' time.

There are no 4x4 excursions from the Rookery or The Neck, but those staying at the Rookery Inn or in the cabin at The Neck will have abundant wildlife on their doorsteps – both areas have large colonies of black-browed albatrosses and rockhopper penguins, plus a variety of other birdlife and the occasional passing seal or dolphin. Visitors staying here will have plenty to see.

Around the settlement The settlement contains the main house, the self-catering accommodation, and a mixture of large and small **sheds**, including the shearing shed that is a hive of activity when the shearing gang are visiting. On an evening walk down to the **jetty**, visitors will sometimes spot a roosting group of rock shags, and a lucky few have seen a whale or two in the distance in late summer.

A short walk (less than a mile along the only track out of the settlement to the southwest) leads you out to the airstrip and then to some pools that have sheltered both silver grebes and white-tufted grebes, a variety of ducks and the occasional black-necked swan. In 1984 the largest of the pools, **Big Pond**, which is the closest to the settlement, accommodated the largest flock of cinnamon teal that the islands have ever seen when around 20 birds were present. It was thought that they bred there that year. As with any island that lies on the west of the Falklands, there is always the chance that an unusual bird or two will have made its way from South America. There are no large colonies of seabirds in these parts other than a few magellanic penguins and some rock shags. Waders, such as blackish oystercatcher and magellanic oystercatcher, make their nests along the shores and some of the islands' songbirds, including the Falkland thrush and Falkland pipit, can be found in the more sheltered places, out of the wind. A few South American terns nest near the airstrip most years and can be seen quite easily as they make a terrific din, driving away marauding Antarctic skuas from their breeding grounds.

The southwestern part of the island that lies beyond these pools is little visited by the majority of visitors owing to the abundance of wildlife at the better-known sites.

The wildlife colonies below Rookery Mountain The main attraction of Saunders Island for wildlife enthusiasts is the large colony of black-browed albatrosses that breed along the cliffs on the north coast below Rookery Mountain. The drive out to the colony as part of a day trip from the settlement takes visitors out through the gathering pens before climbing some rather steep slopes to the northeast, through some of the largest areas of *Blechnum magellanicum* (tall fern) on Falkland before descending to the coast. Depending upon the state of the tide, the track either follows the coastal route or crosses a stream and continues along the beach for a few hundred yards. On the rather low-lying land between this beach and the next, visitors start to see **penguins** for the first time. Small numbers of magellanic penguins nest on the more arid slopes while gentoo penguins have a small colony a short distance back from the second beach. They can often be seen gathering on the beach in small parties. If time permits, this rather scenic part of the island can provide an interesting 10-minute or so stop, as the sight of penguins stood on a white-sand beach against a mountain backdrop is a photographer's dream.

After climbing the steep track at the far side of the second beach, it is approximately a 10–15-minute drive before the **black-browed albatross colony** is reached. Visitors are usually allowed to remain for at least a couple of hours at this spectacular site. The time spent here will be dictated by the weather and if the owners who are driving you out there have other commitments back in the settlement. Upon reaching the site, the owners usually leave visitors to their own devices, though they normally give a quick briefing before allowing you to explore. A diddle-dee heath runs down from the top of Rookery Mountain to the edge of the cliff. Small clumps of tussac grass occur on the steeper sections of cliff where they are out of the reach of grazing sheep. The high cliffs drop straight into the sea and are therefore particularly dangerous on windy days. There are many wet patches where water runs off the hill out to the sea. These can be rather boggy and slippery. There is also a narrow channel of clear water between the kelp beds that surround the shore and the cliff edge.

The albatross colony is situated along the coast on the top section of the cliff. The adults are present between September and April, the eggs are laid during October and fledged young leave the nest between mid-March and early April. The ideal conditions for observing the colony are bright sunshine and an onshore wind. There is then ample opportunity to try and take the ultimate flight shot of these elegant birds as they cruise low over the clifftop. It is possible to sit a few yards from the colony with birds passing low overhead. As with all wildlife, it is advisable to keep a good distance away from these birds (Falklands Conservation's code of conduct states 6m), so that they are not disturbed and therefore allowed to behave naturally. During the incubation period in October and November, the colony is relatively quiet after the noise of the courtship displays at the beginning of the season in September to November. The only sounds are the greetings of these giant birds to each other as they swap over incubation duties. When the young birds are big enough to be left, both parents fly out to sea, gathering food such as lobster krill and squid. These fluffy white young creatures are a comical sight on the mud-pot nests. As some of these nests have been used over many years they have been built up into quite substantial structures. Many of those birds that are not occupied around the actual breeding site can be seen at sea beyond the distant kelp beds. There is constant movement of albatrosses in and out of the colony throughout the day. They have been studied over the years as part of a project to discover more information about these long-lived birds. This is why some of the birds will be noted as having metal rings on their legs, thus enabling researchers to identify individuals. It is thought that they may well live for around 50 years, so some of these ringed birds should be coming back to nest here for many years to come.

As with all seabird colonies, scavengers are ever present. In this case, the scavengers are usually turkey vultures, southern giant petrels and the occasional stray immature striated caracara later in the summer. There is also a constant stream of rock shags and king shags flying past as these birds also have colonies nearby. The main **king shag colony** is to the southwest near The Neck, while small groups of **rock shags** breed on many of the cliffs in the vicinity. Small birds are not common on this exposed site apart from the ubiquitous dark-faced ground-tyrants, which seem to be able to survive in almost any habitat on Falkland. They are usually seen flitting around on the cliff face below the nesting albatrosses.

The flora is not very varied at the site of the albatross colony, although small clumps of berry-lobelia can be found along with pigvine (*Gunnera magellanica*) in the short-grazed turf.

This albatross colony stretches in a westerly direction along the coast until it reaches The Neck in the far distance. By walking along in this direction for half an hour or so, visitors come across a colony of **rockhopper penguin** scattered in three or four satellite sites. All of these birds use the same path to get back to the sea. By remaining discreetly to one side, it is possible to watch these tough little birds porpoising their way through the surf before leaping ashore to begin the arduous climb up the cliff to reach their nest. Many can be seen to have black or red stains on their otherwise gleaming white front. This colour comes from the lobster krill (red) or squid (black) that they have been catching. They are very inquisitive birds and will often come over to investigate anyone or anything unusual near the track. Rockhopper penguin colonies are rather raucous places, as each bird greets its mate on its return from the sea. This din, when combined with the cries of the young, is unforgettable. Most years, during the summer months, **macaroni penguin** turn up at this site, but they do not always stay for the whole season if they remain unpaired. If only one bird is present it is thought that they are pairing up with the rockhoppers and thus producing hybrid young. They can sometimes appear again in late summer, having spent a couple of weeks away from the colony fattening up before coming ashore to moult and grow their new feathers, which can take over three weeks.

The narrow channel between the cliffs and the kelp is occasionally used by **Peale's dolphins**. **Fur seals** and **southern sea lions** have also been seen swimming along this channel.

The return trip to the settlement can either follow the same route, if time is limited, or you can follow an alternative coastal track if there is more time. The longer route takes you past the beaches and around a headland to the **original location of the Port Egmont settlement**. If you park up on the south side of the bay, it is only a short walk of a few yards to see the remains of this historic site. The most visible feature above this shallow valley is the site of the restored **graves of the five Royal Marines** killed at the end of the 1700s. The largest edifice on the other side of the valley is the remains of a large, **stone-built structure** lying parallel to the shore. This was once the living quarters and main building for the British forces stationed here in 1766. Visitors can wander around this small site trying to imagine what it would have been like to be stationed here without any modern amenities. You had to be tough to survive here. Close by is the plaque marking the historical importance of the site, as it was the first British settlement on the Falkland Islands. This little valley, where these original settlers obtained their water, is a good place to look for fachine, one of the few native bushes on Falkland.

The Neck The drive out to The Neck, one of the Falklands' best wildlife sites, takes an hour or so along the track from the settlement, which can be rather rough depending upon the recent weather conditions. This isthmus is only a 10-minute walk, from the foothills of Mount Richards to the southeast and Mount Harston to the northwest. It takes about 5 minutes to cross between the beaches on either side of the isthmus meaning the whole area is very accessible. It can be visited in a day if visitors are staying at the settlement; there is so much to see that it is not really practical to combine it with a trip to the Rookery Mountain site. This is a favoured site for visiting cruise ships as it is possible to land on whichever is the sheltered side of The Neck. The low sandy bank between the hills has been scoured by the wind over many years, making this an ideal breeding site for **gentoo penguins and magellanic penguins**. The gentoo penguins have at least nine satellite sites for this extended colony. Birds seem to be coming and going from both beaches, which can be easily accessed from the gently sloping grassy inclines either side. In the past, a lone chinstrap penguin was occasionally seen mixing with the gentoo penguins. It was a rather shy bird and would soon disappear upon the arrival of humans. Although this was some time ago, chinstrap penguins can occur in any penguin colony at odd times, so keep a lookout. This flat land is also popular with large numbers of roosting gulls, and small flocks of waders have been noted at times.

There is very little variation in the flora due to the sand blasting that occurs during the frequent gales; however, there are some nice clumps of sea cabbage and some of the oreob family are represented on the banks at either end. The grassy banks are home to the small colony of **king penguins**, which started to breed here in the late 1980s and have slowly been increasing over the years. As it is a relatively new colony, disturbance must be kept to a minimum. It is requested that everyone stay outside the markers, which have been placed around the colony.

There is no obvious path beyond the king penguins' territory along the northwest coast but it is worth persevering over some wire fences on the upper slopes. After some 15–20 minutes you will reach a large **rockhopper penguin colony** on the steeper slopes. As with all grassy cliffs on Falkland, this can be dangerous in wet or windy weather. In the past, this colony has also contained a small number of **macaroni penguins**. Large numbers of **king shags** nest in with the rockhopper penguins so that, apart from the comings and goings of the penguins along their track to the water, there is a constant aerial passage of shags dropping in and taking off from the colony. Throughout the breeding season, the shags bring back seaweed to use in nest building, with the constant problem of neighbouring birds stealing much of the material for their own nests. The result is a very vigorous colony.

Only a short distance away, continuing east along the coast, is the start of the elongated **colony of black-browed albatrosses**, which extends all the way to the foot of Rookery Mountain (page 160). The majority of these birds tend not to fly over The Neck itself but keep out over the open sea. Consequently, although it is still easy to watch the birds on the nest, there are not so many birds to be observed flying by at close range. When up on the higher slopes, either here at The Neck or indeed at the Rookery, on calm days in late summer it is worth keeping an eye out for various large **whales**, the most likely being sei whale, which can sometimes be seen feeding in the bay.

Walks from The Neck For people staying at The Neck with more time at their disposal than those arriving on a day trip, there are many enjoyable walks. Elephant seals can be found at **Elephant Point**, the furthest point on the island from the settlement and over 3 miles away from The Neck, when travelling in a straight line. As there are no specific paths, the actual distance walked to reach here will be further, so count on a good day's walk from the cabin. There are some small pools just inland from Elephant Point which have harboured a variety of wildfowl, including the odd scarce species coming in from South America, such as white-winged coot and rosy-billed pochard. Not all the burrows that are widespread on this northern side of Mount Harston belong to magellanic penguins, as rabbits are also found in this area.

For those wanting to head uphill, the view from the top of **Mount Harston** (433m) looks back down to The Neck. On a clear day you can see across to Carcass Island and West Point Island and over to the Jasons away on the northwest horizon. The Neck is less than a mile away from the hill, and although the walk is steep, with no clear route to follow (meaning it can take up to a couple of hours), it's not especially difficult.

From the shore, look out for cetaceans such as Commerson's dolphins in calm weather, which have been seen close inshore all around the island. Meanwhile, southern right whales have been noted in deeper waters, especially in late summer.

KEPPEL ISLAND

Keppel Island has many interesting geographical features and significant figures in the history of the Falkland Islands. There is no airstrip here, so the island can only be accessed by sea, although at present it is not possible to travel to this island as the owners do not allow visitors. Therefore, the only chance visitors have of viewing the wildlife on the island is at a distance, usually from the windows of the plane on the flight between Pebble Island and Saunders Island. The northwestern end of the island has a low cliff along which there is a linear colony of black-browed albatrosses and some colonies of rockhopper penguins. Those islanders who worked on the island until 1992 have described the old settlement – situated on the flatter southeastern side of the island – and its gardens as a good place for smaller birds, including dark-faced ground-tyrants and Falkland thrushes, although the reported presence of feral cats means that there are unlikely to be a wide range of the smaller seabirds nesting nowadays. The flight between the islands can also be an opportunity to look for any cetaceans, such as Commerson's or Peale's dolphins, that happen to be swimming in the shallow water.

The island is named after Admiral Augustus Keppel who was First Lord of the Admiralty in Britain in the 18th century. It has a unique history in the islands due to the establishment of the South American Missionary Society here in the mid 1800s. The present owner, a Mr L Fell, runs it as a private nature reserve. The island is closer to Saunders Island (1 mile away) than to Pebble Island (5 miles away) and extends over approximately 9,600 acres, reaching a peak of 1,122ft (342m) on Mount Keppel. The southwestern part of the island is much higher above sea level than the low-lying land to the northeast. It is in the latter area that pools can be found, depending on recent rainfall.

HISTORY Allen W Gardiner, who was the son of the founder of the South American Missionary Society, leased the island in 1885. It has been described as the first established farm in the western Falklands and soon became a very profitable business. The island was to be a base from which the society could then voyage to Tierra del Fuego to try to Christianise the native inhabitants, the Yaghan (or Yamana) people. The Yaghans were brought to the island to be taught and trained. This mission continued as a farm and training centre for Yaghan people and as a base for missionary work in Tierra del Fuego and Patagonia until the death of the then superintendent, Thomas Bridges, in 1898. During that time the farm had prospered, so that by 1877 it was bringing in £1,000 per annum from its sheep, cattle and extensive vegetable gardens. The remaining Yaghans were taken to a new mission on the South American mainland, which resulted in the closure of the Keppel Mission.

The island continued as a farm until 1911 when it was sold to the Dean brothers, who also owned nearby Pebble Island (page 145). The island was sold again in 1988 to Mr L Fell, and the farm continued to be used until the island was cleared of stock in 1992 to become a nature reserve. One of the largest buildings in the settlement is the farm manager's house and another is the old chapel, which was converted into a shearing shed in the early 1900s. This island was deserted in 1992 and has been uninhabited ever since. Barn owls are taking up residence in the decaying buildings – nature is slowly taking charge again.

10

Carcass Island, West Point Island and New Island

These three islands, lying to the west of West Falkland, are some of the most remote inhabited islands in Falkland. All three are privately owned, yet are open for tourism. Only Carcass takes in staying visitors on a regular basis, but an ever-growing number of tourists call at each of the islands every year on cruise ships. It is possible to visit West Point Island as a day trip on a boat from Carcass Island, but New Island is generally only visited by cruise-ship passengers. All are rather mountainous, with some very impressive cliffs on West Point and New islands. These cliffs are the ideal breeding grounds for large numbers of black-browed albatross and have extensive penguin rookeries. Carcass Island is also home to large numbers of small birds, as neither cats nor rats have become established here.

CARCASS ISLAND

This island, owned by Rob and the late Lorraine McGill, lies at the outer end of Byron Sound, to the northwest of West Falkland. The nearest inhabited settlements are West Point Island, some 7 miles away to the southwest; Dunbar on West Falkland, 8 miles away to the southeast; and Saunders Island, 10 miles to the east. The island lies roughly northwest to southeast and is one of the most picturesque in the Falklands group. The abundance of songbirds, luxuriant growth around the settlement and gently rolling landscape, with rounded hills, give it a very different ambience from any other island in the Falklands. The ridges of these hills extend along the spine of almost all of the 5-mile length of the island, sloping down to beaches on the western shores and to a low cliff on the northeastern side, ending on the flatter areas near the airport in the northwest and finishing at North West Point.

HISTORY The island is named after HMS *Carcass*, a Royal Navy ship under the command of Captain Pattison, which reached the Falkland Islands in 1766. The island has only had three owners in nearly 150 years of inhabitation. It was first inhabited in 1872, when Charles Hanson, a Dane who was looking for land on the Falklands, leased Carcass, the Jasons and some of the smaller islands nearby. He set up a sheep farm on the island, built the settlement in its current location and set up the fencing system. He also planted tussac grass to use as winter feed for his animals when the grass was not as luxurious. He later passed the island on to his son who subsequently sold it to a partnership that included Cecil and Kitty Bertrand, who continued to farm in an environmentally friendly way. They later took on sole ownership of the island, until it was bought by Rob and Lorraine McGill in 1974.

The abundance of small birds is down to the foresight of these owners in having kept the island cat- and rat-free – a remarkable achievement. Nowadays, the island is home to Rob and his staff – usually two or three members during the tourist season. It is still a sheep farm, but their main focus is tourism and they are rightly proud of the fact that they are self-sufficient in meat and dairy produce (they make some wonderful butter) and grow their own organic vegetables.

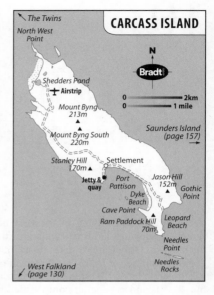

GETTING THERE AND AWAY The **airstrip** that's used by FIGAS (w falklands.gov. fk/aviationservice; £163.32 one-way from Stanley; for booking information, see page 58) is at the north of the island, a 20-minute drive from the settlement. The flight time for those travelling direct from Stanley is roughly 40 minutes, depending on the wind direction. Transport to and from the airstrip is by 4x4, arranged with the lodge (see below), and is included in the cost of your stay there. Although some visitors fly into the island, the majority arrive as passengers on **cruise ships**. Cruise-ship tourists only wanting to see the settlement use the small jetty at Port Pattison – more often used by inter-island boats when landing goods for the settlement – but the majority land on the beaches at the south end of the island in their inflatable dinghies, from where they can visit the penguin colonies. These visitors can later walk up to the settlement for a look around, to sample the famous cakes and to have a tea or coffee in the large kitchen. Those landing at the southern end of the island can land on Leopard Beach, or on Dyke Beach on the northern side of Gothic Point Paddock, depending on which is the most sheltered. There is free **self-drive vehicle** hire available from the accommodation (see below) for those with some off-road experience.

 WHERE TO STAY The tiny settlement, located at the base of Stanley Hill and overlooking Port Pattison, is the only collection of buildings on the island and is therefore where the sole accommodation option is situated, in the island's main house.

Carcass Island House (6 rooms) ✆21374, 41106; ⏱ mid-Oct–late Mar; contact Rob McGill. For those wishing to stay on the island, Carcass Island House is a very comfortable place, with 2 dbl, 3 twin & 1 trpl room. It is situated a 5min walk from the quay in a very sheltered area replete with songbirds. During springtime, the sound of the smaller birds singing is unlike anywhere else in the Falklands, although the 'song' of the magellanic penguins that sometimes breed under the building is less tuneful! This very comfortable lodge is all on 1 floor, with a large dining room, adjoining kitchen & a smaller, comfortable lounge. Some of the rooms are in the main building with the rest in the annex, which was added in the 1990s. The monterey pines that make up the majority of trees surrounding the house create shelter for the hebe & fuchsia hedges that grow in profusion here. The narrow paths between this luxurious vegetation are unique to this settlement. Your hosts are always on hand to answer questions & to help you plan your day. For those who fancy driving themselves around the island, there is a vehicle for hire – just enquire to see if it's available. Cruise-ship visitors also stop in here; the tea & cakes are a well-known attraction. For those staying on the island these are a daily event at *smoko* time, although for the sake of your waistline you shouldn't try *all* the cakes! From b/fast through to dinner, the wholesome food keeps visitors fuelled up for a day of activities. **£££**

WHAT TO SEE AND DO It is possible to walk around the perimeter of the island in one day, although this does not give you a lot of time to explore properly. The main track to the airport is the only route to the northern end of the island that is easy to follow, and there is a similar track over the grass to the southern end. Otherwise, it is possible to walk wherever you like. It is easier to aim for the gates when reaching a fence line, to avoid climbing the wire fence, but it is also possible to step over them. It is usually possible (depending on their commitments) to get dropped off somewhere by the island's owner and then walk back to the lodge. Having reached either end of the island, most visitors will want to explore the surroundings before heading back later in the day.

For those staying on the island, a popular day trip is to take the *SeaQuest* boat to nearby West Point Island. This 40-minute cruise is for up to 12 guests and costs £130 per person. It is booked via Carcass Island House (see opposite). Enquire with them as to when to make this day trip; there will be days when the weather is not fit to sail, so it is best to go at the first opportunity. To do Carcass Island justice, allow at least two days to explore, and another to fit in the day trip to West Point Island.

The oldest house in the settlement is Valley Cottage, which was built in the 1870s and is situated a few minutes' walk up the slope from the accommodation. Like the accommodation, it is situated in the shelter of monterey pines. It is used as residence for the staff working in the accommodation so is not open to the public.

This island does not have the dramatic cliffs of certain other western islands, including West Point or New islands, but it does have many beautiful sandy beaches situated below the gently rolling hills that make up the spine of the island. Leopard Beach and Dyke Beach at the south end of the island (page 168) are flat, sand beaches that are often busy with penguins late in the day, when the air is also full of the piping calls of oystercatchers. The sandy shores at the northern end of the island are broken up with rocky outcrops and are good sites to look for sleeping elephant seals on the washed-up seaweed, or to find the small flocks of white-rumped sandpipers from North America that winter in the Falklands. The luxuriant growth of fuchsia, gorse and cypress around the settlement attracts many small **birds**. Black-chinned siskins, Falkland thrushes and Cobb's wrens are present in great number, all making use of the well-established hedges and trees – which give the settlement an atypical appearance for the Falklands – to build their nests.

The famous colony of black-crowned night herons, once located in the trees around the main house, are now gone, but the birds can still be seen roosting on or near the jetty, a short walk from the settlement along the only track. The striated caracaras, locally known as Johnny Rook, are also very much in evidence around the settlement. They often perch high up in the cypress trees, keeping an eye open for any chance of a quick meal. The sheltered gardens, located uphill of the main house, are a spectacular sight when in full bloom; the yellow of the gorse in springtime can be seen many miles away on West Falkland. They have been temporary homes to all kinds of tired vagrant birds blown in from the South American continent, such as the trio of rufous-collared sparrows in early 2017 or the white-crowned elaenias that have also been noted here over the years.

The hill behind the settlement, Stanley Hill, is a steep 20-minute walk for the very fit, and would take around an hour for those walking at a more leisurely pace.

The summit gives a commanding view across Byron Sound to West Falkland. The military base on Byron Heights is one of the few artificial structures visible from here. Looking back down into Port Pattison, Peale's dolphins can sometimes be seen playing in the beds of kelp that fringe the bay.

South end One of the most popular sites on the island is the **penguin colony** at the south end. An hour's walk from the accommodation takes in the track that runs out through the paddocks around the houses, before continuing along the base of the hills, hugging the coastline, towards Gothic Point Paddock. From the path, as you get nearer to the south end, many ducks and geese can be seen feeding along the shore at low tide. Tussacbirds, intent on finding whatever food is disturbed by walkers, will sometimes accompany you. As the track reaches the base of Jason Hill, about an hour's stroll from the settlement, it climbs slightly around a bank of tussac grass that has been protected from sheep by a wire fence. After the first gate, the first gentoo penguin rookery is soon visible on the hill – this colony tends to move every few years, so its exact location varies. Why some of these birds choose to nest so far from the sea is a mystery. Walking down to the lower-lying ground, you can see that the combination of grass and tussac is also a prime habitat for large numbers of upland geese and smaller numbers of ruddy-headed geese. Late in the summer, the upland geese gather in large flocks on the short grass in the middle of Gothic Point Paddock, for safety while they moult their flight feathers. On the slightly higher ground, many magellanic penguins and their burrows can be seen. The wet areas in the middle of this site can be deep enough to hold small numbers of duck, including the elusive yellow-billed pintail.

The flora of this area is typical of boggy ground on Falkland but does include some nice pink-flowered pimpernel along with the more easily found berry-lobelia. In the early summer the scattered clumps of tussac grass make good singing perches for the displaying white-bridled finches.

There is a gap in the dunes on the south side of this short-grass meadow, in the middle of the area between Dyke Beach and Leopard Beach, which leads out on to the white-sand Leopard Beach. There are invariably small groups of Falkland steamer ducks and both magellanic penguins and gentoo penguins clustered on the sand. There are no southern sea lions breeding on Carcass Island, but they can occasionally be seen swimming through the shallow water close to the shore, on the lookout for an unwary penguin returning to its breeding site. A few minutes' walk, either along the beach or on the short grass behind it, leads you to the rocky crag known as **Ram Paddock Hill**. This is a favoured roost site for the southern caracara, although this shy species rarely allows a close approach. Black-browed albatrosses and southern giant petrels can also be seen, gliding low over Byron Sound. The far side of this paddock has some good stands of tussac grass above some low cliffs, upon which there are some small colonies of rock shags and yet more tussacbirds. The very tip, Needles Point, is a restricted area, allowing South American terns to breed undisturbed. The first section of the walk back can be taken over the flat sandy beach on the north side of this headland. Dyke Beach is a good spot to look for both blackish and magellanic oystercatchers, before aiming for a gap in the tussac on the bank on the far side of the beach, from where you can rejoin the track leading back to the settlement.

North end To visit the north end of Carcass Island it is a good idea to get a lift from the owner to beyond the airstrip – a 20–30-minute drive from the settlement – and to walk back. This can take as little as 90 minutes, but that would not include any time exploring the area. The airstrip makes a good point to start your walk, which first explores the outer northern parts of the island, before later heading back to the settlement. Beyond the fence that marks the northern limit of the grazed land, only a few minutes' walk north from the airstrip, are some narrow bands of tussac grass. Striated caracara have been known to nest on the small rocky outcrops in this area, so it is advisable to keep a lookout for any birds on sentry duty near the nest and keep well clear, as they can be quite aggressive when defending their eggs and young. The flat grasslands before the fence make a good nesting site for Antarctic skuas, locally called 'sea hens', which also have a well-deserved reputation for defending their nest sites. However, skuas tend to ignore visitors as long as a respectful distance is maintained – if the skuas start calling and take off, circling the area, then it's a good idea to back away and find another route.

There is one large shallow pool, known as Shedders Pond, at this end of the island. Having crossed the fence, this is easily seen as you approach the coast. This pool, along with some smaller pools in the tussac grass, are all less than half a mile from the airstrip. Shedders Pond has a good population of geese and other wildfowl including silver grebes and white-tufted grebes. Arrow-leaved marigold, with its large white-green flowers, can be found in the marshy areas nearby. Nearly every pool in this area has good numbers of waterfowl, so it's worth a slow wander around the site to see what is present. Chiloé wigeon, speckled teal and crested duck are all quite numerous here. Snipe can often be found in some of the marshier ground.

The grassy bank at the top of the **beach**, a few feet behind the pool on the seaward side, is the breeding ground for many kelp gulls. The flat grass is the ideal site for the displaying magellanic oystercatchers in the early part of the breeding season. The top of the beach is also a beachcomber's delight, with all sorts of flotsam and jetsam piled up by the latest gales. This area is popular with both Cobb's wrens and grass wrens. Small numbers of southern elephant seal now breed on Carcass, and in late summer this end of the island is also one of the areas favoured when they come out of the water for a few weeks to moult. Typically, they will be sleeping in the banks of washed-up kelp or lying in the tussac-grass-clad dunes. Snores and general grunting noises often tell you that a seal is nearby, even if you can't see it at first.

Along the rocky shore, Falkland steamer ducks are common, along with a scattering of brown-hooded gulls and a few white-rumped sandpipers – the last present from late summer to early autumn. There are plenty of pleasant sites out of the wind suitable for picnic lunches. Striated caracaras waste no time in coming to investigate what is available. Anything left unattended, including cameras and binoculars, is liable to be snatched for inspection. Many other birds will come to survey who has invaded their territory, although most such as white-bridled finches and dark-faced ground-tyrants will soon ignore you and carry on with their days. The small lump of tussac grass a short distance offshore to the northwest is often used by a small group of black-crowned night herons as a roost site around high tide. These can be seen flying in from all directions as the tide comes in.

There are two main routes back to the settlement from the beach area. A third, minor route, with no marked tracks, follows the northeastern coast for a while over the diddle-dee- and white-grass-covered slopes before climbing up over the hills to Port Pattison. However, apart from views over towards Saunders Island in the distance and a few rock shag and king shag colonies, there are more interesting possibilities elsewhere. The same views towards Saunders Island can be seen from the first of the two major routes. To appreciate them, walk past the eastern flanks of the northernmost hill, The Ovens Hill – a rather rocky crag – before heading up towards Mount Byng (213m). This relatively easy climb takes approximately

30 minutes, and you have to find your own route over the diddle-dee. From here, following the ridge back down the island to the settlement takes around 40 minutes. A short stroll south from Mount Byng brings you to the highest point on the island, **Mount Byng South** (220m). Walking the ridge from here is easy going as there is little elevation gained or lost until you begin heading down to the settlement. From these high tops it is possible on a clear day to see as far as the Jasons and Pebble Island on the northwestern side and away to New Island on the other. In late summer there is sometimes some whale activity visible between Carcass and West Point islands as well as out towards Saunders Island to the southwest. The drier ground along the summits produces a different flora, with many more of the berried plants such as tea berry, mountain berry and diddle-dee present. Tucked away in the rocks on the higher slopes, yellow daisy and lady's slipper can be found during late spring and summer. There are not as many birds on the higher slopes as there are lower down, but rufous-chested dotterels like to breed in this habitat and variable hawks and the occasional peregrine falcon can be seen on some of the steeper crags.

The other major route back from the same starting point in the vicinity of the airport follows the lower slopes of the hills for around half a mile, before rejoining

JASON ISLANDS

The group of islands lying to the northwest of the Falklands are collectively known as the Jasons. The most famous of this group is probably Steeple Jason Island, as it is home to a very large colony of black-browed albatrosses, but large colonies are also present on Grand Jason Island. Three of the islands – Steeple Jason Island, Grand Jason Island and Clarke's Islet (close to Grand Jason) – are owned by the Wildlife Conservation Society (WCS; w wcs.org), an organisation based at the Bronx Zoo in New York City. They were bought by the philanthropist Michael Steinhart in the late 1990s and given to WCS along with some money to build a research station on Steeple Jason. This was completed in 2003 and was named after him.

The rest of the group, the largest of which are Elephant Jason Island, Flat Jason Island and South Jason Island, are owned by the Falkland Islands Government.

In the mid 1800s, large numbers of rockhopper and gentoo penguins in the Jasons were killed and boiled for their oil. Other than that, the islands have been little utilised by humans, apart from sheep grazing on some of the larger islands. This began at some point in the 19th century but was gradually phased out during the 1960s–70s, meaning that the islands have now returned to nature.

Apart from the high numbers of nesting seabirds, there is also a large population of the globally endangered striated caracara. Thankfully, the only introduced rodent is the small population of house mice on Steeple Jason, so many small land birds and seabirds are able to breed here.

The only option to land here is via one of the visiting Expedition cruise ships, which will have obtained permission to land from the island's owners. Most will aim to land on Steeple Jason, but the exposed landing sites mean that this is a rare occurrence, with ships often having to land elsewhere in more sheltered locations such as Carcass Island or Saunders Island. Therefore, most visitors to the Falklands will only see the Jasons in the distance from Carcass Island or Pebble Island.

the track back to the settlement. This route can take up to 2 hours, depending on how many stops you make. This track follows the major valley up to a saddle between two hills. Scurvy grass grows in profusion at the base of the first hill, while dark-faced ground-tyrants appear to be perched on every tall rock scattered around the area. The track then crosses a west-facing valley before descending to the settlement. For energetic visitors wanting to experience the views without having to walk along the ridge described in the previous route, it is not too far, merely steep, up to Mount Byng South from the saddle at the end of the first valley. The view is definitely worth the effort of the climb.

WEST POINT ISLAND

West Point Island, owned by the Napier family, is not a big island. Covering 3,630 acres, it is 5 miles long and just under 2 miles at its widest point. The population is just two, who look after the small number of sheep on the island as well as the visiting tourists. Despite the island's size, there is more than enough for walkers and naturalists to see here – whether in a few hours on a stop from a visiting cruise ship, or for a full day when visiting from nearby Carcass Island. West Point is renowned for its huge colonies of black-browed albatrosses on its western side, on some of the most spectacular cliffs in the archipelago. The area around the small settlement, where the island's buildings are, is at its most colourful in springtime when the densely flowered gorse is in bloom. Sheep are still kept here, in managed numbers to ensure there is a good growth of grass, but tourism is the source of most of its income. The highest point on the island is Cliff Mountain at 1,250ft (381m), while nearby Mount Misery stands at 1,211ft (369m) above the albatross cliffs. The channel, located at the narrowest point between West Falkland and West Point, is Woolly Gut, which is strongly tidal before it opens out into West Point Pass to the southwest. The name 'woolly' refers to a sudden down-draught from the nearby cliffs, which in days of sail was a great threat to the safety of the boat.

HISTORY West Point Island was originally known as Albatross Island and has belonged to the same family since the 1860s. It was first part of the Shallow Bay estate on West Falkland before being set up as a separate farm in 1879 by Arthur Felton, the great uncle of the last owner, Roddy Napier, who inherited the island in the 1960s and who did so much for conservation and tourism. It is still owned by the family, with managers on the island keeping everything running. From the 1700s onwards, numerous penguins were killed on West Point for their oil, each penguin yielding about a pint. When meat and fur were among the islands' major exports, sealers came here on a regular basis. The events of the 1982 war passed by this tiny island. The advent of the Expedition cruise-ship market has had a great impact as there can now be over 30 boats calling into the island between November and March

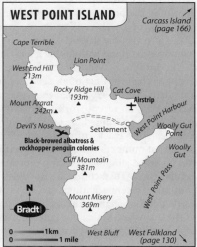

each year. The income generated from tourism is far greater than that from farming sheep, meaning that the managers, who live on the island, are kept very busy.

GETTING THERE AND AWAY This popular island is on many a **cruise-ship** itinerary (page 54). It does have an **airstrip**, but it is small and difficult to use, meaning air travel isn't an option for visitors. It does, however, have a very good **anchorage at West Point Harbour**, just below the settlement. The track from the jetty leads 100yds uphill to the settlement's farmhouse, which is tucked in among some very healthy monterey pine trees. Hundreds of cruise-ship visitors must have passed through the farmhouse lounges on Carcass Island and West Point Island over the years. You get the impression that every subject under the sun has been discussed on these far-flung islands.

For those visitors staying on the Falkland Islands, instead of cruising through them, **day trips** by boat are a popular choice from Carcass Island. The *SeaQuest* carries up to 12 guests on the 40-minute trip across from Port Pattison to West Point Harbour. Generally, the trip from Carcass Island lasts for an entire day, leaving at around 08.30 and returning by late afternoon. If it is a calm day a circumnavigation of West Point Island is possible, from which you can get a different view of the albatross cliffs on the western side of the island. Commerson's dolphin and Peale's dolphin will sometimes come and bow ride as the boat nears the harbours at either end of the trip. In late summer, the trip is also a good opportunity to look out for whales, with sei whale being seen occasionally mid-channel. There is also plenty of birdlife to see from the boat, including both gentoo and rockhopper penguins heading out to sea to fish. Rock and king shags are also seen widely distributed and South American terns can be seen feeding over the bands of kelp. This boat trip is booked with the accommodation on Carcass Island (page 166) and includes *smoko* on arrival and a packed lunch. Once on the island, visitors can either walk up to the colonies at the Devil's Nose or, depending on the managers' other commitments, get a lift there in the 4x4.

It is also possible to **sail** to West Point Island in your own yacht, but it is a good idea to contact the managers in advance and to call them on the radio on arrival to let them know when you would like to come ashore.

WHAT TO SEE AND DO As on the neighbouring island of Carcass, the welcome and afternoon tea provided at the farmhouse for cruise-ship passengers is one of the highlights of a visit to West Point. Even though the main aim of landing on the island is to visit the seabird colonies, the concept of tea and cakes should be high on your agenda, along with taking a look around the settlement.

The **birdlife** of West Point, although not as varied as that on Carcass Island owing to the introduction of cats, rats and mice years ago, is still present, only less abundant. It is now believed that cats have been successfully eradicated and there has been some recent work to remove the rat population around the settlement, resulting in an immediate increase in the number and diversity of smaller birds. Some, such as black-chinned siskin, Falkland thrush and grass wren survived the higher rat numbers quite well by breeding on cliffs inaccessible to rats. These birds can be heard singing on spring mornings with others now being noted on a more regular basis. Tussacbirds are now also being seen regularly and there have been continued recent sightings of Cobb's wren, which is very good news. The lush garden and vegetable patch, close to the farmhouse, are good places to see some of these species. Male long-tailed meadowlark, known locally as military starling, look particularly fine when perched on flowering gorse bushes. Their red breasts stand out from a long way off.

The major attraction is the impressive **black-browed albatross colony** located on the western side of the island. From the settlement, it is about a 5-minute drive to the colony – the managers will be able to give you a lift. Alternatively, the colony is an easy 30–40-minute walk along a grassy track that is marked by red-topped stakes and passes through a series of fields before reaching the inner edge of the tussac grass that grows on the island's periphery, at a safe distance from the local sheep. From where this track ends, which is also where the 4x4 parks, there is a separate path through a gate that leads through the tussac grass out on to a point overlooking the sea in a small valley, which contains some 2,000 pairs of black-browed albatross. The birds situate their mud-pot nests on the top of the slope, so that they can land and take off without too much difficulty. With a wingspan of over 7ft (2.13m), they need plenty of room to get to and from their nest site in safety. The main path leads down to the colonies for a few yards before splitting. You can then follow either path to loop around the colony, walking from one end of it to the other. It is therefore possible to take a circular walk and get wonderful views only a few feet away from the birds. As long as you stay on the path in the tussac, the birds carry on with their daily activities without seeming to be concerned by your presence.

In the past, some of the albatrosses in this colony were ringed as part of a research project to determine the longevity of the species, where the albatrosses went after leaving the island and if they returned here to breed. It seems that this species may live for 50 years or more in favourable conditions, and that they often return to the breeding grounds of their birth. Although noisy when greeting each other on the nest, they are generally silent in flight, often gliding past at a short distance from observers, heads turned ready to scrutinise, before heading back out to sea.

This mass of birds attracts the usual predators including turkey vultures, Antarctic skuas and striated caracara. This last, ever-vigilant species is one of the rarest birds of prey in the world, but it is a forgivable mistake to imagine that they are common here, as they appear to be everywhere. Also nesting here are 500 pairs of **rockhopper penguin**, who make their way up the steep cliff face using only their sharp claws to hang on. The guttural cries of a returning penguin greeting its mate, combined with the eerie sounds that albatrosses make, create a unique atmosphere. For the observer at the sidelines of this impressive seabird colony it is difficult to know where to look, as there is always something happening.

The waters around the island are favoured haunts of **Commerson's dolphin**. They follow many of the boats into the harbour, often playing in the bow wave as the ship enters the harbour. From the westward side of the island it is possible to see the occasional fur seal swimming close inshore, and on very calm days some of the great whales, most commonly sei and southern right whales, have been seen from many locations around this island.

NEW ISLAND

New Island has often been described as one of the most scenic of the Falkland Islands. It is the most southwesterly of the three islands covered in this chapter, and is located over 150 miles from Stanley; its nearest neighbour is Beaver Island (page 183), 3 miles to the south. New Island is about 8 miles (13km) long and half a mile (800m) at its narrowest point.

The highly indented coastline runs for 52 miles in total. The cliffs on the western side of the island rise to 600ft (183m), whereas the eastern shores gently slope into the sea. There are several bays on the eastern side, one of which, Settlement Harbour, once known as Hookers Harbour, is the site of the small jetty where the island's goods are unloaded. The large bay to the south, South Harbour, was the site of the whaling station established in 1908. The highest point on the island is South Hill at 743ft (226m). This island is best known as the home of one of the world's most spectacular seabird colonies, which accommodates large numbers of black-browed albatrosses (29,000 pairs), and rockhopper penguins (13,000 pairs). It is a popular destination for the many tourists who come ashore from passing cruise ships, attracted by the birds and the photogenic scenery. The owners, New Island Conservation Trust, which is now merged with Falklands Conservation, use money derived from the cruise-ship passengers' landing fees and donations to fund their conservation and scientific work. They are looking to provide accommodation

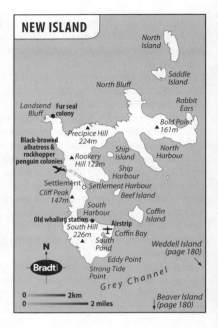

in the future for overseas visitors wishing to stay on the island, but it is presently only open to Falklands' residents.

HISTORY It is thought that American whalers and sealers who were starting to exploit the South Atlantic first visited the island in the late 1700s. One of these men, Charles H Barnard from Hudson, New England, reached New Island in September 1812. He used the island as a base while catching seals around the archipelago in his ship, the *Narnia*. In April 1813 he came across the survivors of the shipwreck of the *Isabella*, which had run aground some nine weeks earlier on Speedwell Island. Upon returning to New Island, Barnard and his crew rowed to nearby Beaver Island to search for provisions. While they were gone, the crew they had rescued took the *Narnia*, meaning that Barnard and his crew were abandoned on New Island when they returned. They managed to survive by building a stone shelter, which is now thought to be in the position of the building at the head of Settlement Harbour, and were rescued by the British ship *Indispensible* in November 1814. Barnard returned home in 1816, alive but penniless. In 1823 a Captain Weddell visited the island to replenish his ships' stocks. He and Barnard wrote detailed descriptions of the island, which have survived to this day, enabling historians to compare those times with now.

In the early 1850s a Captain Campbell, owner of a ship named *Levenside*, thought that the guano on the island was worth collecting. He obtained a licence from the Falkland Islands Government. However, the low value of the guano, and the sinking of his ship at the entrance of Port William on East Falkland, put paid to his venture.

Between 1851 and 1860 a French ship, the *Victor*, came to the islands to collect trypots, presumably to take elsewhere. These three-legged pots were used to render penguins for their oil. There are remains of stone corrals near the penguin rookeries where these birds must have been caught.

The island was leased for the first time in 1860 by the Smith brothers, who were based in South America at Montevideo. The brothers also wanted to exploit the deposits of guano that generations of seabirds had laid on the islands, but this was to be the last time that anybody attempted to make money from these worthless deposits. The Smiths also established a settlement on New Island and a small human population had settled here by 1861, as well as 500 sheep and a small number of cattle. This was the first attempt at introducing sheep to the island, although pigs and rabbits had been brought in during the 1820s. (Sheep numbers peaked in the late 1970s when some 3,300 were grazing on the island.) During the latter part of the 1800s and the early 1900s, sheep farming was the main source of income. The only exception was between 1893 and 1894 when Edward Nilsson, the owner of the island at that time, had a licence to cull 10,000 penguins for their oil. This was the last record of penguins being taken for oil on the islands.

In the early 20th century the southern oceans witnessed the swift expansion of the whaling industry. The first Falkland licence was granted to Alexander Lange, who operated out of New Island in the summer of 1905–06. During that season Lange and his men managed to catch 125 whales. In 1908 a whaling station was set up by Salvesens of Leith in a 30-acre site on the south side of South Harbour. It was ready for operation in January 1909 and its first whale was caught soon after. Four catchers operated out of this station. These boats doubled up as mail and passenger boats around the islands at first, before being replaced by an inter-island boat, the RMS *Columbus*. The products from this whaling operation were used to make margarine, soap and bombs, and the whale bones were ground down and used as fertiliser. By 1916, some 1,188 whales had been caught and processed here. The station's activities were eclipsed by the company's much more profitable operations in South Georgia, with the result that in 1916 the New Island Whaling Company station was closed, and the equipment was dismantled and shipped to South Georgia.

During the whaling years, South Harbour had developed into a busy port, with its own post office and customs officer, when it became a Port of Entry for the islands. The post office closed in 1917, by which time, owing to the general decline of the whaling industry in Falkland itself, the number of boats calling into New Island had decreased significantly. All that remains today are some of the boilers, some rusty metal and some low foundations.

New Island was purchased in 1972 by the New Island Preservation Company with the aim of establishing the island as a nature reserve. This state of affairs continued until 1977, when the company was dissolved and the island became two properties – New Island North and New Island South. New Island North was run as a private nature reserve, owned by Tony Chater. New Island South was run as a reserve by its owner Ian Strange and was recognised as a wildlife sanctuary by the Falkland Islands Government in 1993. In 1988, the New Island South Conservation Trust (w newislandtrust.com) was set up as a registered charity with the aim of promoting the study and appreciation of ecology and conservation. In 2006, the trust gained ownership of the entire island, and in July 2020 merged with Falklands Conservation. They have carried out various wildlife research projects on the island, including studying the breeding biology of the Falkland skua; ringed (banded) birds can often be seen around the main seabird colonies. There have also been projects looking at the numbers of black-browed albatross, the winter distribution of rockhopper penguin, and one mapping the vegetation of the island. In 2013, a feasibility study was undertaken for the eradication of alien invasive vertebrate species.

New Island has been recognised by BirdLife International as an Important Bird Area (IBA) owing to the wide variety of birds nesting here and the black-browed albatross and rockhopper penguin colonies.

10

In recent years there have only been two to four people staying on the island during the summer months, working with the cruise-ship passengers who arrive to visit the seabird colonies. Tourism is the main source of income on the island, with other income coming in the form of donations to the New Island Trust.

GETTING THERE AND AWAY There is a grass **airstrip** on the island, but as it has limited operational conditions, getting to the island by air is not easy. Weather conditions impact the landing site and the plane has a limit of two passengers and luggage. This flight may well be delayed for several days because of adverse weather and as such is only available for those living on the islands, or for scientists, film crews staying for long periods and visitors who are staying in the Falklands for a long time and have more flexibility. Flights are operated by FIGAS (w falklands.gov. fk/aviationservice; £192.99 single; for booking information, see page 58). Therefore, New Island is rarely visited by independent tourists from outside the islands, due to the logistical problems of getting here and away.

The majority of visitors who call in at New Island during the austral summer do so via the **cruise ships** that come into Settlement Harbour. Generally, most ships only visit the island for a maximum of 4–5 hours so either a morning or an afternoon visit is the norm. Permission to land on this reserve must be obtained in advance from Falklands Conservation/New Island Conservation Trust (e newisland@ conservation.org.fk; w newislandtrust.com). For those on a cruise this will have already been organised, as will the £25 per person landing charge. For those in their **own boats**, you can land here once permission to enter the Falklands has been given by customs and immigration officials in Stanley, and also with permission from Falklands Conservation, for a charge of £15 per person per night.

 WHERE TO STAY To stay at any of the below, contact Falklands Conservation/ New Island Conservation Trust (☏ 42317; e newisland@conservation.org.fk; w newislandtrust.com). There is a minimum three-night stay.

North End Hut (1 room) This is basically a hut with 2 bunk beds in 1 room with a separate kitchen & outside toilet – no electricity or shower. It is situated at the northern end of the island, a 50-plus minute drive from the settlement. There is a £100 cost per booking, which includes set up & transit fees. **£££**

Cormorant Cottage (2 rooms) New Island settlement. This triangular-shaped building in the settlement can sleep up to 4. Generally, it is advertised as self-catered but can occasionally be fully catered by prior arrangement. Visitors will need to bring most of their food & any personal items with them. A limited amount of dried &

tinned foods is available in the island's store, depending on how recently the supply ship has visited. There may be space in the manager's freezer to bring frozen food but again this should be arranged prior to arrival. **££** (self-catered); **£££** (catered)

Field Station (4 rooms) New Island settlement. Sleeps 8 upstairs in 4 rooms, each with 2 sgl beds. Not suitable for under 18s & rooms may be shared, as are the 2 showers/toilets & kitchen. **££**

Old Main House (3 rooms) New Island settlement. Sleeps 6 in 2 dbls & 1 twin. This newly restored building looks out over the bay from its large lounge & is also home to the island store. **££**

WHAT TO SEE AND DO The prime aim of a trip to this island is visiting the most accessible **seabird colony**. In the settlement – a small collection of modern houses overlooking the picturesque Settlement Harbour – you'll find the jetty, where those with their own boats land. From here, stroll westwards for 5 minutes, past the house with the blue roof, towards the head of the bay. In this bay lies the **wreck of the *Protector III***, which was beached here in February 1969, having originally been brought to the islands to be used as a sealer based at Albemarle in West Falkland. It is also here where the majority of visitors to the island, arriving via cruise ship, land. The shed at the head of this beach was built towards the end of the 1800s for dealing with sheep and for storage and now houses a small **museum** where stamps and gifts are sold. This robust building contains a mixture of artefacts relating to different aspects of island life – from the ships that have been wrecked around the islands to farming – as well as reflecting on the wildlife that can be found in the area.

The gorse bushes that flank the half-mile-long path from the settlement are a superb sight in springtime and are home to many of the small birds which breed here; dark-faced ground-tyrants and Falkland thrushes are easy to spot. The path then crosses a grassy valley, which has been cropped short by generations of rabbits, before gradually climbing up to the higher, western, side of the island. Once past the stile, the tussac grass increases in density as it reaches the cliff edge. The sounds of the colony greet the visitor before the colony itself is visible on the rocky coast. The cliff is not very high at this point but is chock-full of birds. This colony is a real mixture, with black-browed albatrosses, king shags and rockhopper penguins all jumbled together. The albatrosses and shags tend to be right at the top of the cliff. Even though some penguins do nest with these other species, they also have their own colonies slightly further inland, in the heart of the tussac grass.

Some of these birds are part of the long-term studies (page 48), and therefore their nests may well have individual markers. The study areas are clearly marked out with wooden pegs; it is very important that these pegs are not displaced. By following the path that leads to the south side of this area, it is possible to get to a good observation point without disturbing the birds. This spectacular site has so much going on it is difficult to know where to look and it is definitely one of the most photographed areas on the islands. Birds are coming and going all the time: the albatrosses glide by with a serene grace and the shags hustle and bustle as they crash land next to the nest, while the penguins porpoise their way through the sea to the base of the cliff before living up to their rockhopper name as they clamber up the cliff to their rookery. Above all this, scavengers keep an eye out for an opening: turkey vultures and Antarctic skuas are the most noticeable, while dolphin gulls the most vocal. Striated caracaras create the most havoc as they glide over the colony, as they are the main predator here. Only the albatrosses seem unperturbed by this ace scavenger.

Another recommended site, although rarely visited due to restrictions on time, is the **fur seal colony** that lies to the north of the settlement. A vague track leads from the valley behind the seabird colonies and heads north, upwards past Rookery Hill. After the best part of an hour, you will reach **Landsend Bluff**. Approximately 500 fur seals come back to breed each year on the flat rocky ledges that are found here. The bulls are the first to return in November, the females following a few weeks later once the bulls have laid claim to their patch of rock. Each male then tries to keep his females in his harem until the pups have been born and the females have been mated again. It is not possible or advisable to get down to the colony. The seals can be viewed in safety from the tussac grass at the top of the cliff. There is always something going on in this colony, whether it is the males defending their territory, the females tending their pups or the non-breeding animals playing in the beds of kelp a few yards offshore. Elephant seals do not breed here, but occasionally one or two can be found hauled up on the beach when they have to come ashore to moult. Southern sea lions can also be seen almost anywhere on the island, but usually in small numbers.

The sheltered eastern side of the island is more to the liking of **magellanic penguins** and **gentoo penguins** as it is more low lying than the cliffs of the western side and thus easier for these birds to access. The former make their nests in loose colonies along the shore, avoiding the wetter areas. The gentoo penguins on New Island have large colonies at the north and south end of the eastern side of the island. These are not generally visited, but can easily be seen from a boat. The occasional king penguin will join with the gentoo colonies when they come ashore to moult. There is now also a small southern giant petrel colony on the southern part of this side of the island on the shore north of the airstrip.

The largest pool on the island, South Pond, is beyond **Coffin Bay** at the southwestern end. This is the best place to look for any wildfowl on the island, such as speckled teal, Chiloé wigeon and crested duck. There is also a sizeable gentoo penguin colony on the side of the small hill behind this shallow pool. As on the other islands to the west of Falkland, there is always the chance of vagrant birds reaching these shores, as did the grassland yellow finch and eared dove in 2023.

One of the most numerous birds on the island is the **thin-billed prion**. Approaching the island by boat affords views of these grey-and-white seabirds flitting low over the waves close to the shore. This bird spends most of its time at sea, only coming ashore after dark to elude its predators. Some do not escape, and their corpses can occasionally be found near the narrow burrows in which they have laid their eggs. The peregrine falcons that live on this island appear to have learnt how to catch these elusive birds and can be seen flying over the island from land and sea.

The rich marine life around New Island supplies food for all the aforementioned seabirds and mammals. Large numbers of fur seals have been seen feeding close to the island in recent years, with hundreds often porpoising through the water in one direction. Southern right whales have been seen from boats and from the shore on several occasions in recent years, as have the more common Commerson's dolphins and Peale's dolphins.

11

Weddell, Staats and Beaver islands

These three islands, along with the nearby smaller islets, rocks and New Island, form an archipelago in miniature at the southwestern tip of the Falkland Islands. Weddell Island is by far the largest of this group, with an extremely indented coastline and the highest peak in the area, Mount Weddell, at 1,256ft (383m). The smaller Beaver and Staats islands lie to the west of Weddell. All three of these islands, like many others to the west of Falkland, are much more arid than those to the east, having appreciably less rainfall. There are settlements on Weddell and on Beaver islands and shepherds' shanties on Staats and on nearby Tea Island. The larger islands have been farmed, while some of the smaller islets (such as Little Coffin Island and Stick in the Mud Island) are still covered in tussac grass, having never been grazed. The northwest coastline of Weddell Island can generally be described as relatively level with few high points. The southwestern coastline of the island is very different, characterised by lofty sea cliffs and precipitous rocky islets. Of this group, Weddell Island alone offers accommodation for visitors. Compared with other sites in Falkland, these islands are relatively lacking in diverse wildlife, although there are the ubiquitous penguin colonies and some of the smaller islands are richer in varieties of duck and geese. There is also some magnificent walking to be had on Weddell Island (page 181) (and to some degree on the much smaller Beaver Island), with a different view to be witnessed from every high point.

WEDDELL ISLAND

Weddell Island, comprising some 63,000 acres, is the third-largest island of the Falklands. The southwestern coasts are much higher than the low-lying area to the west of Mount Weddell and are bisected by Chatham Harbour. There are some buildings on the edge of this natural harbour, but the main settlement is on the east side of the island near the smaller, more sheltered Gull Harbour. The airstrip is only a short drive from the settlement.

In recent years this working sheep farm has been upgrading its accommodation for visitors, a project that remains ongoing. At the time this guide went to print, the decision was made to close all the accommodation on the island until a number of outstanding and critical capital works had been completed. As it stands, the timescale as to when they will reopen, and in what format their tourism offering will take in the future, is uncertain.

HISTORY The island has been an active farm for many years. In 1923 the island was bought from the descendants of a Mr and Mrs Williams, the island's first owners in 1871, by John Hamilton, a Scot who moved to the Falkland Islands in the 1880s. Hamilton was responsible for importing many exotic animals and birds to Weddell

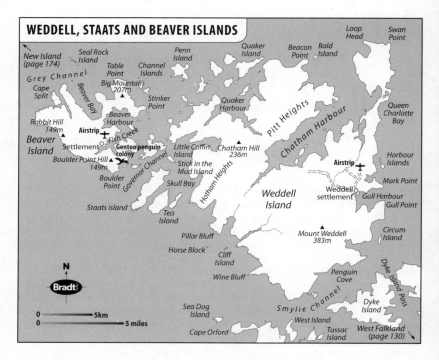

WEDDELL, STAATS AND BEAVER ISLANDS

and to the neighbouring Staats and Beaver islands. During his period of tenure, he brought in parrots, skunks, ibis, rheas, Fuegian otters, Patagonian foxes and guanacos. Only the latter two have definitely survived – Patagonian foxes can be found on Beaver and Weddell islands, and Staats Island still holds a population of guanacos. There have been no sightings of Fuegian otters for many years, but the possibility that they have survived on some remote islands cannot be excluded due to the presence of so much suitable habitat, such as the little rocky islets that can be found in Queen Charlotte and King George bays.

The island was sold by the John Hamilton Estate to Bob Ferguson in 1987 and became an active sheep farm with a 9,000-strong herd. In 2001 it was bought by Richard Visick, a UK lawyer who reduced the sheep population to 200 and encouraged the tourist side of the business to flourish. It changed hands again in 2015, when it was bought by Byron Holdings, a company run by Falkland Islanders Stephen and Lewis Clifton. It is now once again being run as a working sheep farm and is home to 600–700 sheep.

GETTING THERE AND AWAY The only realistic way to reach the island is to **fly** with FIGAS (w falklands.gov.fk/aviationservice; for booking information, see page 58). The current non-resident fare from Stanley is £174.93. Although there is a jetty on the island, it is not possible for visitors to get here on an organised boat trip. It is possible for independent travellers to visit on their own **boat**, but you will have to clear customs and immigration in Stanley beforehand.

 WHERE TO STAY As of mid 2024, all the accommodation is closed. Decisions as to what will happen in the future have yet to be made. For further information contact e weddell@horizon.co.fk.

WHAT TO SEE AND DO The extensive gorse hedges that mark out the edges of the fields around the settlement are a splendid sight in springtime. These lines of yellow are visible from some distance away. The small pine trees, which surround the houses in the settlement, have been home to a small colony of black-crowned night herons in the past. Nowadays, they occasionally contain a roosting heron but no breeding birds. The narrow **Gull Harbour** is a reliable place to look for Commerson's dolphins, which can often be seen moving slowly through the shallow water or playing out in the middle of the bay. There are no large numbers of geese on this island due to the presence of Patagonian foxes. These predators are well camouflaged, as the colour of their coat matches the white grass that covers much of the island. In recent years the number of foxes has declined, making them very hard to find. The island has large numbers of **gentoo penguins**, to the extent that, over 40 years ago, gentoo penguin eggs used to be harvested from here for food in large numbers. This species of penguin likes the easy access to their colonies afforded by the myriad small beaches that are found around the island. The only other penguin that breeds here – the **magellanic penguin** – can be found in typically scattered loose colonies around the lower coastal fringes.

There are no big breeding colonies, but many seabirds, such as black-browed albatrosses, South American terns and a variety of gulls and prions, can be watched from the shore when they are feeding in the strait between West Falkland and Weddell Island. This strait is called **Smylie Channel** and has one of the strongest tidal currents in Falkland. This fast-flowing water brings small fish, squid and plankton to the surface, which feeds a variety of birds. Where the channel opens out at its southern end, many sooty shearwaters and black-browed albatrosses gather in small flocks. Prions can be seen flitting in around the waves in rough weather. In spring and autumn southern fulmars and pintado petrels join in with this seething mass of birds. Rock shags and king shags feed in the calmer water at the edges of the channel. This can also be a good area for cetaceans, but the disturbance of the water caused by the strong current means that it is rarely calm enough to see them.

The scenery on the southern and western edges of the island is dramatic, with many interesting rock formations. One of the more unique lies a mile or so southwest of Pillar Bluff. This is **Horse Block**, a rugged lump of rock some 67m high which at close range appears to have four legs, looking for all the world as though it is standing on the water.

At the western approach to Smylie Channel is **Sea Dog Island**. As it is less than 2 miles offshore, it is easy to see from the southwest coast of Weddell Island. This is thought to be one of very few islands in the archipelago that has never had sheep, or even been landed on, owing to its rocky cliffs. It is thought to be home to many of the smaller seabirds, such as prions and petrels, which can only breed in the absence of any small ground predators such as rats. One such example is the thin-billed prion, which can be seen feeding in Smylie Channel.

Walking on Weddell Island
As there are no footpaths on the island you can walk wherever your fancy takes you but, for a nice 2-hour stroll, head east around the northern side of **Gull Harbour** from the settlement and follow the shore for a while before continuing out to **Mark Point**, which juts out into Queen Charlotte Bay. This is a good spot to look for whales in late summer – both southern right and sei whales have been seen from here. There are also some remains of whale skeletons along the shore. On first glance they look like sections of bleached wood, but on closer inspection curved rib bones and bits of skull can be identified. As for which species they are – that is anyone's guess; DNA work would be needed to identify them.

Another good walk, taking potentially a full day, heads north away from the settlement towards **Loop Head**. The southern sea lion colony at the far end of this headland is about 8 miles away. However, the headland is narrow enough that those looking for a shorter walk can cut across from one side to the other at any point to loop back. At about 5 miles out there is an especially narrow section where the headland is only yards wide. The far end of Loop Head, looking out into Queen Charlotte Bay, provides a nice vantage point from which to watch the whales during mid to late summer. For those wanting an uphill climb, **Mount Weddell** (383m) is a good 3-hour walk from the settlement to the summit. It's fairly steep, but worth it for the view over West Falkland to the east and out to Beaver Island to the west.

In the past, depending on the commitments of the farm managers, it has sometimes been possible to get a lift over towards the inner end of **Chatham Harbour** and to walk back to the settlement. From here, you can walk along the shore of the bay, looking at magellanic penguins and the wading birds that call this area home, including two-banded plovers and magellanic oystercatchers. The walk back brings you through 'The Street' – the fenced area between the larger fields used by the farm to bring the sheep back to the settlement at shearing time.

STAATS AND BEAVER ISLANDS

Despite the lack of visitor accommodation on Staats or Beaver islands, they are worthy of a visit as representatives of the southwestern facet of the Falklands archipelago. These two islands are only accessible for those with their own boat, and cannot be landed on without the permission of the owner, Sally Poncet. However, at present, it isn't possible for visitors to call in at these islands.

STAATS ISLAND Staats is a narrow island with some very impressive cliffs on its southwestern side. The only safe landing point is on the northeast bay below the small shepherd's shanty.

The island does not have a great many breeding birds owing to the presence of the Patagonian foxes that prey on any ground-nesting birds. The complete absence of trees means that the only survivors are those big enough to defend their burrows, for example the magellanic penguins that nest around the low-lying coastline, or those able to nest on the cliffs, such as the rock shags or dark-faced ground-tyrants. Apart from the foxes, this island is best known for the colony of guanacos that was introduced in 1937 and which survives to this day. They can be easily seen from the sea as you sail by the island, as they feed in the valleys. Often observed in small groups, their eerie whinnying cries echo across the valleys.

To the east of Staats Island is **Tea Island**, a smaller version of Staats with another small shanty. Having been grazed in the past, Tea Island is not renowned for its wildlife. There are no organised trips to this island, although those with their own yacht may wish to stop by. As with most of the islands, permission should be sought from the owners to land here (see above).

Independent travellers sailing from Staats Island to the anchorage at Beaver Island pass **Little Coffin Island** and **Stick in the Mud Island**. These are typical tussac-grass islands that have retained their original populations of tussacbird and Cobb's wren, having been undisturbed by humans, cats or rats. Southern sea lions can often be seen basking on the flat rocky ledges at either end of Stick in the Mud Island, although there is a very strong current flowing past the island, making observation difficult.

BEAVER ISLAND The anchorage on Beaver Island is on the northern side of this highly indented coastline, in Fish Creek. A series of low hills traverses the island. The **settlement**, with its sheltered gardens, is on the eastern side of the harbour. In the hinterland most of the habitat is a mixture of grass and diddle-dee with a scattering of gorse bushes. There is a grass airstrip not far from the settlement, but this is rarely used.

This island has a much more varied selection of **wildlife** than Staats or Weddell islands. Assuming permission to land has been granted, visitors land on the eastern arm of the bay from where it is only a short 20-minute walk up the valley to a large **gentoo penguin colony**, which extends around the side of this small valley. There are nearly 3,000 pairs of gentoo penguin on this island along with around 2,000 pairs of magellanic penguin. Many additional birds, including crested duck and the occasional goose, can be seen on the shore or splashing in the shallows around the island. This island once had a population of feral cats until they were eradicated in 1993 – the owners are now trying to remove the Patagonian foxes that were introduced during the 1930s. If the foxes can be completely eradicated, then the wildfowl of the island should have greater success in breeding. The lack of any sizeable ponds or lakes means that there are very few freshwater ducks.

The **south and western coasts** provide useful opportunities for watching seabirds at sea, especially the black-browed albatrosses that breed on nearby New Island (page 177). These coasts are home to large numbers of Falkland steamer ducks and kelp geese. The two species of caracara, southern and striated, are often observed around the island, as are peregrine falcons. The proximity of this island to the South American mainland has resulted in many vagrant birds being found here, usually discovered in sheltered spots around the settlement. Fur seals congregate on the ledges at the base of the western cliffs. From time to time they can be seen elsewhere, but are generally not reliably seen in any other locations.

Appendix 1

■ *Non-breeding* ◆ *Endemic* ◉ *Introduced*

This appendix contains lists of the most common birds, plants and animals that can be seen on the Falkland Islands. The lists are in systematic order and can therefore be used in conjunction with any bird, plant or animal guide for those seeking greater detail on a particular species.

SELECTED FLORA AND FAUNA

BIRDS

king penguin (*Aptenodytes patagonicus*)
gentoo penguin (*Pygoscelis papua*)
erect-crested penguin (*Eudyptes sclateri*) ■
rockhopper penguin (*Eudyptes chrysocome*)
macaroni penguin (*Eudyptes chrysolophus*)
magellanic penguin (*Spheniscus magellanicus*)
white-tufted grebe (*Rollandia rolland rolland*)
silvery grebe (*Podiceps occipitalis*)
southern royal albatross (*Diomedea epomophora epomophora*) ■
black-browed albatross (*Thalassarche melanophris*)
southern giant petrel (*Macronectes giganteus*)
southern/Antarctic fulmar (*Fulmarus glacialoides*) ■
Cape petrel (*Daption capense*) ■
thin-billed prion (*Pachyptila belcheri*)
white-chinned petrel (*Procellaria aequinoctialis*)
great shearwater (*Ardenna gravis*)
sooty shearwater (*Ardenna griseus*)
Wilson's storm-petrel (*Oceanites oceanicus*)
grey-backed storm-petrel (*Garrodia nereis*)
black-bellied storm-petrel (*Fregetta tropica*)
common diving petrel (*Pelecanoides urinatrix*)
rock shag/magellanic cormorant (*Phalacrocorax magellanicus*)
king shag/imperial cormorant (*Phalacrocorax atriceps albiventer*)
black-crowned night heron (*Nycticorax nycticorax falklandicus*)
black-necked swan (*Cygnus melanocoryphus*)
feral domestic goose (*Anser anser domesticus*) ◉
upland goose (*Chloephaga picta leucopta*)
kelp goose (*Chloephaga hybrid malvinarum*)
ashy-headed goose (*Chloephaga poliocephala*) ■
ruddy-headed goose (*Chloephaga rubidiceps*)
flying steamer duck (*Tachyeres patachonicus*)

Falkland steamer duck (*Tachyeres brachypterus*) ◆
Chiloé wigeon (*Mareca sibilatrix*)
speckled teal (*Anas flavirostris flavirostris*)
crested duck (*Lophonetta specularioides*)
yellow-billed pintail (*Anas georgica*)
silver teal (*Spatula versicolor*)
cinnamon teal (*Spatula cyanoptera*) ■
red shoveler (*Spatula platalea*)
turkey vulture (*Cathartes aura*)
variable hawk (*Geranoaetus polyosoma*)
striated caracara (*Phalcoboenus australis*)
southern caracara (*Caracara plancus*)
peregrine falcon (*Falco peregrinus*)
blackish oystercatcher (*Haematopus ater*)
magellanic oystercatcher (*Haematopus leucopodus*)
two-banded plover (*Charadrius falklandicus*)
rufous-chested dotterel (*Charadrius modestus*)
magellanic snipe (*Gallinago paraguaiae*)
white-rumped sandpiper (*Calidris fuscicollis*) ■
snowy sheathbill (*Chionis alba*) ■
brown/Antarctic skua (*Stercorarius antarctica*)
dolphin gull (*Leucophaeus scoresbii*)
kelp gull (*Larus dominicanus*)
brown-hooded gull (*Chroicocephalus maculipennis*)
South American tern (*Sterna hirundinacea*)
barn owl (*Tyto alba tuidara*)
short-eared owl (*Asio flammeus*)
tussacbird (*Cinclodes antarcticus*)
dark-faced ground-tyrant (*Muscisaxicola maclovianus maclovianus*)
barn swallow (*Hirundo rustica*) ■
Chilean swallow (*Tachycineta leucopyga*) ■
Falkland/correndera pipit (*Anthus correndera*)
Falkland grass/sedge wren (*Cistothorus platensis falklandicus*)
Cobb's wren (*Troglodytes cobbi*) ◆
Falkland thrush (*Turdus falcklandii falcklandii*)
long-tailed meadowlark (*Sturnella loyca falklandica*)
black-chinned siskin (*Spinus barbatus*)
white-bridled finch (*Melanodera melanodera*)
house sparrow (*Passer domesticus*) ◉

MAMMALS
southern right whale (*Eubalaena australis*)
orca/killer whale (*Orcinus orca*)
long-finned pilot whale (*Globicephala maleana*)
Peale's dolphin (*Lagenorhynchus australis*)
Commerson's dolphin (*Cephalorhunchus commersonii*)
rabbit (*Oryctolagus cuniculus*) ◉
European/brown hare (*Lepus europaeus*) ◉
house mouse (*Mus musculus*) ◉
brown rat (*Rattus norvegicus*) ◉
black rat (*Rattus rattus*) ◉

Fuegian marine/sea otter (*Lutra felina*) ⊗
South American grey fox (*Lycalopex griseus*) ⊗
southern sea lion (*Otaria flavescens*)
South American fur seal (*Arctocephalus australis australis*)
southern elephant seal (*Mirounga leonina*)
leopard seal (*Hydrurga leptonyx*)
guanaco (*Lama guanicoe*) ⊗

FLOWERING PLANTS AND FERNS
Antarctic hard-fern (*Blechnum penna-marina*)
tall fern (*Blechnum magellanicum*)
curled dock (*Rumex crispus*) ⊗
sheep's sorrel (*Rumex acetosella*) ⊗
mouse-ear chickweed (*Cerastium fontanum*) ⊗
arrow-leaved marigold (*Caltha sagittata*)
silvery buttercup (*Hamadryas argentea*) ◆
Falkland rock cress (*Arabis macloviana*) ◆
shore stonecrop (*Crassula moschata*)
wild Magellan strawberry (*Rubus geoides*)
oval-leaved prickly burr (*Acaena ovalifolia*)
prickly/buzzy burr (*Acaena magellanica*)
yarrow (*Acaena lucida*)
gorse (*Ulex europaea*) ⊗
white clover (*Trifolium repens*) ⊗
hop trefoil (*Trifolium campestre*) ⊗
red clover (*Trifolium pratense*) ⊗
scurvy grass (*Oxalis enneaphylla*)
yellow violet (*Viola maculata*)
field pansy (*Viola arvensis*)
teaberry/cranberry-myrtle (*Myrteola nummularia*)
pigvine (*Gunnera magellanica*)
clubmoss azorella (*Azorella lycopodioides*)
cushion azorella (*Azorella selago*)
balsam bog (*Bolax gummifera*)
Falkland lilaeopsis (*Lilaeopsis macloviana*) ◆
wild celery (*Apium australe*)
mountainberry (*Pernettya pumila*) ⊗
diddle-dee (*Empetrum rubrum*)
Dusty Miller primrose (*Primula magellanica*)
pimpernel (*Anagallis alternifolia*)
Falkland thrift (*Armeria macloviana*)
Antarctic bedstraw (*Galium antarcticum*)
changing forget-me-not (*Myosotis discolor*) ⊗
lady's slipper (*Calceolaria fothergillii*)
boxwood (*Hebe elliptica*)
Antarctic eyebright (*Euphrasia antarctica*)
Moore's plantain (*Plantago moorei*) ◆
berry-lobelia (*Lobelia pratiana*)
Falkland false-plantain (*Nastanthus falklandicus*) ◆
European daisy (*Bellis perennis*) ⊗
marsh daisy (*Symphyotrichum vahlii*)

hairy daisy (*Erigeron incertus*) ◆
Christmas bush (*Baccharis magellanica*)
fachine (*Chiliotrichum diffusum*)
clubmoss cudweed (*Chevreulia lycopodioides*) ◆
Falkland cudweed (*Gamochaeta malvinensis*) ◆
common yarrow (*Achillea millefolium*) ◉
sea cabbage (*Senecio candicans*)
woolly Falkland ragwort (*Senecio littoralis*) ◆
smooth Falkland ragwort (*Senecio vaginatus*) ◆
groundsel (*Senecio vulgaris*) ◉
coastal nassauvia (*Nassauvia gaudichaudii*) ◆
stone run/snakeplant (*Nassauvia serpens*) ◆
vanilla daisy (*Leucheria suaveolens*) ◆
Falkland lavender (*Perezia recurvata*)
Antarctic hawkweed (*Hieracium antarcticum*) ◉
orange hawkweed/fox-and-cubs (*Pilosella aurantiaca*)
common dandelion (*Taraxacum officinale*) ◉
soft camp bog (*Astelia pumila*)
almond flower (*Luzuriaga marginata*)
pale maiden (*Olsynium filifolium*)
greater rush (*Juncus scheuchzerioides*) ◉
brown rush (*Rostkovia magellanica*)
tall/basket rush (*Marsippospermum grandiflorum*)
tussac grass (*Poa flabellata*)
mountain bluegrass (*Poa alopecurus*)
Yorkshire fog (*Holcus lanatus*) ◉
white grass (*Cortaderia pilosa*)
cinnamon grass (*Hierochloe redolens*)
California clubrush/bulrush (*Schoenoplectus californicus*)
yellow orchid (*Gavilea littoralis*)
white dog orchid (*Codonorchis lessonii*)

Appendix 2

FURTHER INFORMATION

BOOKS

Carter, Jen *My Falklands Islands Life; One Family's Very British Adventure* Hope Books, 2017. The story of how a family came to live on the Falklands and how they adapted to the Falkland way of life.

Chater, T *The Falklands* Penna Press, November 1993. An annotated pictorial guide.

Clubbe, Heller, Lewis and Upson *Field Guide to the Plants of the Falkland Islands* Kew Publishing, 2019. This photographic guide is an excellent, up-to-date guide to the islands' flora.

Davis, T H and McAdam, J H *Wild Flowers of the Falkland Islands* Bluntisham Books/Falkland Islands Trust, 1989. An illustrated identification guide to the main breeding flowers on Falkland.

De la Pena, M A and Rumboll, M *Birds of Southern South America and Antarctica* HarperCollins, 1998. An illustrated field guide to the birds of the region.

Important Bird Areas of the Falkland Islands Falklands Conservation, 2006. This summarises the Important Bird Areas (IBAs) on the islands. These designations are assigned by BirdLife International, the worldwide umbrella for various conservation organisations.

Jones, Alexander G *Insects of the Falkland Islands* Falklands Conservation, 2004. This booklet is illustrated with colour photographs of the more common insects of the islands.

Liddle, Ali *Plants of the Falkland Islands* Falklands Conservation, 2007. This small book covers most of the commonly seen plants and includes recipes for the edible ones, such as berries, which are found on the islands.

Middlebrook, Martin *The Falklands War* Pen and Sword Military, 2020. A review of the war in 1982 with many firsthand accounts from those in the military and the Falkland Islanders.

Munroe, Richard *Place Names of the Falkland Islands* Shackleton Scholarship Fund, 1998. This booklet lists alphabetically many of the place names around the Falkland Islands.

Orange, Alan *Lichens of the Falkland Islands* Falklands Conservation, 2016. An illustrated guide to the commoner lichens found on the islands.

Robinson, Gareth *A Curious Legacy...: An idiosyncratic tale of travels around the Falkland Islands* Biddles Books, 2021. The author's account of his many visits to the islands and descriptions of the walks he has done around them and the people he met along the way.

Smith, John *Those Were the Days* Falkland Islands Trust, 1988. A personal view of what life was like in Stanley from the start of the Argentine invasion through to the end of the 1982 Falklands War.

Stone, Aldiss and Edwards *Rocks and Fossils of the Falkland Islands* Falkland Islands Government, 2005. A booklet that gives a lot of useful information about the geology of the islands from the stone runs to the fossils found around the archipelago.

Strange, I J *A Field Guide to the Wildlife of the Falkland Islands and South Georgia* HarperCollins, 1992. A field guide to the birds, flowers, animals and selected other families of wildlife occurring in the area.

Summers, Debbie/Falklands Conservation *A Visitor's Guide to the Falkland Islands* (3rd edition) Falklands Conservation, 2021. A good guide with some very useful maps of the more commonly visited areas and site information.

Woods, R W and Woods, A *Atlas of Breeding Birds of the Falkland Islands* Nelson, 1993. A species-by-species account of the birds that breed on Falkland.

Woods, R W *Native Plant Survey* Falklands Conservation, 1998. An illustrated guide to 26 native plant species.

Woods, Robin W *Flowering Plants of the Falkland Islands* Falklands Conservation, 2000. A useful book for visitors wishing to know more about the plants they will see while walking around the islands.

Woods Robin W and Woods, Anne *Birds and Mammals of the Falkland Islands* (2nd edition) WildGuides, 2018. By far the best book about the islands' bird and animal life, with excellent photos and very informative text.

Woods, Robin W *The Birds of the Falkland Islands* British Ornithologists Club, 2017. An annotated checklist covering the status and distribution of the birds of the islands.

Woodward, S and Robinson, P *One Hundred Days* HarperCollins, 1997. The commander of the British naval forces' account of the Falklands War 1982.

MAGAZINES AND JOURNALS

McAdam J (editor) *The Falkland Islands Journal*. This publication is independent of any organisation and publishes an annual magazine covering a range of subjects from history (particularly maritime history) through to geography and natural history. To access it, contact Jim McAdam (16B Dirnan Rd, Cookstown BT80 9XL; w falklandislandsjournal.org).

Wildlife Conservation in the Falkland Islands. This magazine summarises the recent work done by Falklands Conservation, ranging from penguin and albatross surveys to tussac planting and invasive predator management, through to updates about what unusual birds have been seen on the islands recently. This is available to Falklands Conservation members and is published twice a year.

MAPS For more on maps, see page 59.

Falkland Islands, scale 1:250,000, Ordnance Survey, 1996.

WEBSITES

Chronicle of the Falklands/Malvinas History and War of 1982 w yendor.com/vanished/falklands-war.html. A summary of the history of the islands up to the end of the war in 1982.

CIA – The World Factbook – Falkland Islands w cia.gov/the-world-factbook/countries/falkland-islands-islas-malvinas A summary of information about the islands from the CIA.

Falkland Islands Development Corporation w fidc.co.fk. This website outlines the work of the FIDC in improving the economy of the islands.

Falkland Islands Government w falklands.gov.fk. The website of the islands' government, covering everything from local government to the air service and lots more.

Falkland Islands Tourist Board w falklandislands.com. A good portal to learn more about the islands with information on where to go and what to see.

Falklands Conservation w falklandsconservation.com. The website details their work protecting the islands' wildlife and includes information about what can be seen. They also produce a very useful newsletter for members.

The South Atlantic Medal Association 82 w sama82.org.uk. This website was set up for all those involved in the Falklands War in 1982 who received the South Atlantic Medal. It supports those members in need, organises various events and meetings and helps those who wish to revisit the islands.

NOTES

NOTES

Index

Page numbers in **bold** refer to main entries; those in *italics* refer to maps

1914 Battle Memorial (Stanley) 78–9

accommodation 57, **59–60**
see also individual locations
Actaeon (Stanley) 80
agriculture **17**, 19
air travel
DVT 55
getting there and away 53–4
inter-island 15, **57–8**, 72
Ajax Bay 107
albatrosses **35**, 48, 128, 141, 160–1, 162–3, 173, 174, 177
alcohol 61
area of the Falkland Islands vii, 2
Areguati, Don Pablo 8, 100
Argentina
claims of sovereignty 8, 12–13, 100
see also Falklands War 1982
Argentine Military Cemetery 113
arts and crafts 21, 62–3
Australian Gold Rush 70
avian influenza (bird flu) 34

Barnard, Charles H 174
Beauchêne, Jacques Gouin de 6, 128
Beaver Island 179, *180*, **183**
Beaver Pond 15, **128**
Beaver Shed (Stanley) 79

beer 61
Berkeley Sound 32
berried plants 26
Bertha's Beach 118–20
Betts Pond 151
Big Pond (Bleaker Island) 118
Big Pond (Pebble Island) 150
Big Pond (Saunders Island) 159
Bignone, General Reynaldo 14
Billy Rock 89
binoculars 57
birds **33–45**, 184–5
birds of prey **39–40**, 118
Bleaker Island 25, **116–18**, *116*
blue whales 32
Bluff Cove 14, **120–1**
Boca Wall 113
Bodie Creek Suspension Bridge 114
bog formation 24
see also peat bogs and peat cutting
Bomb Alley 107
Bougainville, Louis-Antoine de 7, 100
Brisbane, Matthew 8, 100, 101
Britain
exploration and colonisation 6, 7, 8–9
military presence 10–12, 15
see also Falklands War 1982
British War Cemetery 108
Broadsword, HMS 145, 147

budgeting 57
Bull Point 114, **115–16**
butterflies and moths 45–6
Byron, John 7, 106, 156
Byron Heights 3
Byron Sound 143, 165, 168

Cable Cottage (Stanley) 78
Californian Gold Rush 9, 70, 113
camp 16, 23
camp life 19, 20
driving 58
where to stay 60
camping 60
Canache 86
Cape Bougainville 105
Cape Dolphin 105–7
Cape Horn route 11, 69, 70
Cape Pembroke 85, **88–9**
lighthouse 89
Cape Tamar 152
Capricorn (Stanley) 79
car hire 59
caracaras **40**, 92, 118, 125, 154, 167, 168, 169, 173, 183
Carcass Island 29, 31–2, 51, **165–71**, *166*
cats, domestic 29, 43, 172
cattle 9, 110
cemetery (Port Howard) 135
charities 17, 47–8, 175
Charles Cooper (Stanley) 80
Chartres River 3, 135, 137
Chatham Harbour 182

Chelsea Pensioners 11, 82
children, travelling with 56
chinstrap penguins 162
Christ Church Cathedral (Stanley) 70, 77, **80**
Christina Bay 89
cinema 63, 76
Cliff Mountain 171
climate 5–6
clothing 56–7
Cochon Island 94
Coffin Bay 178
colonisation 7, 8–9
Commerson's dolphins **32**, 92, 108, 116, 119, 121, 133, 136, 142, 149, 163, 172, 173, 181
communications 15, 21
Community Hall (Goose Green) 113–14
Condors 12
conservation 46–8
corral (Darwin) 112–13
countryside code 47
Coventry, HMS 14, 145, 147, 153
Cow Point 125–6
Cowley, Ambrose 6
Craigie Lea Point 115
Cross of Sacrifice (Stanley) 81
cruise ships 51, **54–5**, 71, 158, 166, 171–2, 174, 176
crustacea 46
cultural etiquette 64–5
culture 20–1
currency 2, **57**
cushion plants 23, **27**

Dampier, William 6
Darwin 110–13
Darwin, Charles 98, 101, 110
Davis, John 6, 16
De L'Isle, Guillaume 7
de Weert, Sebald 6
departure tax 53
dialling code, international 2
Dickson, William 8, 101
disabilities, travellers with 56
dolphins 32–3
  see also individual species

Don Carlos Bay 91
Double Stream 136
drinking water 55
driving 56, **58–9**
ducks **38–9**, 88, 119, 137, 154
Duncan, Silas 8, 100
Dyke Beach 166, 167, **168**

East Falkland *84*, **85–121**, *96–7*, *111*
East Loafers 124, 125, 127
economic exploitation 9–10
economy 15, **16–19**
education 20
Egeria (Stanley) 81
electricity supply 2, 57
Elephant Bay 149
Elephant Beach 24, 25, **149**
Elephant Beach Pond 106
Elephant Corner 126
Elephant Point 163
elephant seals *see* southern elephant seals
embassies 53
emergency services 56
entertainment 63–4
erect-crested penguins 51, 154–5
events 61–2

Falkland Islands Company 9, 17
Falkland Islands Defence Force 11–12
Falkland Islands Interim Conservation and Management Zone (FICZ) 15, 17, 71
Falkland Sound 3, 6
Falklands Conservation **47–8**, 80–1
Falklands War 1982 **13–14**, 81–2, 99, 107–8, 111, 113, 120, 123, 127–8, 132–3, 136, 145, 147, 154, 155
Fanning Head 109
fauna **29–46**, 184–6
feldmark 23
ferries 15, **58**, 112, 133
First Mountain 153
Fish Creek (East Falkland) 99
Fish Creek (Pebble Island) 149

fishing 49, 109, 112, **135**, 139, 140
fishing industry 15, **17–18**, 71
flag, national 16
Fleetwing (Stanley) 81
Floating Interim Port and Storage System (FIPASS) 15, 86
flora vii, **23–9**, 49, 186–7
flowers 27–9
food and drink 61
fossils 3, 115, 137, 144
Fox Bay 50, **136–9**
Fox Bay East 136, **138**
Fox Bay West 136, 139
Freezer Rocks 136
fresh-water formation 24
fur seals 10, **30**, 104, 177, 178, 183

Galtieri, General Leopoldo 13, 14
Garland 113
geese **37–8**, 99, 104, 110, 121
General Belgrano 14
gentoo penguins 10, **33**, 91, 95, 103, 105, 115, 117, 119, 120, 125–6, 138–9, 144, 153, 160, 162, 168, 178, 181, 183
geology and geography 3, 5
Gilbert House (Stanley) 77
glaciation 3, 129
Gladstone Bay 144
golf 63–4, 135
Goose Green 14, 110, **111–14**
government 16
Government House (Stanley) 78
grebes **34–5**, 118
Green Hill Stream 135
Green Pond 151
Green Rincon 153–4
guanacos 29–30, 182
guano 79, 174, 175
Gull Harbour 179, 181
gulls 34, **41–2**, 92, 142, 154
Gypsy Cove 50, **85–8**

habitats 23–5
Haig, Alexander 13
Hamilton, John 179–80

hares 29
Hawkins, Sir Richard 6
Hawk's Nest Ponds 137
health 55
herons **36–7**, 93, 144, 167, 169
highlights 49–51
Hill Cove 50
Hill Cove 'forest' 24, **143**
Historic Dockyard Museum (Stanley) 77
history 6–16
 see also individual locations
Hornby Mountains 3, 129, 136, 139
Horse Block 181
horseriding 112
hotels *see* accommodation
hypothermia 55

industry 2
infrastructure 15, 16, 17–18
insects 45–6
internet 21, **64**
itineraries, suggested 50–1

Jason Islands 47, **170**
Jhelum (Stanley) 79
Johnson's Harbour 99
Jones, Lieutenant Colonel 'H' 14, 111, 113
Jubilee Villas (Stanley) 80

kelp 17, 29
Kelp Point 138
Keppel Island 156, *157*, **163–4**
Kidney Cove 94–5
Kidney Island 25, 47, **90–4**, *90*
killer whales (orcas) **32**, 49, 125
King George Bay 142, 180
king penguins **33**, 95, **102–3**, 105, 120–1, 138, 162

Lady Elizabeth 82, 86, **87**
Lafone, Samuel Fisher 9, 110
Lafonia 3, 5, 9, **114–16**
Lake Hammond 139
Landsend Bluff 177

landslides 70
language 19–20
Leopard Beach 166, 167, **168**
leopard seals 32
Liberation Monument (Stanley) 78
Little Coffin Island 179, 182
Little Wreck Point 149
location of the Falkland Islands vii, 2, *4*
Lombardo, Juan José 12
Long Pond 127
Loop Head 182
Lyn Blake Reserve 137

macaroni penguins **34**, 51, 105, 140, 154, 161, 162
McBride, John 7, 100, 156
Mackintosh Ridge 141
Madariaga, Don Juan Ignacio de 7, 100, 156
Magellan, Fernando de 6
magellanic penguins **34**, 87–8, 95, 103–4, 115, 117, 119, 121, 152, 154, 155, 160, 178, 181, 183
Main Point 142
Main Point House 143
Malo River 139
mammals **29–33**, 185–6
Many Branch Creek 135
maps 59
Marble Mountain 154, 155
Margaret (Stanley) 77
marine algae 29
maritime tussock formation 24
 see also tussac grass
Mark Point 181
Martinez, Juan Crisostomo 7, 100
medical treatment 55, 76
memorial wood (Stanley) 81
Menendez, General Mario 14
Mengeary Point 91
Middle Peak 153
migrant birds 45
minefields 56
mineral resources 16
mobile phones 15, 21, **64**

money 57
Moody, Richard 9, 11, 70, 101
Moody Brook (Stanley) 81–2
Moore, Major General Jeremy 14
Mount Adam 3, 48, 129
Mount Byng 169–70
Mount Emery 140
Mount Fegan 142
Mount Harriet 14, 98
Mount Harston 156, 163
Mount Jock 144
Mount Kent 14, 99
Mount Keppel 163
Mount Longdon 14, 82
Mount Maria 129, 136
Mount Misery 171
Mount Pleasant Airport (MPA) 15, 71, 72
Mount Rees 156
Mount Robinson 48, 129
Mount Rosalie 141
Mount Tumbledown 14, 82, 98
Mount Usborne vii, 3
Mount Weddell 182
music 63

Narrows Island 142
national park proposal 48
natural history 23–48
Neck, The 156, 157, **162–3**
New Island 10, 48, 165, **173–8**, *174*
newspaper 20, 64
North Arm 114, 115
North East Point 126

oceanic heath formation 23–4
oil industry 71
The Ovens Hill 169
owls 42

Pacheco, Don Jorge 8, 100
Packe's Jetty (Stanley) 79
packing 56–7
Paloma Beach 110
passerines 43–5
passports 52
Patagonian foxes 30, 180, 181, 182, 183

Peale's dolphins **32–3**, 91, 92, 116, 119, 121, 138, 141, 168, 172
peat bogs and peat cutting 19, 23, 24, 27, 70, 82, 136
Pebble Island 14, 32, 51, **145–55**, *146*
Pebble Islet 155
penguins **33–4**, 49
penguin oil 10, 126–7
see also individual species
people 19
peregrine falcons (Cassin's falcons) **39–40**, 143, 178
petrels **35–6**, 48, 92, 93, 107, 118, 121, 126, 153
philately 18
Phillips Cove 152
photography **49–50**, 57, **63**
pilot whales 32
Pinedo, Don José María 8, 100–1
Pioneer Row (Stanley) 82
places of worship 77
politics 16
population 2
Porpoise Point 116
Port Edgar 139–40
Port Egmont 7, 161
Port Howard 5, 32, 50, **129**, **132–6**, *132*
Port Louis 7, 8, 99, **100–1**
Port Pattison 166, 169
Port Purvis 141
Port Salvador 5
Port San Carlos 107, **108–10**
Port Stanley *see* Stanley
Port Stephens 140
Post Office Museum 138
prions 36, 39–40, 178, 181
Protector III 176–7
public holidays 61–2
Purvis Pond 141

Queen Charlotte Bay 139, 180

Rabbit Island 155
rabbits 29
radio 20–1, 64
rainfall 5
Ram Paddock Hill 168

rats 29
reading, recommended 188–9
Reagan, Ronald 13
red tape 52–3
religion 2, 19
restaurants 61
see also individual locations
River Plate, Battle of the 11
road travel *see* driving
rockhopper penguins 10, **33–4**, 93, 95, 105, 109, 117, 128, 140, 141, 151, 154, 161, 162, 173, 174
Rogers, Woods 6
Rookery Mountain 156, 157, 159, **160–1**
Ross, Captain 9, 69–70, 101
Ross Road (Stanley) 77, 78–81
Roy Cove 142
Royal Marines memorial (Stanley) 78
Ruiz Puente, Don Felipe 7

safety 55–6
sailing 54, 158, 172, 176
St Mary's Roman Catholic Church (Stanley) 79
Samson 86, **87**
San Carlos 107
San Carlos River 3
San Carlos Water 14, 107, 108
Sapper's Hill (Stanley) 82
SAS 13, 14, 152, 155
Saunders Island 31–2, 51, **156–63**, *157*
Scott, Captain 7, 156
Sea Dog Island 181
Sea Lion Island 31, 50, **122–8**, *123*
sea lions *see* southern sea lions
sea otters 30
sea travel 54–5, 58
see also ferries
seals 30–2
seal oil 10, 31
see also individual species
seashells 46
seasons and when to visit **5–6**, 49

Secretariat (Stanley) 78
sei whales **32**, 94, 141, 172, 173
Settlement Harbour 176
Shag Point 149
shags **36**, 93, 117, 128, 141, 142, 151, 152, 153, 161, 162, 177, 181
Shallow Bay House 143
shearwaters **36**, 91, 93, 94, 128
Shedders Pond 169
sheep farming **9–10**, **17**, 19, 110–11, 114, 132, 145, 157, 180
Sheffield, HMS 14, 127–8
Ship Harbour Pond 152–3
shipwrecks 69, 77, 79, 80, 81, 86, 87, 113, 115, 118–19, 176–7
shopping 62
shrubs and bushes 24, **25–6**
skuas **41**, 104, 125, 142, 169
Smith, Henry 8, 101
Smylie Channel 181
Smylies Creek 110
snowfall 6
Solar System Sculpture (Stanley) 79
South Georgia 10, 13, 18, 34, 80, 103, 141, 175
South Harbour 175
South Hill 174
South Sandwich Islands 13, 14, 18
southern elephant seals 30, **31**, 49, 90, 104, 116, 124–5, 169
southern right whales **32**, 94, 163, 173, 178
southern sea lions **30–1**, 49, 89, 93, 106, 118, 124, 127, 142, 144, 152, 177
sovereignty disputes
Argentinian claims 8, 12–13, 100
early 6–8
Sparrow Cove 88
spiders 45
sport 20
Staats Island 179, *180*, **182**

Stanley 5, 12, 50, **68–83**, *68–9*
city status 71
day trips from 73
driving tour from 85–90
entertainment and nightlife 76
Falklands War 13, 14, 71
getting there and around 71–2
history 69–71
other practicalities 76–7
population 19
post-war 15–16
shopping 76
tourist information and tour operators 72–3
what to see and do 77–83
where to eat and drink 74–5
where to stay 73–4
Stanley Volunteers 11
Stick in the Mud Island 179, 182
stone runs 3, **98**
Strong, John 6, 132
Sturgess Point 149
sun protection 5, 57
Surf Bay 25, **90**
Sussex Mountains 108, 111
Swan Pond (Cape Dolphin) 106–7
Swan Pond (Pebble Island) 151
swans **37**, 107, 119, 137, 151

Tamar Pass 141
Tamar Point 152
taxis 59, 72
Taylor, Flight Lieutenant Nick 111, 113
Tea Island 182
telephones 15, 21, **64**

television 21, 64
temperatures 5
Thatcher, Margaret 78, 113
time zone 2
totem pole 86
tour operators **51–2**, 73
tourism 17, **18–19**
Tourism Recovery Incentive Programme (TRIP) 18
tourist information 72
Town Hall (Stanley) 79
travel
getting around 57–8
getting there and away 53–5
travel clinics 55
travelling positively 65
trees 24
tree planting 17
Turkey Rocks 143
turkey vultures **39**, 92, 143, 154
tussac grass **24**, **25**, 90, 107
Tussac Pond 127
Two Sisters 14, 82

United Kingdom Falkland Islands Trust 17
United Nations 12, 13, 14

vaccinations 55
variable hawks **40**, 137, 138, 143, 154
Vernet, Louis 8, 100
Vespucci, Amerigo 6
Vicar of Bray 113
Victor Creek 150
Victory Green (Stanley) 80
visas 52
Volunteer Beach 99, 103

Volunteer Point 50, **95**, **98–104**

wading birds **40–1**, 137
Walker Creek 114
walking and hiking 55
Warrah River 3, 135
waterfowl **37–9**, 137
weather 5–6
websites 189–90
Weddell Island 179–82, *180*
West Falkland 5, **129–44**, *130–1*
circular tours 140–4
West Point Harbour 172
West Point Island 5, 165, **171–3**, *171*
Whalebone Cove 86, **87**
whales 32
whale oil 10
see also individual species
whaling 10, 175
White Rock 34, 50, 141
Wickham Heights 3, 98, 99
wildlife
conservation 46–8
reserves 47
see also fauna
William Shand (Stanley) 81
wind 5
Wireless Ridge 14, 82
Woodward, Rear Admiral Sandy 13
wool market 10, 15, 16, 17
Woolly Gut 171
World War I 11, 78, 79, 81
World War II 11–12, 81
Wreck Point 152

Yaghan people 6, 164
Yorke Bay 86, 88

INDEX OF ADVERTISERS

Estancia Excursions 83
Falkland Island Holidays inside front cover
Falkland Island Tourist Board inside back cover
International Tours & Travel 3rd colour section
The Falklander 3rd colour section
Wanderlust 190

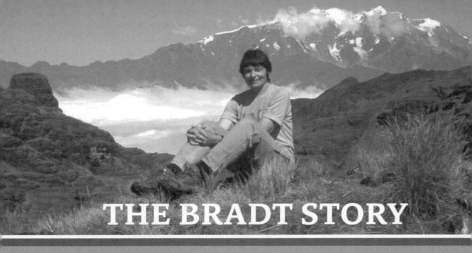

THE BRADT STORY

In the beginning

It all began in 1974 on an Amazon river barge. During an 18-month trip through South America, two adventurous young backpackers – Hilary Bradt and her then husband, George – decided to write about the hiking trails they had discovered through the Andes. *Backpacking Along Ancient Ways in Peru and Bolivia* included the very first descriptions of the Inca Trail. It was the start of a colourful journey to becoming one of the best-loved travel publishers in the world; you can read the full story on our website (**bradtguides. com/ourstory**).

Getting there first

Hilary quickly gained a reputation for being a true travel pioneer, and in the 1980s she started to focus on guides to places overlooked by other publishers. The Bradt Guides list became a roll call of guidebook 'firsts'. We published the first guide to Madagascar, followed by Mauritius, Czechoslovakia and Vietnam. The 1990s saw the beginning of our extensive coverage of Africa: Tanzania, Uganda, South Africa, and Eritrea. Later, post-conflict guides became a feature: Rwanda, Mozambique, Angola, and Sierra Leone, as well as the first standalone guides to the Baltic States following the fall of the Iron Curtain, and the first post-war guides to Bosnia, Kosovo and Albania.

Comprehensive – and with a conscience

Today, we are the world's largest independently owned travel publisher, with more than 200 titles. However, our ethos remains unchanged. Hilary is still keenly involved, and **we still get there first**: two-thirds of Bradt guides have no direct competition.

But we don't just get there first. Our guides are also known for being **more comprehensive** than any other series. We avoid templates and tick-lists. Each guide is a one-of-a-kind expression of an expert author's interests, knowledge and enthusiasm for telling it how it really is.

And a commitment to wildlife, conservation and respect for local communities has always been at the heart of our books. Bradt Guides was **championing sustainable travel** before any other guidebook publisher. We even have a series dedicated to Slow Travel in the UK, award-winning books that explore the country with a passion and depth you'll find nowhere else.

Thank you!

We can only do what we do because of the support of readers like you – people who value less-obvious experiences, less-visited places and a more thoughtful approach to travel. Those who, like us, take travel seriously.

Bradt GUIDES
TRAVEL TAKEN SERIOUSLY